the ESSENTIAL NEW MANAGER'S KIT

Florence Stone

Dearborn™
Trade Publishing
A **Kaplan Professional** Company

This publication is designed to provide accurate and authoritative information in regard to the subject matter covered. It is sold with the understanding that the publisher is not engaged in rendering legal, accounting, or other professional service. If legal advice or other expert assistance is required, the services of a competent professional should be sought.

Vice President and Publisher: Cynthia A. Zigmund
Acquisitions Editor: Jonathan Malysiak
Senior Project Editor: Trey Thoelcke
Interior Design: Lucy Jenkins
Cover Design: KTK Design Associates
Typesetting: the dotted i

© 2004 by Florence Stone
Published by Dearborn Trade Publishing, a Kaplan Professional Company

Printed in the United States of America

04   05   06   10   9   8   7   6   5   4   3   2   1

Library of Congress Cataloging-in-Publication Data

Stone, Florence M.
　　The essential new manager's kit / Florence Stone.
　　　　p.　　cm.
　　Includes index.
　　ISBN 0-7931-7841-X
　　1. Management.　2. Executives—Training of.　3. Supervision of employees.
　4. Executive ability.　I. Title.
　HD31.S69618 2003
　658.4—dc22

2003016190

Contents

Introduction
Managing in Chaotic Times

In recent years, managerial challenges have grown significantly. Consequently, the demands on managers have increased, making the transition to first-line management doubly difficult. If you are a new manager, that's why you picked up this book. You feel pressure to excel in your new position—and to develop the skills and abilities to move beyond your current responsibilities.

You've passed by other books because they offer highfalutin' theory—which you know won't help you. You want practical answers to the daily problems and pressures that came with your promotion.

I've been a new manager, and I can relate to your desire to:

- Gain confidence and experience less stress in your new position
- Improve performance and job satisfaction—your own and your employees'
- Demonstrate the skills, abilities, and knowledge that your manager and all the executives within your organization expect of you
- Grow professionally

Divided into five parts, this book provides how-to information on almost 25 skills that you need to succeed as a first-line manager. In my 30-plus year career as a manager and business writer, I have met with many new managers who tend to fall into certain traps. I don't want that to happen to you, so the advice in this book will help you avoid many of those traps.

In this book, I cover the financial responsibilities, the people skills, the communication abilities, your leadership role—yes, you have one of those, too—and even some endurance skills to help you be successful throughout your career. You'll learn how to undertake planning, something many new managers ignore to their peril (Chapter 1); you'll learn how to survive the hell that comes with the budgeting process (Chapter 2); and you'll learn how planning and budgeting together enable you to track performance. That's only the start.

A full section is devoted to your people management skills (Chapters 4 to 9). You'll learn how to hire and retain the best and ignore the rest. You'll discover a skill even many experienced managers lack: the ability to analyze resumes and screen applicants to hire the most talented employees.

I'll teach you how to delegate work so that it gets done as you want. You will also learn how to empower those employees who have the talent to take on responsibility, thereby freeing you to assume greater responsibility yourself.

I know that not all your employees are capable of empowerment. Many need more direction—even counseling—and you'll learn how to provide regular coaching and also counseling to subpar performers and employees with problems. You will also learn in this book how to handle those awful appraisal interviews. You'll discover what to document and what not to include, how to conduct appraisals, postmeeting recordkeeping, and potential legal pitfalls.

That's still not all. I'll also help you to manage conflicts—those between your employees that you must mediate and even those in which you are a combatant. If you have a troublemaker on staff, this book suggests how to handle that behavior. You'll learn the art of discipline, including how to fire without fear.

Chapters 10 to 14 look at another major area of responsibility: communication. You'll learn in these chapters not only how to listen but also how to hear and how to use body language to communicate more effectively, as well as how to understand what an employee is really trying to convey.

This book will also teach you to be more assertive in your communications; to use communications to build better relationships with your employees, your manager, and your new peers; and to improve the quality of your written communications, on paper and online.

I mentioned that this book will help you better understand your leadership role. Your manager will watch how you handle these responsibilities because your degree of success will signal your capability for advancement. So check out Chapters 15 to 19. You'll learn how to build a sense of teamwork, solve problems, make change happen, negotiate, and manage meetings.

Why are these things called *endurance skills?* They are the fundamentals for a successful career, no matter what, and I've included them in this book to help you grow professionally beyond your current position. For instance, you will learn critical time management skills. Neither this book nor its author promises to give you more than 24 hours in the day, but the book and author will show you how to use those hours more effectively (Chapter 20). Because stress is very much a part of any job, you'll also find help to manage job stress (Chapter 21). Because focusing solely on your career doesn't make for a full life, this book also suggests how you can find more time for family and friends (Chapter 22). Finally, because my own experience has taught me about the importance of strong networking and political skills, I've set aside a full chapter on these (Chapter 23).

As a perfect ending, I have added a chapter on career management, for when you think you are ready to move up to middle management (Chapter 24).

Within the chapters, you'll find checklists and assessment tools as well as tips. All this will be useful in your new job.

I know that you did a great job before your promotion. Otherwise, you wouldn't be in the job you have now. But I want to be sure that you do an outstanding job in your new position.

Let me show you how helpful this book will be. I've written a number of scenarios that show situations new managers are likely to encounter. I've also suggested three ways you can handle each one. Test yourself. You'll find answers to these situations throughout the book.

Good luck.

Self-Assessment

You told Sam that you needed his copy ready for the Web site by Friday. By Wednesday, he hadn't finished the work. You had promised you would have it to the production team before the end of the day, but Sam says he hasn't started yet. "I thought I had other priorities," he says. What do you do?

1. You blame Sam for making it impossible for you to keep your promise to the production team. True, you had asked Sam to complete the work by Friday, so he really hasn't missed the deadline. Still, Sam makes a good patsy for your failure to keep your promise to the production group.
2. You take the work from Sam and hurriedly work on it, putting aside your own tasks since you promised the production team it would get the completed job two days earlier than scheduled.
3. You call the production team and explain that you should have checked the schedule before you made your promise. The team can expect the work on Friday. To ensure that, you speak with Sam to explain how crit-

ical it is that the job be ready to hand off to the production group by 9:00 AM on Friday.

You have been asked to submit a budget for your team. It's your first effort, so you are a little unsure, but you believe you can handle it. How do you begin?

1. You talk to Joe about his costs. His operation is a lot like yours, and the numbers he uses should pretty much work for your unit, too.
2. You copy the budget from last year. Because you are responsible only for costs, no major changes should be needed.
3. You take last year's budget and compare it against actual costs right now. Then you speak with purchasing to see if they anticipate price increases in any of your budget lines. You project actual costs for the year, adding a slight increase based on figures from purchasing.

Your manager has called to ask why your budget shows an overexpenditure in travel and expense (T&E). "How should I know?" you think to yourself, as you scramble to find the source material you used to build your budget over six months ago. What should you do?

1. Go back to the assumptions on which you based your budget. Look them over to see what is costing more than expected.
2. Blame Lynn, who attended a trade conference for your group. Clearly, she spent more than you allotted. It's all her fault, and you will make sure your manager knows that.
3. Tell your manager a little white lie: you had no idea where the trade conference was to be held, and you only learned about the higher cost after the budget had been approved. Because your manager also knew where the conference was and didn't suggest canceling it, you assumed everything was OK.

You have to hire a new clerk for the store. You have over 100 resumes and a real need for help. What should you do?

1. Look through the resumes and find a candidate who is currently unemployed. Talk briefly to that person and, if available right away, make a job offer.
2. Ignore the resumes on your desk. Call a friend who is looking for a job, any job. Your friend should fit in and shouldn't be a problem to supervise.
3. Review the resumes, looking for those candidates with experience in stores like yours. Because salary is an issue, select only those candidates whose

salary demands fit what you can pay. Now arrange to meet with each candidate to discuss the job in detail.

Martha has finished the work, but the quality isn't even close to what you expected. What should you do?

1. Tell Martha that in the future you'll handle such tasks.
2. Sit down with Martha and point to the shortcomings. Ask her to try again, reminding her that if she has any problems, she should speak with you.
3. Ask Sal, Martha's coworker, to take over the job.

Management is encouraging each department to operate as a team. To encourage an attitude of teamwork in your operation, what should you do?

1. Talk to each member of your department about the value of teamwork and hold a meeting to extol the values of closer working relationships.
2. Hold monthly staff meetings where members of the group describe particular activities, share successes and failures, and recognize the accomplishments of individual members.
3. Send a memo to all staff reminding them they are members of a team and that you expect them to pull together no matter what their job responsibilities.

Your new salesperson gets angry with a client and blows up. How should you respond?

1. Blow up at the employee in turn. After all, this is a valuable client.
2. Sit down with the employee and discuss damage control. Coach, pointing out how the problem could have been handled and how to prevent the blowup from happening again. You point out what was done right and what was done wrong.
3. Avoid the employee because you are too angry to discuss the situation. When the client calls, you apologize and reassign the account to another staff member.

You and your staff have just completed a product study. You want to write the report because you think you have identified some key issues that others might miss, but your desk is stacked high with essential paperwork. How do you proceed?

1. Put aside the paperwork to write the report. After all, the report has long-term value.

2. Call the proposed recipient of the report and explain that you have some nifty insights, and ask if the report can wait a week.
3. Share your insights with a team member, who then drafts the report.

You are meeting with your staff to tell them about a new corporate procedure. What do you include in your presentation?

1. Point out how this change has been delayed because the division has not been perceived as a moneymaking operation.
2. Indicate that senior management recognizes the contribution your operation can make and, in keeping with the organization's goal to identify ancillary products, has set up policies and procedures to facilitate that.
3. Inform your staff that they are lucky to be where they are right now— other areas within the operation have had cutbacks. If they don't take up the new challenge, they could be out, too.

Conflict has arisen about whether a relatively new product should be pulled from the market. Management says it is up to you. What do you do?

1. Call an end to the argument and make a decision based on the economic numbers submitted by marketing, disregarding any new information about shifts in the marketplace.
2. Allow the argument to proceed, using the flip chart in the room to capture key points made by both sides.
3. Call on a member of the product group to submit a paper in favor of continuing the product and promise to make a decision based on that.

A colleague has asked you for help to complete a project. Your desk is piled with work. You know you don't have time to help. How do you respond?

1. Agree. You know you won't be able to help, but refusing could be politically unwise in an organization that encourages managerial cooperation.
2. Say no. Explain your own situation.
3. Say no, but ask if one of your employees might be able to help, either by freeing one of your colleague's employees to help your colleague or by directly helping your colleague.

Even if you know the right answers, you need to ask yourself if you would really act that way. Often, what we *should* do hasn't yet become a part of our natural behavior. This book is designed to help you change knee-jerk reactions to management situations into more productive responses—into solutions that will make you stand out among your peers for your management acumen.

1

Planning

Your success as a manager will depend on your skills, ability, and knowledge in a number of areas. Of these, the keystone is planning, followed closely by control. Because budgeting is both the means to finance a plan and to measure progress, Chapters 1 to 3 are good places to start excelling in your new position.

Short-Term Planning

Your focus in planning will primarily be short term, on operational planning. Although you should understand corporate strategic planning, you are less likely to be involved in it than those in top management. I'll address the elements of strategic planning in this chapter, but my major focus here—as yours should be—will be on unit goals and plans that contribute to the overall corporate mission.

To understand the difference between strategic plans and operational plans, think of them from a military perspective. Strategic plans are the basis of a major battle or an entire war, while tactical and operational plans deal with engagements or skirmishes.

Why Plan?

Focused on the day-to-day responsibilities of their jobs, many new managers don't appreciate the need for planning, even operational planning. This is especially so in today's fast-changing world, where the time frames for planning are continually being shortened. Admittedly, your chances of planning effectively in our unpredictable world are greatly diminished if you approach planning as managers have in the past. Still, a rapidly changing environment is no excuse for not planning. Neither is moving forward when the future is unclear a matter of substituting gut instinct for analytic rigor. Rigor is still needed, but it needs to be more flexible than that of the past. More than in the relatively tranquil past, failure to plan—whether a year, three months, or even a month ahead—can cause confusion and, ultimately, crises in your unit.

In terms of the bigger picture, because your unit's efforts should support the overall corporate mission, it can make the corporate master plan work—or not. The inability of your unit to fulfill its commitment because of poor planning can mean *not*.

The Big Picture

To understand your role in the planning process, let's begin at the top of your organization, with its mission.

A corporate mission statement is the starting place in planning. It articulates the company's vision—what the company will evolve into. It gives direction to all within the firm. It tells everyone who they are, what they are, and, most importantly, what they are striving to become. The more succinct the statement of mission, the clearer it may be. Henry Ford used eight words to describe his company's mission in 1903: "I will build a motorcar for the multitude."

SWOT Analysis

The next step is a SWOT analysis. SWOT is an acronym for Strengths, Weaknesses, Opportunities, and Threats. It is merely a guide for organizing one's thinking about a company and the environment in which it operates. In conducting a SWOT analysis, your company's senior management will be examining the firm's external and internal environment. External considerations might include customer attitudes, competition, technology, and economic conditions; the internal environment might encompass employees' skills, abilities, and knowledge, product and service offerings, and support services.

After this analysis, senior management will ask some serious questions. Do we have the resources and capabilities to take advantage of the opportunities in the external environment and neutralize the threats we have identified? How many competitors have the same strengths and management competencies as we? Does our company lack a particular resource or capability that we can't afford to acquire? On the other hand, if we have this resource or capability, can we make something of it to grow the business? Answers will enable top management to come up with workable strategies.

Top-Down Planning

Corporate strategies are the broad goals designed to grow the business. These strategies are vital because they will give each and every manager within the organization, including you, a focus. The mission will be achieved when these strategies (think *objectives*) are accomplished. These strategies or objectives, built around the organization's mission and the demands of the marketplace, cascade down within the organization, translated at each level into goals that support the strategies.

Tactical goals—broad goals designed to achieve the strategies—are generally developed by middle managers. Line managers and staffs typically create operational goals, whose purpose is to facilitate tactical steps.

This top-down approach to planning continues to be used more often than the bottom-up approach, in which the organization sets broad corporate aims and then asks managers and their staffs at lower levels to specify what they can do to achieve them. Although the bottom-up approach is far more effective at ensuring that unit goals are realistic and at gaining staff commitment, it can be time consuming, calling for several cycles of decisions and revision.

So you and your team may have goals imposed on you, or you may set them yourselves, or you may find yourself somewhere between those two extremes. Goals (tactical and operational) cover output, quality, and allowable expenditures, as well as employee-related issues like recruitment and retention (think *turnover*), pay and benefits, and safety issues. The goals may be qualitative (described with such words as *improve, maintain, good,* or *better*), they may be quantitative (tied to number of pieces completed or dollars saved or earned), or they may be both. The kind of goals you set depends on your unit's work.

Start from the Start

Your unit planning begins similarly to the strategic planning done at the corporate level. For instance, before setting final goals, you and your unit should consider your strengths and weaknesses and your threats and opportunities in light of your company's mission and strategic and tactical goals. This SWOT analysis will influence both your goals and your plans to reach them.

SMART Goals

Once you have completed this analysis, you are ready to commit to your unit's goals.

These goals should be defined so that they are SMART; that is, they are Specific, Measurable, Agreed, Realistic, and Time based. In other words, the outputs should be clearly defined (specific) so that performance can be quantified (measurable), agreed upon between you and your staff (agreed), achievable within the constraints of time and resources (realistic), and have an achievable target date (time-based).

All five criteria are important. Certainly, the motivational and practical reasons for agreement among those responsible for achieving the plan should be clear. Likewise, you should understand why so much emphasis is placed on realistic, measurable goals. Goals are of little value unless they are achieved, and the only way to achieve them is if they are realistic, and the only way to know they have been achieved is if they are measurable (see Chapter 3).

You can identify goals and make plans to achieve them alone, but the experience of other managers suggests that you should involve your staff members in the process. Their job experience can add insight into how to get effectively and efficiently from Point A (corporate objectives) to Point B (your unit's goals). That's what planning is all about.

Questions to Ask

Goal setting is critical for effective planning. Perceptions about what is important may differ, and unless time is spent in discussing and mutually agreeing on the unit's goals, time may be wasted on the wrong activities. Such discussion begins with you and your manager and then proceeds down to include your staff.

Well-written goals also enable you and your team to check your progress. By comparing results to the goals, you can determine how effective operations have been and take needed steps if improvement is called for. In this way, goals play a control function, along with your budget (see Chapter 3).

When you and your unit sit down to agree on goals, you need to consider the following:

- What are the corporate goals?
- What demands will be made of the work group in the future?
- What conditions will affect our work in the future?
- What do we need to accomplish?
- What desirable results can we identify?
- What results should we look for along the way?

By involving your employees in setting or finalizing your unit's goals, you benefit in three ways:

1. The goals are based on the best information available to the unit.
2. Employees will understand how their work fits into the bigger corporate picture, thereby feeling more job satisfaction and taking more responsibility for achieving results.
3. Your employees will learn more about each other, which should support collaboration and cooperation.

The Planning Process

Once goals are identified, you and your team need to undertake your planning. First, you will identify all intermediate steps and resources necessary (see Chapter 2 on budgeting), then you will determine the sequence in which these steps must be performed, and finally you will assign the appropriate people to assure task completion.

As you and your team set about planning, you should be aware of certain human tendencies, for they can interfere with even the best-laid plans. For instance, you may focus solely on the short term, giving little attention to the period beyond. Or you and your team may be too optimistic, believing that performance will improve over current levels.

You and your group may also oversimplify the internal or external environment. For instance, you may plan to find more distributors for your firm's product line, ignoring the likely reality that your competitors will see what your firm is up to and do likewise. Maybe your own sales force may see an expanded distribution network as competition and put obstacles in your way.

If significant change within your unit will be needed to enact a plan, you may even get opposition during planning. If the plan might threaten job security, your staff may not want to face that tough issue.

Actually, your staff may be a major obstacle to operational planning. You will have to sell some individuals on the idea that planning can make achievement of goals more likely—that it isn't just time consuming.

The support you can expect from your staff will influence how detailed your plan will need to be. If your staff members have been involved in planning in the past, you can keep your plans relatively broad. Other factors that will influence the nature of your plans are the difficulty of the plans and the ability of those involved to follow them.

If this is your first time planning, I'd advise you to be more specific than you think you need to be. Also, don't get so wrapped up in the planning that you lose sight of where you are trying to go. Keep in mind that the plan is a means, not an end. Remember, too, that as you work your plans, you may encounter problems. Spend time with your team identifying the kinds of problems you may encounter and how you can respond to these.

Keep in mind that the most important factor in the success of the planning process is the plan itself. To ensure you have a well-constructed plan, ask your employees:

- Is it clear? Do you understand it? How about your peers?
- Does it agree with the values and purpose of the organization?
- Does the plan deal effectively with both threats and opportunities, those identified by top management for the organization and by the unit?
- Does it identify the items of importance to our work unit?
- To what extent does it contain specific, measurable goals and objectives?
- Is the plan a real basis for action?
- Does the plan contain contingencies in case of a serious internal or outside event?
- Does the plan include a way of obtaining feedback on its success?
- Is the plan flexible in case it needs to be changed?

In essence, you want a plan that is workable, because an impossible goal does not motivate. You also want a plan that is flexible so that you can adjust to changes beyond your control. And you want to tie your plans to corporate objectives and tactical goals. Your manager's involvement in building the plan may be considerable at first, until you demonstrate your ability to manage this responsibility on your own.

You need to be ready to tell your manager who will be responsible for what aspect of the plan. Pin down assignments. Put numbers and dates on everything you can, too. Plans work best when employees know *how much* or *how many* are required. Because plans are for the future—tomorrow, next week, or next month—due dates are essential.

Once you have completed your plan, you will review it with your manager to assess its completeness and accuracy. Your manager, in turn, will review your plan with a supervisor. Top-down planning begins at the top, cascades down to the smallest units, and then goes upward for final review.

To ensure that your staff is committed to your unit goals, you should align their performance goals to your unit plans (see Chapter 7, "Performance Appraisals"). The final plan will include the following:

- The deliverables (the goal)
- Processes to achieve the goal or a plan to develop processes
- Constraints
- Tasks involved
- Involvement of others
- Budget needs (see Chapter 2)
- Staff requirements

Project Planning

Among your plans may be one that addresses the completion of a single project. A project entails planning very similar to that for your unit. Besides goals for the project, you will need to identify who within your unit is responsible for what. You also will need to put together a schedule for completion of the project (milestones).

Let me share with you some tools you can use to set milestones. These tools also may work in setting completion dates for unit plans.

Scenario Planning

This process builds three or four descriptions of potential future conditions and develops a plan that will succeed regardless of which scenario actually comes to pass.

Backwards Planning

This is exactly what it sounds like. You begin with the desired result, or objective, of the plan. Then you and your team back up in a sequential manner from the final project result, identifying each required prior action. As each preceding task is completed, the time required to achieve it is estimated. The process continues, working backwards from each task, until all tasks are identified and the interval for completion of each is determined.

Determining the starting date is then simple, as it merely requires adding the times required for each task.

PERT Planning

PERT stands for Program Evaluation and Review Technique and was developed in the late 1950s. It continues to be used today for projects from cross-functional situations to smaller, department projects. It is a version of backwards planning but a little more sophisticated, in that it shows graphically both the time frame and interrelationships between tasks.

Like backwards planning, PERT identifies each milestone, their interrelationships, and finally any bottlenecks that can occur when a problem arises. The last is referred to as a *critical path,* and it is shown graphically. The various steps in the plan are also depicted as they will look if all goes smoothly.

Gantt Chart

This shows the time-phasing and scheduling of events necessary to reach an objective. A bar chart format is used. It is good for tracking progress on a plan after either PERT or backwards planning is used to dissect a plan into its various stages.

If you find yourself in charge of a project outside your unit, you should become comfortable with using all four techniques. For traditional planning, they are less necessary. Based on conversations with your staff and your peers, you should be able to identify the activities and time each plan will take. But before you share your plans with your manager, you may want to review your goals and plans with colleagues who are skilled in planning. If time, money, or equipment are essential to your plans, you may also want to talk to an experienced planner to be sure that you have made accurate estimates.

Tips

- Identify the steps and the roles needed to successfully implement your plan.

- Review your unit's goals and plans for compatibility with your organization's strategic and tactical plans.

- Identify the business processes involved in achieving each goal. Then identify process owners for each process. These individuals should be included in your planning if possible.

- Include vendors and suppliers when their commitments are necessary and cannot be taken for granted—for example, when a plan depends on new technology.

- Set aside time each day to review progress toward plan objectives and to revise plans accordingly.

See Also

Bangs, David H., Jr. *The Business Planning Guide* (9th Edition). Dearborn Trade, 2001.

Bittel, Lester R. and John W. Newstrom. *What Every Supervisor Should Know* (6th Edition). McGraw-Hill, 1995.

Petersen, Steven D. and Peter E. Jaret. *Business Plans Kit for Dummies*. For Dummies, 2001.

Pinson, Linda. *Anatomy of a Business Plan* (5th Edition). Dearborn Trade, 2001.

2

Budgeting

Once you have developed your plan, you need to determine how much it will cost. That brings us to your responsibility for budgeting.

Admittedly, budgeting increases paperwork and can be a drain on your time. On the other hand, budgets can help you achieve planned goals. Having a budget improves the performance of the entire organization and each of its parts. It enables all levels of management to predict results and needs and to keep score.

In budgeting, the overall period is 12 months, usually aligned with the calendar year. Reduced to essentials, the budgeting process asks, "What will it cost to achieve your operating plan next year, and what will the financial return be, if any?"

The answer to this question begins with a study of this year's costs, followed by another question, "How will next year's costs and revenue projections be different from this year's?" Make assumptions for those outputs that are unknown, uncertain, and/or uncontrollable.

Your operating plan included all activities critical to achievement of your goals. For your budget, it offers answers to the question *when*. The expenditures and revenue are the *how much* in the budget. If you think that once you fill out your budget spreadsheet, you are done with budgeting for the year, you are wrong. Far from being a once-a-year activity, budgeting requires continuous maintenance of budgeted and actual figures.

Every month, you will be asked to compare your actual expenses and revenue against forecast figures for this year and for several years—the year just gone, the current year, and the year to come (see Chapter 3).

Putting Together a Budget

What's the best organizational approach to budgeting? Most executives would answer: the one that works best. There are three effective approaches to developing budgets.

Top-Down

In this approach, budgets are prepared by top management and imposed on the lower layers of the organization, generally without any consultation or involvement of the lower layers. Top-down budgets clearly express the corporate strategies and expectations of top management. These budgets, however, are often unrealistic because they do not incorporate the input of the very individuals who will be responsible for implementing them.

Bottom-Up

Most organizations use the bottom-up approach. In bottom-up budgeting, supervisors and middle managers are asked to prepare the budgets and then forward them up the chain of command for review and approval. Because middle managers and those first-line managers who report to them have a clear view of the organization and its financial performance, bottom-up budgets tend to be more accurate than top-down budgets.

Bottom-up budgets can also have a positive impact on employee morale, because employees assume an active role in the process.

Zero-Based Budgeting

In this process, each manager prepares estimates of proposed expenses for a period of time as though the plan was being performed for the first time. In other words, each activity starts from a budget base of zero. By starting from scratch at each budget cycle, managers are required to take a close look at all their expenses and justify them to top management, thereby minimizing unnecessary expenses.

The zero-based budget is based on the assumption that managers will spend money if allocated to them, whether it's necessary or not.

Coming Up with Numbers

You are sitting before your computer with your spreadsheet on the screen. How do you begin? There are three main ways to come up with numbers for your budget.

Historical Approach

This approach bases the numbers on the cost of similar past work. If your unit is doing work that is essentially similar to that done year after year, this approach can work reasonably well. By estimating increased charges or costs, or additional staffing needs, you should be able to incorporate significant cost changes.

Task-Based Approach

The idea here is to take your plan, break it into the major tasks, estimate the cost of each task, and then add the costs to calculate the total. This is the best approach to estimate costs of a project that is completely new to your unit or your organization.

Combined Historical/Task-Based Approach

Here you combine the previously mentioned approaches. First, each approach is used to estimate the budget. Then the numbers are compared. If there are large cost differences, more analysis is required. Even when cost differences are minimal, it's a good idea to compare the new efforts to past ones to identify any areas that might increase costs or allow savings.

What's Coming In, What's Going Out

Look at your budgeting worksheet. Are you responsible for both income and expense projections? Are you responsible for generating funds? If so, is revenue coming from various products or services, and can you influence the amount?

Now look at expected costs. Check out the different budget lines. Cost headings usually include personnel (staffing, wages, pensions, training, etc.); overhead (rent, office space, computers, etc.); and materials and equipment (from stationery to telephones to raw materials).

Some of these costs will be *fixed*—that is, costs you have no control over (e.g., permanent staff costs). Others will be *variable* and depend on the organization's work output (e.g., raw materials or advertising costs). If you are unsure which figures are variable and which ones fixed, you may want to check with your accounting department. Because the state of your firm's business can impact variable costs, you will want to adjust these costs during periods of prosperity and during economic downturns.

Mistakes to Avoid

Over the years, I have spoken to many new managers after their first budgeting experience. Many encountered the same problems. For one, they inflated their estimates. Often, this wasn't deliberate. Some managers did it out of fear, worried that there might be contingencies they hadn't anticipated.

Sometimes, overestimating costs, and even revenue, was due to lack of information about past expenditures or income streams. These new managers just didn't have the information they needed to make more accurate estimates of either costs or revenue. They seemed to think that they would look unprepared for their new responsibilities if they sought advice from others—members of their group, their manager, or other first-time managers with similar responsibilities. After the fact, one manager told me, "It was dumb not to use the resources available to me—and that included my own boss."

On a few occasions, new managers' estimates were too low, often for the same reasons. The manager just didn't know what the job would really cost. Some overestimates of revenue were due to overoptimism.

Some new managers admitted that they were so anxious to impress their manager, they came up with numbers that, in hindsight, they had to admit were unrealistic—and caused problems in achieving unit plans. For example, one new manager underestimated the cost of training his staff on a new software package. Consequently, he had to rethink his plan. Instead of an on-site training program, which had been planned, he sent only three staff members to a public seminar. These three then were responsible for helping the rest of the unit, slowing the transfer to the new software. Another manager made the mistake of projecting more sales than his sales force could realistically bring in. Because he couldn't hire a new salesperson, his department had to report a shortfall.

The Budgeting Climate

Budgeting can be very emotional. It can also put unit managers through high-pressure cycles of "hurry up and wait." One company calls its budgeting time "hell month." The term is apropos, especially for first timers.

Emotions stem, first, from time pressure. Many budgeting processes can be aptly described by the adage, "There is never enough time to do it right, but always time to do it over." Budget spreadsheets flow up and down an organization. As one level after another reviews your budget, you will have to sit back and wait. Then you will be asked to make a modification—quickly, quickly. And then you will resubmit the budget, only to find yourself waiting again to hear.

At each step, you may be asked to justify your figures. Your manager has to undergo this kind of review, too. Indeed, one of the reasons you may experience pressure is that your boss is both a reviewer of your budget and a submitter of a budget, which also has be approved, and on and upward. Consequently, you, your manager, and your manager's boss may get emotional under pressure. There are many "can, cannot" discussions before formal budgeting begins and even more once it starts.

As a first-time player in this multidimensional guessing game, you need to appreciate the emotional pressure everyone is under and try to remain as calm and collected as you can.

During this period of unrest, the following precautions will help you:

- *Keep careful notes of the assumptions, reasoning, and calculations behind your budget submissions.* You may have to make several adjustments, and a few weeks after the fact, when a particular number is attacked in a new review, you will be expected to remember how you arrived at it.
- *Put your budgeting form on a computer spreadsheet.* This will make it easier to track each revision and the reasoning behind it. If done right, it also eliminates arithmetic and multiple-entry errors. Don't underestimate the potential for embarrassing math mistakes.
- *Expect the costs in your first submission to be cut.* Depending on your organization's financial situation, the first cut may not be the last, either.

Therefore, fight back if you are pressured to cut a cost to the bone. If your costs are cut beyond what is required to do the job, say so.

Budget Reviews

Let's look at some of the reworks you can expect.

I mentioned that your manager may make cuts in your budget. Peers are also developing their budgets, and they may have different needs than your unit. As your manager weighs your needs against others, you will need to recalculate costs, and possibly even reconsider your initial plan.

Your manager's manager will also want to put in two cents. Finally, your company's chief financial officer will meet to review the budget. You may be present at this meeting. During this session, you should clearly grasp the agendas of each member of the budget committee, understanding why they are there and what they are trying to achieve.

Certainly, each reviewer will expect you to justify all your numbers. So be prepared with forceful arguments for all proposed plans. Share the assumptions on which the plan and subsequent budget are based—if asked. If your numbers are questioned and you are told to redo the numbers based on the group's thinking, you should do so.

If your unit is responsible for producing revenue, you may be pressured to forecast a significantly higher income number than you first wrote down. You may also be expected to cut back on cost projections, even where you have argued the consequences of such cuts on unit performance. If you get either request, you will have to amend your budget accordingly, but tactfully remind your manager or other executive that you are making the adjustment at their request. This reminder frees you somewhat from responsibility if your original forecast turns out to be more accurate.

Some experienced managers have told me about burying some added money in the budget to cope with anticipated budget cuts. I have mixed feelings about this. Padding is clearly the enemy of good budgeting. On the other hand, a manager's first responsibility is to get approval of the resources needed to do next year's required work. Often, if you have a good relationship with your manager, indiscriminate cuts can be avoided.

I had a supervisor who seemed to have a knack of getting through budget reviews with minimal changes. First, Ernie would review his budget with his own manager, and they would agree on the numbers. He then could come to budget reviews with our chief financial group knowing that his manager was behind him.

But Ernie went further. He brought with him stacks of documentation to justify his assumptions. Asked a question, he always had a ready and lucid response. He had learned over the years what were the hot button issues, current problems, and priorities, and he had reviewed his budget beforehand to anticipate questions and prepare good answers.

He didn't do poorly, either, when it came to his projections. Ernie's presentation of his budget was impressive. He recognized that to get the budget through, he had to sell it to our financial group. He never assumed it would be accepted without supporting arguments. Nor did he think he could flim-flam our financial staff. So he could make a case for every dollar he promised to make or every dollar he needed to run our division.

I learned one thing very early in my own budgeting experience by making a mistake: never volunteer information. Wait until you are asked about something, then reply clearly and succinctly. After volunteering information on one occasion, I found myself redoing several budget lines.

I watched Ernie's style, and I learned from it. I also learned why he increasingly wasn't questioned about his revenue forecasts or cost predictions. He built a reputation for doing what he promised. Further, he had proven over time how knowledgeable he was about his data. Consequently, budget reviews went relatively smoothly.

This is not to say that Ernie wasn't asked to cut costs or increase revenue projections. But he was heard out when asked to make cuts, and often senior management agreed to compromise. Such are the benefits of building a reputation as a skilled budgeter, a reputation you want to gain.

Dos and Don'ts for Drawing Up a Budget

Do:

- Be realistic.
- Take last year's budget and actual results into account.
- Be aware of fixed and variable costs.
- Develop budget lines that reflect your operational plans and responsibilities.
- Gather complete information.
- Decide whether to base your budget on historical facts, or to use a zero-based approach, or a little of both.

Don't:

- Make overoptimistic projections.
- Leave too little time to complete your budget—accept that it is time-consuming work.
- Draw up a budget without involving your employees and others who can offer insights.

Always Question Trends

The use of trends to generate numbers carries an implicit assumption that the trend will continue. Therein lies a problem. Few trends of any kind last for years—the world changes too fast for the conditions that defined the trend to stay the same.

The Realities of Budgeting

I wish I could tell you that budgeting is straightforward and done in a businesslike manner. Not so. For instance, if resources are scarce, there will be competition for resources, which can often lead to deliberate overestimates. Many turf-oriented managers may argue that they represent major revenue sources and consequently need funds that can only be cut from your budget. Don't get caught up in this budgetary game-playing if you can. Come prepared to defend your needs, but be prepared to amend your budget, prioritizing how funds will be spent as a consequence. The operational plan may have to be revised.

■ Tips

- Allow for the impact of inflation on expenses.

- Check last year's budget to make sure you've included all the operating costs.

- If you have objections, consult with those involved in changes to the budget—but be tactful.

■ See Also

Fields, Edward. *The Essentials of Finance and Accounting for Nonfinancial Managers.* AMACOM, 2002.

Godin, Seth and Paul Lim. *If You're Clueless about Accounting and Finance and Want to Know More.* Dearborn Trade, 1998.

Rachlin, Robert and Allen Sweeney. *Accounting and Financial Fundamentals for Nonfinancial Executives.* AMACOM, 1996.

3

Controls

An effective control system identifies variances from budget and signals when plans are not working. Monitoring results may take time, but failure to detect gaps between plans and actual results can cost money. Ideally, the control systems you impose should balance the cost of monitoring with the cost of failing to catch problems in time.

Writing a budget without using it to monitor performance uses only half of its purpose.

The thinking behind monitoring operations via your budget is simple: when your costs are under or equal to budget, or income is over or equal to budget, you are in control. When your costs are over budget, or your income is below budget, you must exert control to bring the numbers back into line.

Control is achieved through continuous review of actual progress and expenses relative to plans—in essence, comparing input-output relationships. Of course, managers can control internal factors more than external factors.

Discrepancies (Variances)

No matter how careful you were in planning your budget, you should expect discrepancies or variances. We can't predict everything that is likely to happen—particularly in today's environment of rapid change. Some differences can be ignored if they will correct themselves the following month, but other discrepancies or variances, no matter how small, need to be understood. A difference that seems small in your mind and to your unit could be crucial to the whole organization, especially if other departments are not meeting their budgets. By assessing why discrepancies have occurred, you may be able to reduce their recurrence as well as provide insights to help the rest of your organization.

The control cycle is monthly and begins when you get your hands on spreadsheets that reflect your expenditures and any income received. That spreadsheet covers actual results. It not only alerts you to variances between your budget and your actual experiences but also guides you in taking corrective action if necessary. If no remedial action is possible, then to get back on budget, you will be expected to redo the budget for the remainder of the budgeting period in light of current information.

Variance Reports

The variances and their cause are written up in what is traditionally called a variance report. Overspending is an adverse variance and underspending is a positive variance. You will prepare a variance report for your manager, who will then review it and forward it to the next level of management.

As you look at the spreadsheet, determine those variances that are most critical to your operation's plans. Also, identify those that are controllable or most likely to recur. These should be the focus of your variance report.

In selecting the variances you will examine, don't focus solely on large discrepancies. Smaller ones may hide insights into operational issues that could save money or increase revenue once changes are made.

There is no specific rule about how variance reports should be laid out. Their format reflects your company's budgeting practices and your department's function. So a report done in one company's marketing department might look very different from one prepared in another organization's customer service department. But all variance reports have one thing in common: they use the original budget and the assumptions that were its basis as the means of explaining discrepancies between the set budget and real one. You will want to indicate not only the difference in dollars but also the percentage difference between budget and actual costs or income. Depending on the budget, you may also want to compare the current year's variances against those from last year.

Assumptions

Often, you will find that variances are due to errors in the original budget set. Analysis may show that the assumptions made in creating the budget were inaccurate. Let's assume, for instance, that you estimated a 10 percent increase in cost of office supplies but your supplier actually raised costs by 15 percent. To save money over the long haul, you might want to meet with your supplier to see if you can work out a better deal. If not, then you might want to consider purchasing from another firm.

You might also have underestimated some costs, thereby saving your company some money. These positive variances have to be reported, too.

Analyzing Expenses

Use a step-by-step approach to identify variances in costs. The following questions should direct your thinking:

- Is the price paid for items more or less than budgeted? If more, what are the financial consequences? What can you do to eliminate the variance?
- Are the amounts purchased more or less than budgeted? Where this is the case, you need to consider the cause. Are operations down? This could explain a reduction in expense for items critical to work. Likewise, an increase in activities could mean an increase in items purchased.
- Is there an expenditure timing difference? That is, did you budget to purchase next month but needed to expend this month? Is this likely to happen again? How will this impact the year as a whole?

Studying Income

Income variances against actual results are harder to remedy than expense variances. It is also tougher to identify the reason behind such differences. Again, you need to ask yourself some key questions:

- Is there a price variance—that is, are you selling for more or fewer dollars than expected? If so, what has been the impact on the budget? If you have had to cut prices, what can you do to make up for the deficit? What is the long-term impact?

- Are you selling more or fewer items or providing a service more often or less than anticipated? If reality differs from your original assumptions, how is actual revenue affected?
- Are buyers paying late? If the economy is experiencing a downturn, some purchasers may hold off paying until the very last minute. Delays can impact your income projections—particularly cash flow.

You can see how variances in income projections can help you determine the progress of your staff in a variety of planned efforts and also alert you to the kinds of remedial actions you will need to take to get the revenue stream to the level anticipated. While foresight is admittedly better than hindsight, once you've analyzed variances and determined their cause, you need to take action.

Finger-Pointing

Often, when variances are negative to plan, managers may look for some other part of the organization to blame for the variance. "It's not our fault that costs are higher for raw materials than we projected. We were misled by purchasing," or, "Marketing didn't get ads out in time for the holiday purchases," or, "Customers aren't happy with service support, and it's affecting repeat business." I don't need to tell you how unproductive such an approach is. Look beyond apportioning blame. Dig for real causes and seek actions to address controllable variances.

Sometimes, where the problem demands actions by many managers from different parts of the organization, forming a cross-functional team may be more effective than pointing fingers. If your department is one of those accountable, talk to your manager about the problem and get approval to put together a corporate team to remedy it.

The point is: once unexpected variances have been identified, you and your unit can do a lot about them, either alone or in cooperation with other parts of the organization. Whether a negative variance lies in costs or income, senior management will expect you and your peers to do something about the situation.

If we're talking about controllable costs, and if you can't reduce the dollars spent by seeking a cheaper alternative, you may want to look at the budget as a whole, choosing not to spend money elsewhere. Possible examples include training, travel, or technology. During the recent economic downturn, for instance, many managers held off purchasing new computer equipment, putting money into maintenance until sufficient funds to purchase new hardware and software became available.

Redoing the Budget

If conditions change dramatically after you prepare the original budget, management may ask you to redo your budget entirely. This situation is not unusual. In the recent downturn, many firms redid their budgets several times to reflect changing circumstances.

The revised budget should contain more valid assumptions based on existing conditions. In Chapter 2, in offering advice on budget preparation, I warned against excessive optimistic or pessimism. This is important, if not more so, when revising a budget.

In tough economic times, where revenue is down, you may have to make tough calls about how to spend money. You may have to postpone filling a vacancy or curtail, or even discontinue, a project effort until more money is available. Some costs are better to cut than others. Reducing travel and luncheon expense (T&E), for instance, may make more sense than cutting staff training, because losing a development opportunity could demotivate your team.

If you can, involve your employees in discussions about the new budget. Working together, see if you can identify ways to get work done at less cost. Don't cut costs yet keep targets high, unless there truly is a way to achieve those kinds of results. Shakespeare said, "Balance is all." Balance what is achievable with funds that are available.

Looking to the Future

At the end of each quarter, you may want to look back over your efforts at budgeting and other supervisory activities to get a measure of your performance. How well did you and your unit do? Sometimes, both the plan and budget are synchronous or show only minor discrepancies that are financially insignificant and do not reflect poorly on staff. Where differences are at 10 percent or more, you need to ask yourself what happened, starting with the planning phase. Look again at your goals. Were they too aggressive? In budgeting, were some costs or income more difficult to forecast than others? You might even ask yourself how well you did in monitoring the budget. Looking back, do you now realize that you unconsciously either overestimated or underestimated revenues and costs to make results more achievable and expenditures easier to control?

A former colleague of mine used to budget income at 10 percent less than she anticipated and expenses at 10 percent higher than trends indicated. She made budget, and indeed she looked good the first year or so—until people got wise to her approach.

The point is to learn from your effort at budgeting so that next year's budget will be more accurate.

Cost Control or Cost Reduction

So far, I've been talking about cost control as it relates to your budget. Right after cost control in importance comes cost reduction, particularly in tight economic times. As a manager, you may be asked to find ways to help your company save money.

At the very least, you may be asked to find out where expenses are leaking through the controls and to plug them immediately. For instance, financial records may show that for several months you have relied on overtime to make scheduled deliveries. Senior management might now tell you to plug that leak by developing better schedules.

Sometimes, you may be asked to postpone spending. Deferred maintenance work is the most common of these postponed costs. A machine that is not lubricated today may need a new bearing tomorrow, but the company's cash flow may be such that there isn't enough money to consider the long-term implications of the short-term decision. You may be asked to restrict your spending to necessities. Worse still, you may be told to do without, which could mean scuttling hiring plans or cutting talented employees.

Fortunately, while cost reduction is sometimes euphemistically called "cost improvement," you can avoid the impact that belt-tightening programs might have on department morale by finding opportunities to improve fiscal management. Rather than cut costs, sit down with your staff members to identify how your unit can spend more wisely. Your workers probably know more about the ins and outs of the job than you. You can hold a problem-solving meeting in which you solicit ideas for cutting production corners or for reducing waste. As a group, your unit also may come up with ways to step up the amount of work done, thereby reducing unit costs and helping your organization achieve a competitive advantage with lower prices.

Because cost reduction or even "cost improvement" efforts can raise employee concern about job security, you may want to talk to your employees about costs in a manner that will cut through employee resistance and build support for identifying opportunities for savings. Explain the situation to your employees in terms they can understand. For instance: "Sales have fallen off by 50 percent. Last quarter, we processed 10,000 forms; this quarter our schedule calls for only half as many to be handled." Next, set specific goals. Don't just tell the staff that the unit has to cut costs to the bone.

If you have a specific program in mind, let your employees know the goal you have in mind. Let's assume that one of your staff members, Myrna, has retired, bringing your staff down to five employees. You had planned to replace Myrna. However, now you have decided to reorganize the work to get keyboarding tasks done by your current five employees. "I've decided not to replace Myrna," you can tell your staff. "So we need to come up with methods to get the work done with one less person."

Let your employees know that you need their help—and that means more than cooperation. Tell them you need their thoughts and will welcome their suggestions. The reasons for cutbacks in expenditures should be explained, of course. Unless you can sell cost improvement to your employees, they are likely to be indifferent at best, rebellious at worst.

Tips

- Learn from each year's budget so that next year's budget is more accurate.

- Only spend time on those variances that you can do something about.

- Once you have identified the reason for a variance, take action.

- Focus action plans on the root of a variance problem.

- Keep in mind that some things just happen—not all variances have a logical basis.

Once you come up with some action steps to reduce costs, monitor the results.

If your unit can influence sales, a similar effort should be undertaken to identify new opportunities for revenue, and actions should be taken to implement these ideas.

Just as you have controls to manage your plans and budget, you need to monitor progress on your cost improvement efforts. You should also keep your manager alerted to your unit's efforts to cut costs, to increase revenue, or both.

■ See Also

Hope, Jeremy and Robin Fraser. *Beyond Budgeting: How Managers Can Break Free from the Annual Performance Trap.* Harvard Business School Press, 2003.

Oliver, Lianabel. *The Cost Management Toolbox.* AMACOM, 1999.

4

Hiring, Orienting, and Retaining Employees

While you may want to move quickly to fill a vacancy in your department so workflow isn't disrupted, you should recognize a key fact about recruitment: a job interview rarely lasts longer than an hour, but its consequences may last for years. So you need to be sure that you hire someone who not only fits the job but also is a good fit within your work unit.

How do you begin?

Review the Job Description

The first step is to have a timely job description that reflects the job now and, perhaps, in the near future based on future department plans. If you are filling a new position, you will have to write one. If you are filling a current position, you need to review the current job description. What changes should you make?

To answer that question, you should talk to the current job incumbent. If you have others in a similar job, watch them at work to see if critical aspects of their work aren't included in the requirements on the current document. Talk, too, to people with whom the incumbents interact—including coworkers and customers. The more you know about the job, the clearer you are about the job's key responsibilities, the types of problems the employees need to solve, the interactions they have with others, the most difficult part of the job, and the skills and abilities necessary for success.

There may also be opportunity to redesign your operation, redistributing responsibilities of the vacant job to current staff members, and perhaps creating a different but needed position.

But let's assume that you decide to fill the current position, which is a customer service representative. Besides the job title, the updated document would include:

- *Statement of objectives.* Here's where you would indicate how the position supports your department's mission or the strategy of the whole company. For instance, your unit supports Marketing/Sales by handling customer questions and complaints and making appointments for salespeople to meet with prospective clients.
- *Major responsibilities.* You would list all the tasks, beginning with the most important. The higher the job position, the broader the responsibilities. For instance, your responsibility as the head of customer service would be both to bring in new revenue and ensure current customers are delighted with their products. A service rep, on the other hand, would be responsible for both phone and in-person complaints and sales leads.
- *Prospect criteria.* List here specific education and experience required. For instance, your customer rep might need at least two years' college education, certainly a high school diploma, and maybe two years' experience in customer service. Ideally, you might also want someone who has done customer service work in your industry.
- *Reporting relationships.* To whom will the jobholder report? The employee might report to you as head of the customer service department. The individual would be part of the Customer Service Unit within the Marketing/Sales Division.

Promotion from Within

Before you place an advertisement for the position, you may want to look within your organization for qualified candidates. Actually, your firm may have a policy that demands you post the position for consideration by current employees. Even if you want to hire from outside, you may have no choice but to consider inside candidates.

Let's assume that you get some internal applicants. You will likely have to hold formal interviews with each one, even those whom you know are unsuitable for the job. Some candidates might fit the position, so you need to determine if these individuals would be willing and capable of learning skills they currently lack. How about familiarity with the product line and company? An interested and involved employee can compensate for lack of job experience with corporate and industry knowledge.

If you like one of your internal candidates, you may also want to review that person's past appraisals and even talk to the individual's current manager. Listen between the lines to be sure that you are being told the truth. Some managers may lie to keep a talented worker; others may lie to get rid of a troublemaker.

Advertising Your Opening

What if you don't find anyone within your organization to fill the position? You will need to work with the human resources department to create an ad to place in career Web sites and local newspapers. You may also want to extend the search beyond these traditional sources. If the position is entry level, you may want to advertise in local high school or college job placement offices and job fairs. If you are looking for an experienced professional, you may want to advertise in a professional association group's trade magazine as well as list the position with an executive recruiter.

If you work in a large organization, you won't be the first person to see the resumes that are received in answer to the ad. Most HR managers will prescreen incoming applications, dividing them into two piles: possibles and impossibles. A resume will wind up in the impossible pile if the applicant lacks critical skills, education, or experience; is vastly overqualified or underqualified for the position; or asks for a specific salary or opportunities for advancement that cannot be met.

If your firm doesn't have an HR professional to review incoming resumes, the task of reviewing replies may be yours. It can be time consuming, depending on the number of replies.

However you get your pile of possible applicants, read carefully both their covering letters and resumes. Be alert to four key elements: work history, education, technical competence, and motivation. Look, too, for gaps and inconsistencies in the resumes. Breaks in chronology and inconsistencies in the facts provided may be due to simple error, or they could be clues to a candidate's attempt to falsify or hide information. Check the resume to see if any periods of time are unaccounted for. Do periods of employment overlap with periods in education? Be prepared to give candidates the benefit of the doubt, but compile a list of questions to help clarify any inconsistencies you discover.

As you review the resumes, consider not only how well the candidates will fit the job but also how well they will fit your organization. Even if your staff members work independently of each other, they still are part of a group.

As you look through your stack, you may want to cull it by making some phone calls to the applicants. Because resumes generally don't tell the whole story for most candidates, it is not a bad idea to further prescreen all potential interviewees by asking a few questions over the phone.

Before you pick up the phone, prepare questions that address areas that are not clearly enough laid out in the resume. List your questions with room to write the responses. For instance, the resume says, "Improved productivity by 15 percent." Ask, "How did you do this?" Then tell the applicant a little about the job (not too much, just enough to expand on the ad). If you are both interested in having an interview, then you can invite the applicant to come in.

Whatever your decision, you need not mention it on the phone. Thank individuals for their time and promise to get back to them.

Meeting with Candidates

Let's assume that you wind up with five applicants who look good on paper. Prepare for interviews with each candidate by reviewing the resume. Write down the questions that you'll need to ask to flesh out your understanding of the candidate's background. Be prepared to greet the applicant at the reception area and even to take the interviewee on a tour of the work space before sitting down in your office. You want to make the individual feel at ease.

For the meetings, you should find a quiet place where you won't be interrupted. The location can have a material effect on the proceedings. Rather than hold the interviews in your office, you might want to meet in a conference room with comfortable seats and softer lighting.

Once you sit down, you might open the conversation with a noncontroversial question such as, "Did you have trouble finding our building?" If the candidate was referred by a friend or a business associate, you might want to talk a bit about that person. The resume or application may also suggest a means of breaking the ice. For instance, "I notice you went to New York University? Did you ever meet Professor Austin, in charge of communications?" or, "I see you live in the 50s in New York City. Have you ever eaten at Olympia Kitchen?"

Referring to past successes noted in the resume, either in previous jobs or outside the work field, also helps set the candidate at ease.

The one thing you shouldn't do is to ask the applicant, "So, why do you think I should give this job to you?" You would put the applicant on the defensive. Thereafter, to find out more about the candidate, you would have to drill like a dentist, a procedure pleasant for neither you nor your prospect.

Interviewing Applicants

What questions should you ask? To begin with, you might ask candidates about what they consider their most significant accomplishment. You might follow up this question to determine how significant the accomplishment was. Do you need someone with lots of energy? Ask whether handling multiple priorities would represent a problem. Ask about instances in which the applicant had to address tight deadlines. If the job requires making critical decisions, ask candidates about the most important decisions they have made and how they turned out. If you want to learn about their work values, you might try this question: "If you could start all over, what would you do?" If the person has visions of winning the lottery and going into business with the winning funds, you might want to look elsewhere for that steady, reliable employee you need.

Find out about past companies in which the candidates worked. What did they like about these firms? What didn't they like? Don't forget to ask about past supervisors, either. Ask the applicant, "Of all the managers you worked for, describe the supervisory methods of the one you enjoyed working for most." Follow up this question with, "You told me about the managers you best liked to work for. Who were the worst?" If the applicant has had only one former supervisor, ask for a description of that manager's methods and how the candidate felt about them. Answers to these questions will tell you how the candidate's style of working fits with your own.

Of course, your questions should also identify candidates' skills, abilities, knowledge, and attitudes, all of which are critical to their success on the job. However, experience has shown that results-oriented questions are most indicative of an individual's subsequent behavior in a job. What did they accomplish? How did they go about it? Based on the discussion with you, where would they focus their attention at first?

Ask questions about areas of past jobs that were likely to have caused problems. Find out how the individual handled them. For example:

- What aspects of your previous jobs gave you the most trouble?
- What are some disappointments you had in your last job?

- In what areas did you need help or guidance from your supervisor?
- For what things have your managers complimented you? Criticized you?
- What did you like most about your past jobs? How about the things you liked least?

If you feel that an applicant is holding something back in answer to a question, don't ask further questions. Rather, be quiet. It is difficult for most people to tolerate silence. If you don't respond immediately, the candidate may keep talking. After listening to the applicant's response to the question, wait about five seconds before asking the next question. You will be surprised at how often an applicant fills in the silence with something—positive or negative.

You and the Law

As you develop your list of questions to ask candidates, keep in mind that all questions must be strictly job related. Avoid questioning applicants about such subjects as race, color, ethnic background, family history, or membership in ethnic or other organizations; marital status, children, or childcare arrangements; spouse's occupation; church membership or religious beliefs and practices; sexual orientation or preferences; medical history; and age. Also, you cannot ask questions of applicants of one gender that you don't ask applicants of the other—for instance, you cannot ask only your female candidates if they can type.

Reasonable Accommodation

Let's assume that one of your candidates is disabled. What does this mean in terms of your task to hire the best qualified person for the job? The answer is: nothing. According to the Americans with Disabilities Act, you can't ask, "Are you disabled?" or, "Will you need any sort of accommodation or special equipment to perform the job duties?" On the other hand, you can ask, "Can you perform the essential functions of this job with or without accommodation?" A qualified individual with a disability is one who, with or without reasonable accommodation, has the skills, experience, education, and other requirements of the job and can perform the *essential functions of the job* without endangering his health and safety or that of others.

Your firm can make numerous reasonable accommodations to assist qualified individuals with disabilities to perform the position's essential functions. For instance, it might be possible to make the workplace more accessible by installing a ramp or automatic doors. The job might be restructured so a candidate does not have to walk. If the employee is receiving physical therapy, the position might be offered on a modified work schedule so the employee can continue therapy during the workweek.

Concerns about hiring a person with a disability often center on the person's ability to perform the job's tasks and meet attendance demands. While discussing this issue with someone disabled may seem awkward, the situation can be made manageable if you develop and use a standard set of questions to identify whether or not each applicant can perform the essential job functions. For instance, if a job requires lifting heavy objects, the list of questions might include, "In this job, you will need to lift 50-pound bags of concrete. Can you meet this requirement?" The interviewer simply reads each job function and asks the applicant if he or she can perform the function with or without accommodation. If the candidate indicates the need for an accommodation, the interviewer writes down a detailed description.

As you can see from the above, the ADA guidelines allow employers to ask how an individual will perform essential job functions. However, under the ADA, the employer is never allowed to ask an applicant about the disability itself. The ADA strictly prohibits inquiries about an applicant's disability during preemployment to prevent individuals from being screened out before you determine if they can do the work.

Other issues that should not be addressed: the need for special leave because of the disability; past worker compensation claims; past, present, or future treatment by a medical doctor; use of prescription drugs; treatment for alcohol or drug abuse; and current state of mental or physical heath.

Employment at Will

It is also important to avoid making statements during the interview process that could be alleged to create a contract of employment. When describing the job, don't use terms like *permanent, career job opportunity,* or *long term.* Don't promise job security, either. If the employee subsequently is laid off due to personnel cutbacks, a breach of contract could be charged, claiming that termination is illegal unless you can prove the individual couldn't do a "good job."

Courts have held that such promises made during interviews create contracts of employment.

Keeping Track

A lot of information will come from the interviews, and you may forget who said what. So keep a record of what you learned from the applicants. For instance, you may discover that Joe knows COBOL, speaks Spanish, and has supervised 6 people; whereas Lynn has worked 3 years with COBOL, knows conversational Spanish, and has supervised 12 people.

Intangibles are more difficult to note. Stay away from vague comments. List specifics. Instead of observing that Joe is creative, list examples of his creativity in previous jobs. If appearance is a job-related factor, don't write *sloppy* or *rumpled.* Those comments are subjective. Note, instead, "clothes unpressed, dog hairs, shoes not shined."

Personality factors may also be important to the final decision. Once again, avoid subjective comments. "Applicant appears to lack self-confidence," is an opinion, but the statement, "Applicant looked down at the floor during the entire interview and was hesitant in answering questions," is a fact.

Wait until after an interview to record the information you discovered about the candidate. Give yourself 10 to 15 minutes between interviews to summarize your impressions.

Making Your Choice

Let's assume that you interviewed six candidates: Tony, Sara, Laura, Harry, Phil, and Dennis. Of the six, you have chosen Sara as your new customer service rep. She is currently unemployed, and she can come to work as soon as you can put through the paperwork—next Monday.

Before you offer her the job, you may want to do a reference check. Work history and education are perhaps the easiest qualifications to verify. Deciding that candidates wouldn't lie about something that could easily be checked, many managers don't bother checking references, and consequently, false claims on resumes go undetected.

Do check references, including such basics as education and job experience. Bill, a good friend, hired a young editor who claimed to have a degree from Harvard. Maybe the job candidate was at Harvard, but it was as a visitor to the campus—he had never attended the school. His lie was discovered two months later when further discrepancies caused the HR department to investigate his background extensively. He had made up some of his personal references, his

Harvard degree, the death of a fiancée so he could take a week off immediately upon being hired, and the name of the hospital where he supposedly stayed after being mugged.

Needless to say, he was terminated as soon as the organization uncovered his trail of lies.

Unlike my friend Bill's hire, the candidate you hire—Sara—passes the reference check, and, as planned, she is scheduled to come to work on Monday. What should you do next?

Monday Morning

You know that Sara will spend about an hour with your HR manager reviewing your firm's compensation and benefits programs. About 10:00 AM, she enters your office. You could take Sara to her work desk and leave her there with a stack of brochures about the company and its products. But that wouldn't be fair to Sara—she needs to know more about her job, how it fits into the work done by your unit, and how the unit in turn contributes to the corporation's mission. Yes, you probably covered a lot of this during the interview, but you should go over the information to ensure that she has a clear idea about her job, the department's values and mission, and the corporation's strategic goals.

You also should have some assignments to acclimate Sara to her new job. For instance, you might want to leave Sara with customer correspondence to answer, or you might sit her at the customer service desk. Because she isn't ready to answer many questions, you might have one of your other customer reps, Joyce, stay with her to help as the need arises. Should she have any questions, she can ask Joyce or you about the work.

At the end of the day, you should visit with Sara to see how things went. Does she need more help? Did Joyce help her? Because Joyce has a great track record with your department, knows the job backward and forward, and is patient with new workers, she was your choice to be Sara's buddy for the first few weeks on the job—and you discover that you chose well.

You may want to talk to Sara about the standards by which her performance will be measured. Rather than talk about your expectations over the next year, break the time frame into manageable units—first a few days, then a few weeks, then months, and so forth. Establish periodic reviews to track progress and do them as scheduled. Keep performance problems from developing by being alert to any training needs or confusion about the work to be done. If your interview with Sara identified some development areas, now is the time to schedule such training before the lack impedes her job performance.

Don't limit the time you spend with your new hire to the first day. Praise, encouragement, two-way communication, and feedback will help keep the new hire committed.

Turnover

Let's assume that Sara works out well in her new job. On the other hand, another of your workers decides he can do better elsewhere and finds a job with a competitor. You've talked with the departing employee to see if he would reconsider, but he explained that he saw more opportunity for advancement with the other firm. There is nothing you can do about the situation, and fortunately such departures have been rare in your department.

Generally, companies monitor department turnover. As you think about it, you realize that one or two managers in your firm have high turnover rates. The company is aware of this. Turnover—the number of separations from the department during a given time period—is monitored because finding replacements costs dollars, time, and productivity.

Employee turnover is generally considered to be the best single measure of morale: good morale equals low turnover; poor morale equals high turnover. This isn't to say that companies want no turnover in employees. When employees leave a company, they are replaced with others who bring new knowledge, practice, experience, and skills into the organization. Employees with large salaries may be replaceable with less expensive but equally qualified newcomers. Some positions may be eliminated, merged, or automated.

Through turnover, too, an organization can rid itself of marginal performers or people who are difficult to work with.

On the other hand, recruiting, selecting, and training new employees can be expensive. Exit interviews, severance benefits, and outplacement services also cost. Until someone is hired, temporary help may be needed. Then there is the cost of lost productivity while a position remains vacant.

No one can ignore the disruption on workflow from the loss of a key employee. Remaining employees have to take on more work. Some projects may have to be delayed. If the person who leaves is well liked, department morale may be affected. Other employees may decide to leave, either to join a former colleague at the new employer or to find a comparable position elsewhere.

So some turnover is acceptable, but you don't want it to get out of control.

The question, "How do I reduce turnover?" raises a more basic question, "What makes most employees leave their jobs?" Many managers will tell you that employees leave to make more money elsewhere, but the truth is, money is rarely the only motivator. It may not even be the primary motivator in most cases. Evidence has shown a high correlation between employee job satisfaction and the management style of their immediate supervisor. Employees want to feel that their manager won't have favorites; will promote open, honest communication; will provide opportunities for them to increase their employability; and will offer opportunities to share their ideas. They also want work that is fun, interesting, and exciting.

Employee Retention

As a manager, you can influence personally the turnover within your organization by doing, or not doing, the following:

- *Carefully assess the job or applicant.* All too often, we idealize a job, hoping to lure a potential candidate on board. Similarly, we frequently aim for credentials that sound impressive but have little to do with what the employee really needs for the job. In short, people are hired on false pretenses and offered quick advancement and varied assignments, even when this will not be the case. A job candidate who discovers the truth may remain for a while but, in time, may begin to search for another job.
- *Provide training.* We can all stand to learn. But for the new employee, or any employee with a change in responsibilities, training is critical. If you don't offer this training or training that offers increased employability, then you're setting up your employees for frustration and failure.
- *Clarify goals.* Too often, employees are overwhelmed by conflicting demands or infuriated by requirements that appear only when it's too late to incorporate them into their work. People have to know their responsibilities and the priorities that affect them. Have you communicated with your employees? Stop and ask what they think the priorities are—you may be surprised. If they aren't clear, take the time to communicate so that there's no confusion.
- *Offer clear, consistent instructions.* Don't assume employees will do the job according to your expectations. Make sure you have told them the parameters to which they must adhere.

- *Provide feedback.* Employees want to know when they're doing well and want to receive helpful redirection when they're not. You are the major source of that feedback.

■ You and the Law

The five federal EEO statutes that have had the greatest impact on hiring practices are:

- *Title VII of the Civil Rights Act (1964).* It protects individuals against employment discrimination on the basis of race and color, national origin, gender, or religion. It was the first federal statute to protect against discrimination in employment, and it continues to have significant impact on hiring practices today, prohibiting both intentional discrimination and the use of seemingly neutral hiring practices that disproportionately exclude minorities and that are not job related.

- *The Age Discrimination in Employment Act (1967).* It prohibits discrimination in employment for individuals age 40 and over. While the statute does not specifically prohibit employers from asking an applicant's age or date of birth, this type of inquiry may indicate a possible intent to discriminate and would be closely scrutinized for its relevance to the job.

- *The Immigration Reform and Control Act (1990).* It prohibits discrimination based on national origin but also requires employers to obtain verification of an applicant's right to work in the United States. Note that U.S. citizenship is not required in most cases. If you impose citizenship requirements or give preference to U.S. citizens in hiring or employment opportunities, you may be in violation of IRCA unless a particular job has a legal requirement.

- *The Americans with Disabilities Act (1990).* This act prohibits discrimination against a qualified individual with a disability, if the individual can perform the essential functions of the job with or without reasonable accommodation. The ADA covers both physical and mental impairments.

- *The Civil Rights Act (1991).* It allows an applicant to seek compensatory and punitive damages for willful discrimination—for discrimination based on gender, religion, and disability. It also provides for a jury trial for the plaintiff. This act does not extend protection to any characteristics not already covered under Title VII, but it does create steeper consequences—via a jury trial—for employers who violate the law.

◼ Tips

- Be sure to avoid all interruptions during interviews.

- During interviews, spend 75 percent of the time listening, 25 percent of the time talking. You have two ears and one mouth—listen twice as much as you talk.

- Ask open-ended questions—that is, those that require more than a simple yes or no answer.

- Assume that resumes involve some creative writing. Probe for the facts. Invite employees to meet with final candidates to get their perspective on applicants if you feel such a process will encourage teamwork once the final choice comes on board.

◼ See Also

Arthur, Diane. *Recruiting, Interviewing, Selecting & Orienting New Employees* (3rd Edition). AMACOM, 1998.

Falcone, Paul. *The Hiring and Firing Question and Answer Book.* AMACOM, 2001.

Levin, Robert and Joseph Rosse. *Talent Flow: A Strategic Approach to Keeping Good Employees, Helping Them Grow, and Letting Them Go.* Jossey-Bass, 2001.

Mercer, Michael W. *Hire the Best . . . and Avoid the Rest.* AMACOM, 1993.

Outlaw, Wayne. *Smart Staffing.* Dearborn Trade, 1998.

5

From Delegating to Empowering

"If you want something done right, do it yourself." Many first-time managers believe that, and to a large extent, it is true. However, no one can do everything. Besides, delegating and empowering employees has positive benefits. Both build employee abilities, experience, and confidence.

Yes, delegation and empowerment take time in preparation and follow-through, but the costs of avoiding it are high. A manager who does neither or does them poorly will seem disorganized and will spend a lot of time on catching up on work. If you try to do everything yourself, you will wind up exhausted, while your staff will have too much free time. Work will be bottlenecked, maybe deadlines will be missed, and work quality will be poor.

Why do managers resist delegating work to their employees or empowering their workers? Resistance may be greater to empowerment than to delegation, because empowerment entails more than assigning a task—it involves giving authority over the task. But in both instances, a major reason for opposition is managers' concern that delegation and empowerment mean they are abdicating responsibility. Not so. Consider the definitions of both words.

Delegation involves giving an employee the responsibility for part of your job and the authority to carry it out, while retaining control and accountability. *Empowerment* involves not only giving responsibility and accountability for a task but also the responsibility and authority to make decisions tied to the assignment while, again, retaining control and accountability. *Retaining control and accountability* is the critical phrase in both definitions. It means that you avoid two managerial mistakes. The first is to dump a task, walking away and for-getting about it. The second is to appear to delegate or empower but stay so close to the employee that you are practically hovering over the shoulder. One of your goals in either delegation or empowerment is to set up a means by which you can monitor what is happening without stifling initiative.

Other concerns managers have about delegation and empowerment are:

- *Lack of trust.* Managers who don't delegate or empower worry that their employees won't be able to do the job right. Better that they do it them-selves and ensure that the work is done correctly, they think. But if you give the right instructions, you needn't worry that the work won't meet your expectations.
- *Loss of control.* Another reason managers don't delegate or empower is that they fear that the employees to whom they give the work won't do it the same way they would. But no one says that there is only one way to get something done. Often, employees find more effective or efficient ways to do work previously done by their manager.
- *Fear of loss of position.* Some managers who refuse to delegate or em-power admit to a worry that an employee may show them up and take their job. They fear that the employee will demonstrate more skill at doing the work and making decisions tied to the chore than the manager—and the manager doesn't want that to happen. But managers who don't dele-gate or empower are showing their higher-ups that they can't effectively manage the people who report to them. After all, management is getting work done through others—which is what delegation and empowerment are all about.

Admittedly, problems can arise when we delegate or empower. You can ex-pect mistakes to happen. Our responsibility, through training and coaching, is to minimize them. We can also minimize troubles if we do both right. That's why I use the term *thoughtful* when referring to both practices.

Let me start by describing how to avoid problems when delegating tasks.

Delegation—Doing It Right

When you think about how delegating will save you time—how it will free you to focus on your many other tasks—you may be less leery about it. To ensure that things go smoothly, you should:

- *Set standards.* By making your expectations clear to your employees—the quality of the work, the time frame for its completion, and the like—you will increase the chances that the finished work will be satisfactory.
- *Train your employees to handle the assignment.* Spend time up front preparing your employees to handle the task well. Because delegated work is generally task oriented, the training is usually skill based.
- *Build employee confidence.* Employees with previous experience under managers who dislike delegating often are unwilling to take on other assignments. After all, who would want to have someone hovering over the shoulder and criticizing every move made? Because some employees have been burned, you will have to demonstrate that you will give them a fair chance to show what they are capable of doing.

Praise them for previous work and point up their knowledge and skills. Your staff members need to know that you chose them to do a task because of their competence—and, most importantly, because you trust them to do the job well.

Six Questions

Now, to get down to the actual delegation, you need to consider six questions: who, what, when, where, why, and how.

Who

Choosing the right person for a task requires careful assessment of experience and abilities. Different tasks require different skills. For example, you may need someone who is good at organizing schedules and budgets, or who is an enthusiastic and cooperative team player, or who can work well under tight deadlines, or who can take initiative. Consider the qualities of all your staff members and think about which individuals have the right skills, abilities, knowledge, and attitude to take on the work.

Not all of your employees will be able to take on the added work. They may lack the skills or knowledge about the work that would make it possible to do the job well. While delegation can be used to train and develop talented employees' range and depth of skills, you need to be sure that you have the time to support the delegates until they can operate independently. Alternatively, to prepare for the next opportunity for delegation, you may want to offer training or coaching in areas where the individual has deficiencies (see Chapter 6).

What if you have someone capable and willing but who is too busy to do more? Reshuffle tasks among staff members, freeing the potential delegate to take on the task by giving some of the employee's previous work to coworkers without full workloads.

Not all staff will agree to take on the added work. Some will say no because of a perceived lack of autonomy. Others will say no because they doubt their ability to do the work well. In both of these instances, you need to give honest reassurances. To reassure the former, address the employee more as partner than as subordinate, presenting the task as an opportunity to develop skills and experience. In the latter case, discuss the support, both formal and informal, that the individual can call on.

What if an employee refuses to take on the work and disagrees that the work fits within his or her job description? The employee offers to do the work, but only if you come up with a generous raise or an offer of a promotion. You might want to say yes, but don't. At best, offer to mention the additional work in the employee's performance assessment. If the employee isn't satisfied, then the answer is the same: the year-end appraisal will reflect the person's response.

What if the person still says no? Cut your losses and look for someone else.

What

What you decide to delegate to your employees can have a great deal of range. Typically, it is safe to delegate:

- *Paperwork.* Many administrative duties can be delegated to employees. This not only saves you time but also gives an employee a better understanding of how the department runs.
- *Routine.* Tasks done on a regular basis can be shared or rotated among your employees, again giving them an opportunity to understand workflow better.
- *Technical issues.* Delegating responsibility for technical matters is a good way to recognize an employee's aptitudes.
- *Tasks that offer learning opportunities.* Any assignment that provides your employees with the chance to learn new things, to acquire skills, or to exercise their creativity is a desirable assignment to delegate.

What shouldn't you delegate to your employees?

- *Personnel matters.* Hiring, firing, mediating team conflicts, counseling, handling grievances, and discussing salary issues are all managerial responsibilities that should never be delegated to staff.

- *Confidential matters.* Anything that requires secrecy should not be delegated. Even secretarial and clerical tasks involving issues that cannot be shared—for instance, performance assessments—should be done by you.
- *Crises.* In a crisis situation, you won't have time to explain what needs to be done. You are the only one capable of taking immediate action. Your level of authority may also be needed to resolve the situation.
- *Tasks assigned to you.* Anything that your own manager asks you to handle yourself should not be delegated to an employee, no matter how capable.

When

Knowing when to delegate added responsibility is just as important as knowing what and to whom to delegate.

If you want to use the new assignment as a reward for improved or outstanding work, make the assignment at the same time that you are praising the employee. If the employee is still under a lot of work pressure at that time, you can offer congratulations on earning the new assignment but assure the worker that the new task will not have to be started until the current project is completed or much further along.

Where

Where is closely related to when in thoughtful delegation.

For instance, you might announce that you are assigning one of your employees a high-visibility task. The announcement recognizes past work. Also, making the new responsibility public will ensure that the employee has the support of coworkers and other managers in getting the work done.

In other cases, a private meeting is best suited for delegating a new assignment or task to an employee. Perhaps you are assigning the employee the work on a trial basis, or that employee is unsure about assuming the new responsibility. Use your judgment with each situation.

Why

Besides the *whys* for delegation and empowerment mentioned above, here's another reason for delegation: delegation will set a positive tone in your team. Employees know that you will be looking for assignments to give them that will allow them to develop their skills and help them increase their employability. Reporting to you, your employees will know that they will not stagnate in repetitive jobs, because you periodically give them opportunities to take on new challenges.

How

The way in which you delegate can have as much influence on whether the employee succeeds or fails as the employee's own ability. Successful delegation requires the following five steps with each assignment to every employee:

1. *Give complete instructions.* Do not assume that the employee already has the information to do the work. The employee must understand what results are expected, what the limits of authority are, why he or she was selected for the assignment, where and when the work is to be done, who is involved in the task, and any methods that are mandatory in completing the task.

2. *Grant sufficient authority.* Make certain that your employee has the necessary clearance to obtain and use needed materials or equipment. Inform others that the employee is in charge of the job and has the authority to make decisions. Each time a job is delegated, the amount of authority your delegate has should be clearly identified.

3. *Maintain communications.* Many managers mistakenly believe that they no longer need to be involved with a project once they have delegated authority or given an employee an assignment. They make the error of giving an employee a sink or swim test, rather than maintaining contact with the employee and being accessible to make sure no crises develop. Your coaching sessions are an ideal occasion to review progress on assignments, discuss problems, and offer criticism, which is Step #4.

4. *Make constructive criticism.* Delegation is a learning experience for your employee, so mistakes will be made. When that happens, focus on the problem, not the person. Don't say, "I can't believe what you did!" Say instead, "Let's look at what happened." Employee mistakes should not be seen as reason for chastising but as a further opportunity for learning. Keep in mind that learning is a lifelong experience not only for you but also for your employees.

   Certainly, don't take back an assignment once it is given. You may have to be involved more than you expected, but in the end, the employee should have a valuable learning experience. You may then want to reevaluate your own methods for choosing that individual for that particular assignment. However, keep in mind that selecting the right person is your problem, not your employee's.

5. *Reward success.* When one of your employees successfully completes an assignment, don't forget to say thanks for a job well done and to congratulate the employee on a significant accomplishment. Make a concerted effort to praise the employee—don't try to slip the compliment into another conversation: "By the way, that was a good job on the Jones deal."

Reverse the Reverse Delegation

I mentioned that you shouldn't take back a delegated assignment when it becomes evident that your employee is experiencing problems. Reverse delegation occurs when an employee returns the task to the manager who assigned it. The buck passing often goes unnoticed by managers, because it often happens very informally. For instance, an employee may say, "Boy, have I had a rough time today," which prompts the manager to ask, "What kind of help do you need?" or to offer, "Tell me about it." Either way, the manager is hooked. Before he or she knows it, the manager has resumed responsibility for the task. Told the nature of the problem, the manager might say, "Let me think about it, and I'll get back to you," or, "I can see your problem. Let me see what I can do about it." The employee may want to give up the task, or the manager may like to feel needed. Whatever the reason, the end result is the same: the manager is now stuck with the "delegated" task.

If you, over time, delegate work but then see yourself stuck with it, you may want to reverse the reverse delegation. The secret is to stop the process right at the start. Don't take on the problem. Rather, ask the employee to think further about the situation and come back with some potential solutions. You might even add, "Thank you for making me aware of the problem." You leave the responsibility for the task with the employee.

True Empowerment

Empowerment is very similar to delegation and, consequently, demands the same management approach. Empowered employees suffer, however, when their managers haven't prepared them to make wise decisions. A manager says, "I'd like to empower you to do so and so," then walks away. The employee makes decisions, but too often they are the wrong ones. Upon failure, the manager comes down on the employee.

Empowering without preparation—that is, removing the safety net (yourself) without first preparing your employees—is like letting a young child cross the street alone without first explaining the difference between red and green lights. Employees are very likely to get into trouble if they don't know what they should and shouldn't do. They'll fall flat on their faces, which will discourage them from trying again—and discourage you from letting them try again, despite all the benefits you could gain if you provided a little grounding in the needed skills.

Making Empowerment Work

If you want to empower your employees—truly empower them—you need to do the following:

- *Invest in your employees' knowledge, skills, and ability.* Failure to train is shortsighted, whether your goal is to delegate or empower. When you delegate, you want to be sure that the employee is capable of handling the responsibility. In the case of empowerment, training can not only enable your employees to handle the work but also contribute to increased self-esteem, which will make employees more comfortable with greater responsibility.

    Training should involve not only the skills, abilities, and knowledge your empowered employee will need but also corporate values and business finance. The training in financial management shouldn't be so complex that only an economist could understand it. I know of one company that built its financial management training around the idea of a children's lemonade stand, a model easily understood by the plant's managers. The company found a way to put complex ideas into simple words and graphs and pie charts, and you can do the same for your work unit.
- *Believe in your employees' ability to be successful.* You have to trust your employees to do a job well when you empower, just as when you delegate. Your workers will know that you have faith in them to make the right decisions.
- *Be clear about your expectations.* Your employees need insights into your goals, beyond just task completion. Be sure they know about the importance you place on quality or customer service or market share. Your priorities should influence their decisions.

- *Provide a safety net.* Set up management controls to ensure that you hear about problems before they grow beyond control. There are limits to what empowered employees can do, and they need to know them. One example might be modifying work procedures without getting approval from those responsible for initially setting them.
- *Identify those who can and those who can't be empowered.* Those with the capability to be empowered should be asked if they have seen problems that they would like to address or decisions they would like to handle. Not only does this query demonstrate your desire to empower your employees, it demonstrates your interest in your staff's growth and development, something that can't help but motivate your employees. Those unable to handle empowerment may still handle delegation.
- *Share information.* Empowered employees need to know the situation from a micro and macro perspective. "They don't really care about the organization's goals or objectives," you say. If you're right, then the blame rests with you. A caring attitude is something you as a manager need to create in your employees.
- *Put peer pressure to work.* Recognition helps ensure that delegated work gets done. It also ensures that employees fully utilize the opportunity that comes with empowerment. Let employees' peers know when their co-workers have broken sales records, identified new product offerings, or found ways to reduce accident levels. Demonstrate the respect they have earned, so that their peers will want the same opportunity.

As a new manager, you may have to overcome bad experiences your employees may have had with managers who talked about empowering their staff

---

▪ Tips

- Use delegation and empowerment to train your staff members.

- Pick delegates who are confident enough to admit they are encountering problems.

- Make sure that those empowered to oversee tasks are not limited by lack of others' support, both within and outside your unit.

members but did nothing more than heap more work upon them. When you use the term empowerment, you have to mean it. You have to demonstrate to your workers by your actions that empowerment isn't just the latest management buzzword. Otherwise, you will wind up with disappointed, demoralized employees.

Expect delegates to achieve performance at least equal to your own. Otherwise, coaching is in order.

■ Yes or No

How many of these statements reflect your thinking?

- I use my failures to learn valuable lessons for future delegating and empowering.

- I make opportunities to recognize employees who have taken on delegated or empowered responsibilities.

- I ensure that I am accessible to provide feedback to employees with delegated and empowered responsibilities.

- I keep an up-to-date log of which tasks I have delegated and which ones I have empowered, and to whom.

- I encourage delegates and empowered employees to use their initiative when confronted with problems.

- I ensure that my employees understand the extent of their accountability from delegation and empowerment.

- I monitor progress but don't constantly intervene.

- I see that staff members are trained in the skills, abilities, or knowledge associated with tasks delegated or empowered.

- I keep notes of errors made and lessons learned for future reference.

- I recognize the effort that my employees put into completion of a delegated or empowered task and reward them for it.

■ **Did You Know?**

Delegation and empowerment are done more freely in the United States than in Japan, where failure is considered shameful. Germany is similar to Japan. Actually, in most highly structured cultures, managers retain more control of tasks, delegating and empowering less.

■ **See Also**

Bellman, Geoffry M. *Getting Things Done When You Are Not in Charge.* Simon & Schuster, 1992.

Benfari, Robert C. *Understanding and Changing Your Management Style.* Jossey-Bass, 1999.

Blanchard, Ken and John C. Carls and Alan Randolph. *The 3 Keys to Empowerment: Release the Power within People for Astonishing Results.* Berrett-Koehler Publications, 1999.

Cox, Jeff and William C. Byham. *Zapp! The Lightning of Empowerment: How to Improve Productivity, Quality, and Employee Satisfaction.* Fawcett Books, 1998.

Imundo, Louis V. *Effective Supervisor's Handbook.* AMACOM, 1996.

Straub, Joseph T. *The Agile Manager's Guide to Motivating People.* Velocity Press, 1997.

6

Coaching and Counseling Employees

Ideally, you want employees who do their jobs well and maybe a little more and who can adapt as your organization shifts directions. You don't want individuals who do less than they are expected to do, but you may be willing to give them the chance to improve. On the other hand, if you see no sign of improvement after a short period, you want to be able to fire them without worrying about any legal ramifications.

We're talking about two of your responsibilities toward your employees and your organization: coaching and counseling. Part of your responsibilities in performance management, they are offshoots of your performance appraisal skills and abilities.

Understanding Your Coaching Role

Coaching, in the context of performance management, means bringing the right people onto your staff and developing them continually so that they do their jobs well all the time. Think in terms of baseball, football, or volleyball coaches. They recruit the right people, assess training and development needs, and work to improve the skills of all. You're a coach in just the same way.

As a coach, for instance, one of your jobs is to hire top talent. Then, if at any point your employees lack the skills they need to do their jobs well, your job is to train them. Analyzing training needs is, in fact, an ongoing responsibility, because skill needs change as the demands of the workplace change.

Besides making sure your employees have the skills they need, as coach you need to ensure they understand your organization's values and mission. Otherwise, your employees may create problems for themselves or for you.

This belief is critical to coaching: employees like to do a good job, and they want to get positive feedback and encouragement. Sitting down with a worker to discuss recent efforts doesn't have to be demoralizing. If done tactfully, the conversation can move individuals to a point where they can do a good job and where, consequently, they'll get the positive feedback and encouragement they want.

To make this happen, you have to tell employees exactly what you want and why. Present the big picture and their role in it. For example: "I get calls from customers when they don't hear from us about the status of their orders. Keeping them abreast of the status of their orders is a promise we make to our customers. Your responsibility is to process this information and send e-mail updates to them. Because I got a few calls this morning, I am assuming that you haven't sent out all the letters yet. Is that so?"

If an employee says yes, then you might explore the reasons for delays. More important, together with the employee, you would come up with a plan to address any obstacles in completing the work on schedule. In the meantime, you might suggest, "Make print copies of the information. If a customer calls, I'll be able to answer any questions. Given our plan, I should be able to assure the client that in the future a call won't be necessary."

If the employee needs to learn a new skill, you might want to both tell and show the person what to do. As the employee is learning, you should be there as personal cheerleader—assuming that you believe the individual can handle the job. If you have some doubts, go back and offer further training. Effective coaches don't leave their employees to sink or swim. They recognize that there is a learning curve, and they make a point to help employees who are on it. Interestingly, as a coach, you need to accept that your employees will make mistakes and—most important—that they can learn much through the process of getting it wrong and then finding out how to put it right. Your role is to be there and congratulate them when they get it right.

Coaching Like a Pro

Coaching is something you begin from the first day an employee arrives on the job, when you discuss the individual's responsibilities, your expectations, the unit's role in the bigger corporate picture, and the company's mission and strategy. Thereafter, schedule to meet with the employee one-on-one at least once a month. See the sample coaching worksheet in Figure 6.1.

Many managers argue that they don't have time to coach each and every one of their employees on a regular basis. But ask yourself, "What will it cost in time or money if my employees don't have a clear view of operating priorities or plans, or lack critical skills, or encounter problems that impede progress?" The cost in time and money will be considerably more than the time you'd spend in coaching. In other words, coaching is preventative maintenance.

FIGURE 6.1
Sample Coaching Worksheet

Employee Name: _____

Position: _____

Date: _____

1. What does the employee think he or she did well?

   _____

   _____

2. What could the employee have done better? Were expectations clear?

   _____

   _____

   _____

3. Are there obstacles to the employee doing his or her work? If so, what did you agree to for overcoming these obstacles?

   _____

   _____

   _____

4. Are there skill gaps? What training is needed? What additional training does the employee want?

   _____

   _____

   _____

While coaching mostly involves one-on-one meetings, bear in mind that it can also take the form of group sessions. The intent of these meetings is the same as one-on-one sessions—to prepare employees to do their jobs better. Group sessions can thus provide information on action plans, focus on skill-building activities, or remedy small group performance difficulties before they grow beyond control.

How can you go about coaching your employees?

Question employees about work in progress. Give feedback. There is no such thing as too much feedback about job performance. Praise for a job well done reinforces that behavior and increases the likelihood of its continuation. Suggestions for improvement tell employees you think they are capable of doing better.

Should you see any problems, ask open-ended questions. "What's keeping you from doing an even better job than you are now?" Or, "Is there anything we need to talk about?" And, most important, "How can I help you?"

Once you have developed the knack of asking such questions in a non-threatening way, you should be able to uncover problems that may not otherwise come to light. You might identify a skill deficiency. Sometimes, too, you may discover more about an employee's interests and aspirations. This may suggest ways to redesign the job and thereby stimulate above-standard performance.

Besides being a skilled listener (see Chapter 10), you should be alert to what's happening on the plant, service, or office floor. Practice management by walking around, and then discuss what you observed with the employee. Jot down casual comments or follow-up thoughts you can discuss during one-on-one meetings you hold with staff members each month.

Your Training Responsibilities

No new hire comes fully qualified to take on the job. Nor do jobs remain the same. Assessing training needs is one of a coach's ongoing responsibilities. Be alert to new abilities staff members need to do their current jobs well, then provide needed training—or see that it is provided.

Sometimes, one or two employees, whose jobs have changed, need to attend a public seminar or university course. Other times, you might want your entire staff to take training. If you feel confident enough to do so, you might even provide the group training yourself. Many managers handle the following topics on their own.

Interpersonal Communications Skills

If your employees interact with employees in other departments or clients, give a periodic review of methods for dealing with others. You can make this a part of department meetings.

Open the session by using an example, perhaps from your own experience. Share a story about a complaint or a request you received from a coworker or a client and ask for suggestions on how you could have responded. Discuss how different responses would have affected the quality of your work or your ongoing relationship with that person. Ask your employees to share any experiences they have had with others in which they weren't sure how to best respond.

Because there are no exact answers to these questions, employees should be encouraged to offer their opinions.

Telephone Skills

All of us have had a few bad experiences when doing business by phone. Use your own and your employees' peeves to teach how best to serve both your internal and external customers.

Written Communication

Let your staff know the approved style for writing memos, reports, and other forms of business correspondence. Written communications should be clear and precise. Use examples to illustrate how this can be achieved.

Technology Tune-Ups

To introduce new technology without proper training is asking for trouble. Get training for yourself, and either bring your training to the department or have an employee, a coworker, or an outside trainer do the training. Once the training is given, check to see if any employees are having difficulty. Are some employees not using all the capabilities of the technology? They may need reinforcement sessions to improve their skills.

As part of your coaching efforts, such tune-ups should be given six months after the system is in use, because it takes time to identify what the technology is capable of doing and what an employee isn't getting right. Such sessions can be offered one-on-one with a specialist or in a users' group.

Coaching Assessment

Are you doing your job as a coach? To find out, ask yourself these questions.

- Am I keeping my staff members informed on how well they are doing?
- Do I frequently offer insights so employees can make the best decisions?
- Do I communicate trust and confidence in my employees?
- Are my staff members clear about project priorities?
- Are both department goals and the organization mission clear to staff? If they see conflicts, have I taken the time to resolve them in employees' minds?
- Do I seek out information from staff about obstacles or barriers they are encountering in doing their jobs and what might help?
- Do I give my staff my full attention when we sit down to talk?
- Do I keep a record of my meetings with staff?

The last question is worthy of further discussion. Keep notes of your coaching sessions. A memo to yourself may be sufficient. If the information is critical to the employee's development, then share the memo with that employee.

Alternatively, you may want to develop a form in which you jot down key points discussed during the coaching session, an extension of the records you keep on employee performance for assessment sessions—a critical incident notebook. After each coaching session, jot down key points. These might include training needs and plans, solutions to problems, answers to routine questions, scheduling items, or insights and ideas shared.

Coaching Problems

Through the years, I've met with many new managers. They have told me about problems they've encountered as coaches. Let me share with you their problems and, more important, suggestions about how you can address them.

For one, managers tell me that they don't undertake a needs assessment to identify skill shortcomings. They let it slide as they get their new recruit to work. Consequently, problems arise in the new hire's job performance. The solution is relatively simple: as a part of the orientation session, conduct a training needs assessment, follow through on skill-building exercises, and make sure that new hires understand the organization's mission and what it takes to succeed.

Another mistake is to make promises to workers—either during their orientation session or subsequent coaching meeting. One new manager made the mistake of saying, "If you take on this assignment, I know you will be qualified for a promotion. I'll certainly work to get you a big raise." Needless to say, the employee worked day and night to complete the extra task. But when it came time for that promotion or raise, none was forthcoming. The disappointment put a huge wedge in the relationship between the manager and his worker. "It took me a long time," the manager told me, "to regain my credibility with him."

Promotions and raises aren't the only promises that managers make but don't keep. Some managers offer help and do not deliver it. The only advice here is: do what you say you will do, or don't offer. If you promise to arrange for training, intervene with another manager, remove roadblocks to good work, or what have you, then you need to do just that.

I'm seen some tough managers do a good job of coaching. They are honest and open in communications and consequently earn their workers' trust. Part of their secret is that they truly believe that their workers are capable of what they are asking of them. Some managers forget that one of the purposes of coaching is to demonstrate to employees their belief in their capabilities. A good coach avoids *never* or *always* to suggest that the employee never does such and such correctly or, along the same lines, always does such and such wrong. Further, the manager doesn't blame employees for 100 percent of the problem, but instead considers the possibility of personal involvement in the problem and is ready to work to change the situation.

Counseling

All managers must deal with employees who don't meet standards or objectives. Certainly, it's best to deal with budding problems as soon as possible through coaching, but should the problem continue, a counseling session with the employee may be needed. Counseling is a five-step process.

1. Alert employees about problems in their work.
2. Make them understand that poor performance cannot be tolerated.
3. Develop an action plan to turn around poor performance.
4. Document the discussion to ensure—and to prove—that you made a reasonable effort to help the employee perform well.
5. Should no effort to improve performance seem likely, take steps to rid your organization of the individual.

Counseling Like a Pro

Your role as coach focuses primarily on your employees' knowledge and skills. When one of your workers is doing well, your goal is to help build on job strengths. When the employee isn't doing well, your intent is to further clarify what's expected, help the employee acquire the knowledge and skill needed to improve job performance, and step in and address any external obstacles that may be impeding performance.

Sometimes, however, coaching just won't work. After you've made several attempts to solve the problem to no avail, then something other than lack of knowledge or skill is evidently behind the problem. At this point, you need to move from being a coach to being a counselor.

There are obvious reasons to engage in counseling. For instance, a poor performer is often half as productive as an average worker. Bringing this person up to average productivity can improve your department's performance considerably. Besides, left to fester, performance problems can demoralize your staff. Your employees will lose respect for you and begin to doubt the fairness of your performance assessments (see Chapter 7). Either their performance will decline, or they will move on to another company. Worse, some managers have told me that their failure to confront poor performers has sometimes affected their own self-confidence. They may use worries about the legal consequences or time commitment as reasons for ignoring the problem, but in time they begin to think less of themselves as managers.

Some fears are understandable. Unless you have a clear idea about how to counsel a marginal performer, you may have cause to worry about losing control of the discussion, particularly if the employee becomes emotional and starts to cry or shout. Then there is a real danger of landing in court if counseling isn't done correctly.

The secret to good counseling is accomplishing the following objectives during a one-on-one interview:

- Get the employee to agree that the quality of job performance needs to change.
- Identify the nature of the problem in the employee's performance.
- Reach agreement on the specific actions that the employee will take to improve performance.
- Follow up regularly to ensure that the employee is reaching the goals you both have set.

To reinforce continued improvement, recognize efforts by the employee to improve performance.

Of these four steps, the most difficult may be the first. For counseling to work, the employee must agree that yes, indeed, a problem in performance exists and that the employee is responsible. This is where documentation of employee job performance is critical. Not only must it describe the nature of the problem but also how the problem affects the performance of the whole department.

A secret in gaining employee agreement lies in demonstrating a willingness to hear the employee's explanation. To prompt a response, you might say, "Tell me about it," or, "Is my understanding correct?" or, "Is there more I need to know about what happened?"

If reasons for the problem lie beyond the employee's performance, then the matter should be over. If you have doubts about the employee's explanation, share them then and there or offer to look further into the matter and get back to the employee. Often, if the employee is stalling, either approach will be sufficient to get the employee to say something like, "Gee, I guess I could have handled the situation better," or, "I might be responsible—a little—for what happened. What would you have wanted me to do?"

Getting buy-in to the solution is important to the success of the counseling session, but perhaps even more important is clarifying the cause of the problem.

Many different situations lie behind problem performance. The cause might be due to stress within or outside the workplace, unclear priorities (more attributable to the employee's manager than the employee), or poor time or task management on the employee's part. Personal problems also create work-related problems, distracting employees and making them unproductive and maybe argumentative and uncooperative.

Whatever the cause, once you identify it, you are better able to develop an action plan to turn the performance around. But keep in mind: the action plan works only if the employee has played a major role in its development. Helping to create the plan increases the likelihood of buy-in.

Once the plan is in action, monitor the employee's performance. Meet at set times to review progress.

To measure yourself as a counselor, ask yourself these questions.

- Am I making allowances for some poor work? Consequently, is performance slipping within the department?
- Am I using my busy schedule as an excuse to avoid confronting the performance problem?

- When I meet with an employee to discuss poor performance, am I clear about the purpose of the meeting?
- Do I describe clearly the performance that troubles me, pointing to documentation I've maintained?
- Do I plan the one-on-one meeting in advance, even preparing a list of questions I might be asked—and my answers—to ensure that I maintain the focus of the meeting?
- Do I give an employee in counseling the opportunity to tell the other side of the story without interruption?
- Do I allow the employee to identify several alternative solutions to the problem and to share feelings about each of the alternatives before settling on a single solution?
- Do I demonstrate to the employee that I am truly listening by paraphrasing what has been said?
- Do I use open-ended questions to stimulate discussion?
- Do I keep from making judgments about the employee, like "lazy," "difficult to work with," or "loser"?
- Do I refer employees with personal problems to the Employee Assistance Program (EAP), human resources manager, or some community program to enable them to address the nonwork part of the problem? At the same time, do I make it clear to the employee that having a personal problem is no excuse for failure to do the job well?
- Am I clear about the specific work that must be improved?
- Did I offer to help to ensure the change?
- Am I ready to meet with the employee as agreed in the improvement plan?

A no to one or more of the questions here could create problems for you in counseling.

Counseling Mistakes

The biggest mistake you can make with poor performance is, of course, ignoring the problem. If you allow it to continue over a long period of time—some managers admit to years—addressing the problem at some late date becomes fraught with legal ramifications.

It also makes other actions difficult. For instance, let's assume you have a problem performer who applies for a promotion. He's not doing his current job well as is, and you have no intention of letting him be promoted. So you turn him down and choose another employee—perhaps someone newer in the company—for the position.

Guess what? The poor performer sues for discrimination, claiming either a gender, age, or racial bias. Because you never addressed the issue of performance, raising it at this point is unlikely to justify your action. What would you say in court? Sometimes, employees reach the warning stage yet claim they had no knowledge about a problem. In some instances, they are just making an excuse. In others, unfortunately, the manager never made clear the nature of the problem and the consequences if they did not improve.

That's why you must be very specific about the existence of the problem, its nature, and—most important—the consequences if the employee does nothing to remedy the situation. Further, you need to document this session and share a copy with the problem performer, including the agreed-on action plan to address the problem. Documenting incidents that justify counseling will make it easier to prove that a problem does, indeed, exist.

Your management of performance appraisals will certainly support the need for counseling, as will the standards against which you measure job performance. Appraisals and standards are discussed in the next chapter.

For now, let me share some communication mistakes to avoid during the counseling session. For instance, you shouldn't dominate the meeting. Practice the 20/80 rule—speak only 20 percent of the time and listen 80 percent of the time.

Focus, too, on the problem. Don't bring emotions into the discussion by dwelling on how the problem performance is making you feel. Stick to the facts. You may understand how the problem could have developed, you may even empathize with the employee if it stems from personal problems, but you have to remain objective. If your staff member senses that you are sympathetic, they may be less motivated to change their behavior.

Don't dictate a solution to the employee. As mentioned, the employee must truly be involved in creating the plan for it to work.

Finally, spend sufficient time on identifying the nature of the problem. Don't think you can save time by jumping quickly into the problem-solving phase. Indeed, any employee being counseled needs to feel that the manager is willing to give the needed time to the problem.

Keeping Performance High

Sometimes, an employee in counseling will improve, then slip back to the previous level of performance. Why does this happen? What can you do to prevent it?

Generally, an underachiever fails long-term to improve for two reasons. One is that the counseling did not stick—once the extra attention was withdrawn, the employee fell back into old ways. The second reason is that an additional problem is affecting the employee's performance, such as a personality conflict with you or with one of the employee's coworkers. It may also be that the employee cannot sustain interest in the job at hand and has not been able to find motivation to continue to improve.

Dealing with this situation can be exasperating—so acknowledge your own personal feelings, then put them aside. You need to focus on what, if any, further constructive measures you can take to get the employee back on the right track. It may be time to make the tough decision to terminate the employee, if the employee doesn't realize that both mind and body need to come to work.

■ Tips

- Ensure that your employees meet your expectations by communicating them.

- If employees slip up, discuss it as part of your monthly coaching session. If they continue to foul up, call them in for counseling.

- If a task is difficult, break it into pieces. Use the one-on-one coaching meeting to teach one step at a time and build your employee's self-confidence.

- Encourage employees to discover new and better ways of doing things. When they find better methods, praise them for their new ideas.

- Troubled employees are no different from employees with poor attitudes or skill deficiencies in that they must improve their performance, after a given period, or be terminated. Managers should not assume the role of psychologist or medical doctor. Rather, they should encourage the troubled employee to seek proper professional help.

Directive versus Indirective Counseling

When counseling employees, you may use one of two approaches. In directive counseling, you ask pointed questions about the problem. When you feel that you have a good idea of what is behind the problem, then you suggest steps that the employee might take to overcome it. In nondirective counseling, you assume the role of listener, encouraging the employee to talk about any ongoing problems. Slowly, using open-ended questions, you move the discussion to the situation for which counseling is needed. Done correctly, indirective counseling is usually more effective than directive counseling, because the employee is first to recognize the need for change and comes up with solutions to accomplish it.

■ Did You Know . . . ?

Employee assistance programs have been found effective. A study by the U.S. Department of Labor found that EAPs return as much as $5 to $16 for every $1 invested.

■ See Also

Aldisert, Lisa M. *Valuing People*. Dearborn Trade, 2002.

Bell, Arthur H. and Dayle M. Smith. *Winning with Difficult People*. Barrons Educational Series, 1997.

Delpo, Amy and Lisa Guerin and Janet Portman. *Dealing with Problem Employees: A Legal Guide*. Nolo Press, 2001.

Gonthier, Giovinella and Kevin Morrissey. *Rude Awakenings: Overcoming the Civility Crisis in the Workplace*. Dearborn Trade, 2002.

Linkemer, Bobbi. *Solving People Problems*. AMACOM, 2000.

Topchik, Gary S. *Managing Workplace Negativity*. AMACOM, 2000.

7

Performance Appraisals

I recently attended a meeting of managers. One manager asked me an important question: "My company doesn't have the funds to give out raises this year. So why should I be spending valuable time preparing assessments of my employees, when it won't get them anything?"

As I explained to the manager, he was wrong. All employees want to know how they stand—even if it isn't good. Information from the review will let them know more about their strengths and weaknesses and identify areas where training and development are needed. If an employee has plateaued in a position, the appraisal can renew the individual's commitment to the job. But the benefits of performance appraisals don't end there.

The manager gains, too.

The review ensures that employees receive feedback continuously, whether positive or negative. Ongoing feedback improves morale, because employees know exactly where they stand, and it enables managers to express concerns rather than store them up. The development part of the review—and there should be such an element—pinpoints what needs to be done now to prepare them for responsibilities to come.

From a negative viewpoint, it can affirm the need for an employee to undergo formal counseling.

Finally, because appraisals are formalized, such assessments are taken seriously—not only by your employees but also by you. You might stop an employee who is late and mention his tardiness—one of many times he is late. Alternatively, you might visit an employee and compliment her on research for a team project. But such comments, transferred to an appraisal template, carry considerable weight both in the employees' minds and your own.

Such importance may explain why neither employees nor their managers enjoy the appraisal process. On one side, employees worry because of the consequences. Raises and promotions, sometimes even their job security, are at stake. Managers don't like them, for they have to sit in judgment of others, whose cooperation and support are necessary to bottom-line success. Besides, they know negative comments will alienate workers. Appraisals may be seen by employees as just another way managers exert control over them.

How can you make appraisals go smoothly and effectively?

Standards or Goals

The process begins with the standards or objectives you set, in cooperation with your employees.

Review the employee's job description. Analyze, too, department or corporate plans. Together, they should enable you and the employee to set standards, goals, or needed results—whatever is the basis for your firm's appraisal program.

Different appraisal systems use different measurements. Some firms use standards, others objectives, and still others results. Performance goals are often results that are critical to the department's operation. Standards are usually tied to output and are frequently the same for each employee in the same job. For instance, a standard for copy editors might be to "edit no fewer than 12 manuscript pages per hour." For a customer service rep, it might be to "handle no fewer than 20 phone calls per hour." Results are specific ends to be accomplished, like developing a new product, improving delivery of customer orders, or increasing sales by 5 percent.

Increasingly, organizations also include developmental goals along with performance goals, results, or standards. Developmental objectives reflect skills, abilities, or knowledge deficiencies that need shoring up. Let's assume that an employee lacks know-how in statistical analysis. So you might set as a goal for the employee to "complete a course on statistical analysis by year-end." In determining development objectives, consider what you want an employee to be able to do by the end of the year that will improve job performance.

If your organization promulgates a number of values, you may want to tie these to your appraisal as well. For instance, your firm might expect its employees to show initiative. This is a value. For a department administrator, the value-related goal tied to showing initiative could be, "Develop a user's group to increase workers' knowledge of search engines and identify those most useful for competitive research." For an engineer, it might be, "To identify less expensive ways to manufacture existing products to increase profit margin." If the performance factor is collaboration, you could measure it by an administrative assistant's ability to, "Fill in when colleagues are either ill or away on vacation." For the engineer, collaboration might be measured by the ability, "To participate in cross-functional projects so they are completed on schedule."

Whether you work with goals, standards, or results, the statement needs to include the outcome, the time frame or deadline, and a means of measurement. For example, interview four experts to produce one article monthly in time for the midmonth production copy date, to ensure magazine production and delivery to subscribers on schedule." Another: "Review office procedures by July 15 to identify ways to streamline operations." Still another: "Update software programs on schedule as provided by marketing and customer demands."

Ideally, you should have from five to eight objectives. You wouldn't want fewer than five—there wouldn't be sufficient challenge. Nor would you want more than eight; your employee would be running every which way. If you really do identify eight things you would like your employee to achieve, prioritize them and reserve three for later use.

During the year, you will offer feedback—criticism and praise—to your employees hundreds of times. If you practice what I have preached so far, you will also meet in coaching sessions, once a month, with each of your employees, with an emphasis on employee development and day-to-day performance (see Chapter 6). But you will also meet as often as four times a year to review progress toward the standards, goals, or results.

During these interim sessions, you will review the standards or objectives to determine if they are still relevant. If the economy has suddenly taken a deep dip, you and your employee may agree that working toward a 15 percent increase in sales is unrealistic and, consequently, may drop the figure to 5 percent. If the company has decided to discontinue a newsletter for customers, a goal to improve the quality of its content is no longer relevant, but finding an alternative method of communicating with your customers makes a lot of sense.

Working Together

It occurred to me that the phrase *working together* might seem cavalier—it's not always easy to get employees to sit down with you to set objectives. If it might work better, suggest that your employees come to the goal-setting meetings with their own objectives. Those closest to the work often know goals as well or better than you do, and you honor them by asking them to participate in setting yearly objectives. Asking for their ideas can also be an excellent way to engage indifferent workers in their jobs.

You might also consider having you and your employees set objectives independently, then meeting to compare and agree upon the final list. If an employee is way off base in what she thinks is important, you can discuss the misconceptions and clarify your expectations.

Take a look at the standards or objectives you have currently for your employees. How do they compare to those from the previous year? Have the demands on your employees increased? A mistake that many new managers make is to use the job description as the basis for the standards, literally reproducing the job requirements as standards year after year and never stretching their employees.

What do I mean by *stretching?* Every year, there should be an increase in the expected performance or results. You don't want to set standards that reflect the same level of performance over the last few years or that demand minimal performance. Of course, the more stretch you put into an objective, the more resistance you may encounter from an employee. Don't let this discourage you. Just be sure that the stretch is realistic. Too much stretch means that objectives won't be feasible, and employees won't even try to achieve them.

Once you have set the standards, your responsibility is to monitor the employee's progress toward the goals.

Legal Issues

Because appraisals can influence compensation, promotions, staff cutbacks, and termination for cause, they are covered by employment laws. Applicable laws include Title VII of the Civil Rights Act, which makes it illegal for a manager to discriminate against an employee because of race, color, sex, creed, or national origin; the Equal Pay Act, which stipulates that employees who perform similar jobs must be paid equally; the Age Discrimination in Employment Act (ADEA), which protects employees more than 40 years of age in hiring and promotion decisions; Section 508 of the Rehabilitation Act, which prohibits managers from discriminating in promoting the handicapped; the Vietnam Era Veterans Readjustment Assistance Act, which protects disabled veterans and veterans of the Vietnam era; and the Americans with Disabilities Act (ADA), which makes it illegal to discriminate in hiring, in job assignments, and in the treatment of employees because of a disability.

The last doesn't affect evaluations directly, but it should be considered if you are giving a poor evaluation to someone with a disability. Could it land you in court? Maybe, but it probably won't. The law doesn't allow disabled individuals—no matter the disability—to get away with not doing their work. But every reasonable effort must be made to accommodate an employee's work to the disability, and you need to prove that you've done so. This brings us to the important subject of documentation.

Documentation

Most lawsuits related to performance appraisals are based on a manager's failure to support an evaluation. This is why it is important to keep a written record of employees' behavior during the year. Potential lawsuits aren't the only reason for good documentation. It also ensures that you conduct an accurate and effective appraisal discussion. For instance, you may have a worker who did a spectacular job on a team project but a mediocre job otherwise. Without documentation for the entire year, you might give a higher rating than the employee deserves.

You need to keep records on each and every employee—not only those who are driving you to distraction. Should a disgruntled employee bring a charge of discrimination against you, the court will check for critical incident reports on all employees—poor, average, and outstanding. If you have documentation only on your troublemaker, you will seem to be setting up the individual for termination, whether deserved or not.

Too much documentation can backfire, too. It provides more fertile ground a lawyer can plow to dig up an instance of discrimination.

The court will ask to read your documentation. So you need to be sure that your records don't include hearsay; e.g., "Larry says Beth is starting to drink at lunch time." Nor should they include opinions, even your own; e.g., "I don't think Herb has what it takes to work here long term." Your conclusion may be justified, but as a valid record it means nothing.

What is good documentation? It is a record of events that will enable a third party, someone not familiar with the situation, to come to the same conclusion you have. So you need to provide detailed descriptions of specific incidents and facts. It's written because you can't be expected to remember what happened nine or six or even one month before. (See Figure 7.1.)

FIGURE 7.1
Sample Critical Incident Log

Employee Name: _____

Position: _____

Date	Event	Action	Result

Be sure to maintain a separate incident log for each of your staff members.

Here are some don'ts when documenting an employee's performance.

- *Don't document rumors.* You shouldn't use them to evaluate an employee, so they don't belong in your employee log.
- *Don't include personal comments about employees.* Elaine dresses like a gothic heroine, and her hair is so stringy that she resembles pictures of Medusa. That has nothing to do with her job performance, unless her job involves a lot of contact with clients.
- *Don't quote others.* Harry thinks Lucy is lazy. That shouldn't go into your notes. However, you can report that Harry Reid reported that Lucy refused to lend a hand to colleagues faced with tight deadlines. She completed her work and then waited for her next assignment or walked about socializing rather than seeking out work.

The most important things you should be documenting are concrete successes, skills learned, problems solved, or—the reverse—careless mistakes, knowledge and skill gaps, or problems caused. Include observations from other managers who have worked with the employee, describing specifically what happened according to the third party.

Keep a record, too, of remarks—good and bad—from customers, clients, or others outside the firm.

The records you keep should reflect the standards against which the employees' performance will be measured. That these standards are work related is something that the courts will expect. Courts will also investigate your goals and standards to be sure they are realistic. The Equal Employment Opportunity Commission's Uniform Guidelines on Employee Selection demand that standards be "valid," or job related and, beyond that, that your firm's appraisal system measures job performance accurately.

Interim Meetings

Depending on your company's program, you may meet every three or four months with each of your employees to discuss work performance. These interim reviews check that the milestones for standards are being achieved. The goal is to clarify any expectations that remain unclear, set plans for the next quarter to ensure continuation of current progress or get the employee back on track, and leave both you and the employee in agreement about the employee's performance for the year to date.

These sessions also let you remind your employees about the department's goals or broader, corporate values.

I don't think I need to remind you that you have to level with your employees. If there are problems in their performance, you have to tell them. Failure to be up front with them about their work will only get you into trouble over the longer term—when you find you have no choice but to tell an employee that there's a problem and he points out—rightly—that this is the first time he's heard about it. Don't wait until the end of the year, or until the employee is turned down for a promotion and you have to justify your decision.

If shortcomings are found, these meetings can evolve into problem-solving sessions to determine the reason behind the gap. If the employee has made significant accomplishments during the past quarter, you should congratulate her. On the other hand, if the session involved some change in goals or development of an action plan to address some performance weaknesses, you can wind it up by assuring the employee that you think she is capable of accomplishing the new or renewed goals.

Always aim to begin every one of your interim meetings (as well as the end-of-year assessment) with a strong motivational statement and an easy question to help the employee relax. As you review the employee's performance, provide the chance for comment first, with questions such as, "How do you think your performance went in this area?"

You will have your documentation in front of you. However, by allowing the employee to speak first, you encourage the process of self-assessment. In identifying where you have different perceptions, you can explore why.

Of course, give your employees time to prepare for these meetings. They will be better able to discuss their performance if they have had time to think objectively about their work.

If there are problems in an employee's performance, encourage the employee to come up with a plan to deal with them. Offer your own ideas only if necessary. If you have identified serious or expansive problems in the employee's performance, you may want to undertake counseling to give the employee the opportunity to turn around the situation before termination becomes necessary (see Chapter 6).

Of course, before you can correct a problem, the employee must acknowledge that one exists. It is important that the employee realizes the adverse impact of behavior on the unit's workload; otherwise, the employee won't truly commit to solving the problem. Explain how the performance has affected your unit or the organization as a whole. Ask questions to check that the employee has now accepted that there is a problem. Make sure that he or she fully understands what is wrong and the impact of allowing the situation to continue. If an employee questions the review, be prepared to show the documentation or notes you have maintained about the employee. Generally, well-reported incidents will convince your employee that your assessment is accurate.

Write up your conclusions at the end of the meeting, including agreed-on action plans.

Appraisal Mistakes

Before you meet with your employees for their year-end assessments, review your documentation on each of your employees. You don't want to commit either of two errors that many managers make. They either assess an employee as outstanding because of one very impressive trait or accomplishment, on the assumption that other accomplishments were equally impressive, or they become very critical of the employee because of a recent incident, forgetting all those past incidents in which the same employee did well.

In the latter situation, the employee can do nothing to convince the manager that he or she is a good worker. Maybe the employee began the year poorly and then turned the performance around, but the supervisor lets the employee's early mistakes override the significant improvement.

A good employee who associates with mediocre or average employees may also never be rated above average due to those friendships. Despite differences in the level of their performances, the manager rates the employee the same as the employee's buddies.

The Annual Review

The year-end appraisal meeting is similar to the other assessment meetings, in that you will discuss performance and chart progress toward the standards or objectives set. But the conclusions at this meeting will determine the employee's rating for the year and likely any salary increase, bonus, or other financial reward. So it will demand more preparation by you to counter any objections to your conclusions. You will also complete forms.

Both determining pay and filling out the forms are simpler with documentation in hand. Using the documentation, compare the employee's performance to the standards or goals set. Use the language of the goals to show a clear relationship between the work done, the goals, and the ratings you've given.

Before your meeting, review the appraisal form and documentation. Because you and your employees have been meeting throughout the year to discuss performance, they shouldn't be surprised about your conclusions, right? Not so. An employee may suddenly become aware of the final evaluation's impact on his or her career or realize that the assessment will become a part of a permanent record. The employee may become upset—even refuse to sign the document. Even stars whose ratings aren't as high as expected may balk.

Faced with disagreement over ratings, don't compromise to avoid litigation. However, hear out such employees. You must leave the meeting with the employee feeling that there was an open and honest communication between you.

The employee may even be right—there may be cause to reassess the year's performance. If you do decide to revise what you wrote, edit in the employee's presence to provide assurance that you have revised the appraisal. If you still feel strongly that your assessment is correct as is, then say so and provide evidence for your case. That's usually enough to quiet most employees. If you have met regularly and provided ongoing feedback, maintained records about performance, and used that documentation to prepare logical arguments for your assessments, most staff members will acknowledge the fairness of your assessment and sign the form.

At the same time that you share your year-end written appraisal of an employee, lay the groundwork for the next year's performance by working out an employee development plan.

The year-end appraisal can be the most intimidating to a new manager, so let me share this five-step process to help.

1. *Prepare yourself for the meeting.* Suggest that your employee also do some soul searching about performance during the year.
2. *Compare accomplishments with specific targets.* Once you have made the employee comfortable, discuss one standard after another. Don't be vague or resort to generalizations. Be specific about what was expected and how close the employee came to meeting these expectations.
3. *Give credit for what the employee has accomplished.* It is tempting to get through the appraisal by concentrating on the deficiencies, taking for granted those things done well. A fair assessment has to cover both.
4. *Review those tasks that have not been done.* Emphasize where improvements were needed, how they can be done, and why they're important.
5. *Avoid giving the impression that you're passing judgment on the employee.* Don't talk in terms of mistakes or faults. Stick to a mutual explanation of the facts and how you see the employee's performance for the year.

Depending on your firm's procedures, you may not be able to share your final rating of the employee. On the other hand, if the work was well done, you should share that positive feeling. If problems exist, you should discuss what more the employee should do to turn around the situation. If serious problems exist and counseling is called for, you should bring that up.

Employee Development

Too often, managers talk only about the financial consequences of the employee's performance and pay lip service to the developmental side of the appraisal process. But the year-end meeting is an excellent time to discuss skill weaknesses evident in the employee's performance and create action plans to strengthen these areas. (See Figure 7.2.)

FIGURE 7.2
Sample Employee Progress Report

Employee Name: _____

Position/Grade:_____

Date	Nature of Project/Training	Assessment (problems, successes)

This tool can be used to maintain a record of each employee's development and professional growth.

Employee development is for outstanding performers, too. If an employee has consistently exceeded expectations for several years, she is probably frustrated with the lack of opportunities for promotion or new challenges. During the appraisal, then, you can discuss training programs that would develop skills and increase employability.

If opportunities for promotion don't exist within your organization, or are of little interest to the employee, then you may want to discuss new assignments that would be challenging. If the employees are not interested in new responsibilities, discuss ways they can operate more independently.

For outstanding employees, your mutual goal is to answer the question, "What can we do to help you accomplish more?" For other employees, the goal is another question: "How can we make it easier for you to meet and exceed this year's goals?"

The Issue of Money

Money shouldn't be discussed during either your interim meetings or the year-end reviews. Keep the issue separate from discussing performance to ensure that the employee is focused on performance quality. Your company may even have managers hold off on discussing dollars to make sure all the paperwork has been processed and senior management is in agreement with the final assessment. If you give one rating to the employee, with the concomitant raise, and then management lowers the rating and pay increase, you are in an awkward situation.

At the same time that you discuss money, you will also want to schedule the next meeting to set objectives for the new year. This ongoing process makes performance appraisals beneficial to all.

- Your employees learn about their strengths and know you will help them with their weaknesses.
- Your employees actively participate in both the goal setting and evaluation process, which empowers them.
- Your employees know that you are concerned about their performance.
- Your employees have a better sense of their fit within the department and company as a whole, based on the standards and objectives you mutually set. You and your staff become a team working toward a common, agreed-on organizational mission.

■ The ABCs of Documentation

- *A: Accurate.* Record only objective facts, job-related behavior, and direct observations (not hearsay) as they occur rather than from memory.

- *B: Behavior.* Describe specific behavior. Don't make evaluative statements or discuss the employee's personality.

- *C: Consistent.* Record both positive and negative behaviors rather than emphasizing either.

■ Tips

- Document as soon after a critical event as possible. The longer the delay, the less accurate the documentation.

- Rehearse what you will say where poor performance is involved. You want to accomplish three goals: preserve your relationship with the employee, protect the individual's self-esteem, and increase the likelihood that the employee will change.

- If an employee hints at a personal problem during an assessment meeting, address it immediately.

- Keep the tone of appraisal meetings relaxed, but avoid time-wasting chitchat.

- If you spot doubts in the employee's mind that a performance problem exists or an action plan will work, ask questions until you are sure the employee is committed to the need to improve performance.

- Be prepared to spend time on appraisals. They shouldn't be rushed if you want to do them right.

- Ensure no interruptions when you hold appraisal interviews. Choose a room where you won't be disturbed and can give the interview your undivided attention.

When Feedback Is Most Useful

Your feedback will be most useful to the employee when it is:

- *Specific and descriptive, not evaluative.* Effective feedback describes specifically what the person did rather than make a judgment or broad generalization.
- *Aimed at behavior under the employee's control.* Every action people take may be under their control, but some are more difficult, perhaps impossible, to change. Physical or personality characteristics are good examples.
- *Well-timed.* Receiving feedback about last month's behavior is like putting a cast on an arm broken the month before. Immediate feedback is best. Feedback should be delayed only to avoid embarrassing an employee before coworkers or to get more information.

• *Constructive.* The manager should be seen as helping, not as attacking. Toward that end, your feedback should show the employee how performance could have been better.

Putting Appraisals in Writing

Most appraisal systems demand that you put your conclusions in writing. Write a paragraph for each goal that explains how you arrived at your assessment. Along with any forms you have to complete, you may want to include a summary statement about the employee's performance during the year.

Here are three points to keep in mind as you prepare your first draft.

1. *Be as specific as possible.* Use the active voice, not the passive voice, because the passive voice can cloud who did what. Further, in describing what an employee did, be as precise as possible. Avoid empty phrases like "maintains good production records" or "caused a significant loss in time." Write, instead, that the employee "achieved 90 percent accurate production records" or "slowed work by 50 percent on a project by not. . . ."

2. *Compare the employee's performance to the standards or goals set.* Don't compare performance to that of other employees. Even if you have people with the same goals, such comparison means little. However, where a standard is applicable to all employees, and where all employees except one have met or exceeded that standard, use this fact to counter the problem performer's argument that the standard is too high.

3. *Use the language of the goals to show a clear relationship between the work done, the goals, and the rating.* This supports your assessment.

■ **See Also**

Grote, Dick. *The Performance Appraisal Question and Answer Book: A Survival Guide for Managers.* AMACOM, 2002.

Marshall, Don R. *The Four Elements of Successful Management: Select, Direct, Evaluate, Reward.* AMACOM, 1998.

Saunders, Rebecca M. *The Agile Manager's Guide to Effective Performance Appraisals.* Velocity Press, 2000.

8

Conflict Management

Gilbert and Sullivan, whose operettas still play the stage after more than a century, worked together for more than 25 years. Gilbert knew instinctively which words would work best with Sullivan's music, and Sullivan was unerring in his choice of music to fit Gilbert's libretti. Yet the two men's dislike for each other was so strong that they were never on a first-name basis.

Another case in point: the Wright brothers. Orville and Wilbur Wright were known for their personal loyalty, but they also had very different personality styles that led to numerous disagreements. Initially, their arguments lasted days, but over time, they learned how to harness their emotions and argue in a constructive manner. The result: the first airplane.

Conflict is a natural consequence of human interaction. Put two or more individuals in an office for a significant amount of time, and a difference of opinion is likely to arise. When individuals clash, combatants can become so concerned with defending their viewpoints that they cease communicating. Mutual distrust builds. In the workplace, working relationships are threatened.

This isn't to say that conflicts per se are bad. Disagreements can be productive and can even motivate people to excel. Conflict can generate constructive dialogue, from which new ideas are developed, refined, and successfully implemented. Whereas conflicts can impede change and undermine a sense of teamwork within your work unit or organization, they can also help build relationships. This may sound contradictory, but it's true.

As a manager, you can use conflicts productively, converting them into opportunities for creative problem solving (the task of reconciling conflicting visions forces us to think creatively) and improving decision-making skills (entertaining other points of views to make better-informed choices). Conflict can be an excellent way to identify problems before they grow larger and more disruptive. More importantly, conflict helps us find effective, efficient solutions. Consequently, rather than focus in this chapter solely on *conflict resolution,* I'd like to talk about *conflict management.*

Your responsibility is to encourage this positive or constructive kind of conflict. What does that entail on your part?

- *Identification of common goals.* As differences arise, remind the parties of their common goal or mission. Stay away from personality issues. Rather, ask the individuals to review their goals to focus solely on shared or compatible ones. Once the goals have been identified, the group can move on to discuss how these goals can be shared.
- *Clarify, sort, and value differences.* While contrasting viewpoints will surface, so will evidence that the participants have much in common. This commonality should be emphasized.
- *Gain commitment to change.* Goals may be shared, but the preferred means of reaching them may vary. You want to reach consensus on the best way to move forward toward achieving shared goals.

When new ideas are presented to your team, encourage members to play devil's advocate. Run meetings so that participants don't feel uneasy about pointing out what is wrong with a favored idea. Attendees should feel an obligation to identify anything that may be wrong before a plan gets final approval.

When you suspect an employee is afraid to disagree with you, say that you would like to hear their ideas. Don't kill the messenger who carries bad news. On the contrary, make heroes out of employees who spot challenges before you do.

Your goal as a manager is to prevent a conflict from becoming a disruptive force, not to prevent conflicts. Whereas positive conflict can generate new solutions to existing problems, disruptive conflict can create problems such as:

- *Added tension.* This may cause high turnover. After all, who wants to work in a stressful work environment?
- *Poor decisions.* If not properly managed, conflicts can make someone blind to facts or deaf to a logical argument. People's good sense can be shelved because either a desire to prove themselves right or a dislike of

the other individual prompts them to look for "facts" to prove their pre-conceived point.

- *Lack of implementation of a decision, whether good or bad.* Ideas, whether right or wrong, are worthless if they aren't implemented. Dis-agreements can mean that the most creative thinking or the best ideas are never acted upon.
- *A "get-even" attitude.* Ill feelings are harbored, and employees later retali-ate against each other.
- *Destruction of professionalism.* Arguments between managers and their employees disrupt department morale and overall workflow. Conflicts across departments factionalize an organization.

What Causes Trouble?

With people from so many different backgrounds working together, aren't conflicts inevitable? It may surprise you to know what does and doesn't cause most workplace conflicts.

Differences in age, gender, religion, economic background, and race do not usually spell trouble in the workplace. In fact, if you take a look at the friendships that form in the workplace, you will often see alliances between persons from remarkably different backgrounds. Differences in age, sex, color, and national ori-gin normally take a back seat in the workplace. What is most important is the at-titude we have toward the work we are doing, the amount of cooperation we give to our coworkers, and the skills we bring to the job.

Often, our responsibilities demand that we work very closely with others. This in itself is enough to open up opportunities for personality conflicts, par-ticularly if the work itself is very demanding or must be completed under a tight deadline. When colleagues disagree on methods for accomplishing the work or on the sense of urgency for finishing the task, even small differences can erupt into major confrontations.

Communication, or rather the lack of it, can also cause disagreements. Con-flicts may arise because of unfamiliar language or terminology and ambiguous or incomplete information. Words may be misunderstood, leading to anger, or the simple frustration from trying to communicate may ignite the conflict.

Of course, work conflicts are often the result of true personality differ-ences. People often have incompatible personal goals, and these can trigger dis-agreements. For instance, a team has a specific objective, but one member of the group wants to focus on achieving technical excellence, while another is satisfied with present levels. Another common issue on which people clash is action. Some people prefer to approach everything slowly and methodically. Others want to get things done quickly and correct mistakes later. The dangers of both extremes are evident: too much caution could jeopardize a project by making it late; a quick job, on the other hand, may have so many mistakes that it would be prohibitively expensive to correct them, even if there was time. Yet, put two people like this together on the same team, and they may well dig in their heels and become more unbending in their views. It would be bad enough if only these two people were affected, but ultimately their stubbornness can hurt the entire group.

Personal conflicts are also determined by people's interpersonal behavior—how they behave in a conflict situation. Do they fight or do they run? Do they look for potential disagreements? How do they fight? Do they call names, shout, go for the throat? These behaviors are generally learned in elementary school. Certainly, when two individuals who are used to winning by force disagree, conflicts will arise. Neither will want to back down, and as tempers flare, the disagreement will become louder and louder.

No one wants to work in conditions like these. As a manager, your responsibility is to see that no one has to.

Acting as Mediator

Often, managers will be asked to act as mediators between two of their disputing employees. The request may come from your own manager or it may come from one or both of the disputants.

When playing this role, be sure to use proven mediation techniques as opposed to trying to convince both parties to settle the matter with common sense. The latter can get you into a very sticky situation, because each party may have a different perception of common sense. Ultimately, the disputants may come to agree on only one thing—they dislike your intervention in their affairs.

Let's review how the mediation process works.

To establish the proper environment, a mediator should stress that no one is there to judge guilt or innocence. The intent of the mediation is to help those in conflict get to the root of the problem and devise an acceptable solution. In keeping with this goal, the mediator should stress that the parties' focus should be on the future, not on the past. From this point on, all will concentrate on their future working relationship. This makes for more positive communications because no one may accuse the other of wrongdoing. You must also emphasize the importance of flexibility.

The goal of the mediation process is an agreement between the two parties that gives both a basis upon which to solve their problem and avoid future ones. Although a basically informal process, to be successful, mediation must follow five specific steps.

1. *Opening statement.* At the start of the meeting, you need to explain in detail the mediation process and answer any questions that arise. You also have to stress the confidentiality of the mediation session.

2. *Forum.* Next, each individual is given an opportunity to speak. No one is permitted to interrupt at this time. Not surprisingly, this phase is sometimes emotional and time consuming, depending on the conflict. But letting the parties vent their emotions is extremely important, because they will be more receptive to discussion later on.

3. *Caucuses.* After each person has stated a position, the mediator meets individually with the parties. Again, these are confidential sessions. There is no limit to the number of caucuses, as you go from one individual to the other in an effort to reach an agreement. In the process, you will share each person's comments as permitted by the disputants.

4. *Problem-solving/joint session.* When points of agreement become apparent, you should write them down. If there appear to be a number of these, or further group discussion is needed, then you may want to bring both parties together. It may be time to iron out any further differences. Any points where agreement is not possible should be separated out. The two disputants may have to agree to disagree on these issues.

5. *Written agreement.* With the help of the parties, you should finalize the settlement in writing. The agreement is reviewed and signed by everyone, including you as the mediator. The written agreement is a reminder of what each party has agreed to do in order to resolve the mutual problem.

The worksheet in Figure 8.1 may help you accomplish this process.

The benefits of the mediation process should be clear. The process boosts morale by helping to put an end to the disagreement and get past the disputants' pent-up emotions. You, as mediator, should come away from the experience perceived as a wise peacemaker.

Not everyone can take on the role of a mediator. The position demands someone who is an active listener, able to pay attention to both words and body language.

FIGURE 8.1
Sample Mediator Worksheet

1. Who are the parties to the dispute?
   _____
   _____

2. When did the disagreement become evident?
   _____
   _____

3. How did it become evident?
   _____
   _____

4. What is the nature of the disagreement?
   _____
   _____

5. What are the three or four most important issues?
   _____
   _____

6. What are potential areas of agreement?
   _____
   _____

7. Where is there room for compromise?
   _____
   _____

8. What actions to date have been taken to resolve the conflict?
   _____
   _____

9. What further actions will be taken (prioritize these)?
   _____
   _____

10. What actions will be taken if there is no resolution of the conflict?
    _____
    _____

A Party to the Conflict

Sometimes, you may not be an observer but rather a disputant in a conflict. If the dispute is between you and someone whose work you supervise, then it will be almost impossible for you to be objective. You may want to turn to the human resources department or to your own manager for assistance. It is wise to talk about the situation to determine if the clash is due to a personality conflict with your employee or a job performance problem. It may be either, and the latter is more easily solved.

A personality conflict occurs when you and your employee don't agree with each other. But it can go further than this. Besides a difference of viewpoints, a strained relationship may prompt destructive action by the employee. Your staff member may work in an acceptable manner but may question you at every turn of events. Worse, the employee may be sullen or unpleasant in speaking to you, ignore your instructions, and gossip against you. Under these circumstances, you will find it hard to be polite and civil to the individual. It only makes it doubly difficult for you if the individual is friendly with and respected by coworkers.

Under these circumstances, what should you do?

Once you determine that a personality conflict exists, you need to work to reduce or resolve the conflict. Even in this situation, where conflict involves just two individuals, you're really still in the middle. As the employee's supervisor, you have to judge not only the employee's behavior but also your own. Ask yourself, "Am I contributing to this problem?"

It's very easy to forget that our behavior, which seems quite acceptable to us, might upset, even infuriate another person. For instance, a manager committing "halo effect" appraisal error judges an employee's total work by only one characteristic, the individual's neat desk. The employee with a very messy workstation may be labeled a poor worker, when in reality this person may be a top performer. If you maintain a neat office, you may have a skewed perspective on the office pack rat.

Take another situation. A manager who gets angry and upset easily may not realize that what feels like "blowing off a little steam" can be intimidating, rude, or incendiary to one of the staff members. Or take a manager who is always in a hurry. An employee who needs time to question the manager about work assignments may feel frustrated, even alienated.

Only after determining to what extent, if at all, you contribute to a personality conflict can you determine how to resolve the difference. Here are some actions you can take.

- *Focus on the work.* Don't feel that you need to socialize with your employee. It is best to stick to matters of work so that the staff member will have no reason to feel that you are being either invasive or unnaturally friendly.
- *Accentuate the positive.* When you see evidence of positive performance from the employee, acknowledge it as such. Let your staff member know that such job performance is appreciated.
- *Communicate with care.* An employee who does not like a manager often looks for ways to use the manager's own words to make "mistakes" by "following the directions." Likewise, very smart people can become very stupid when they're reading instructions they don't want to follow. You shouldn't give your troublesome staff member cause to do either.
- *Treat everyone the same.* You have to be careful not to treat your other staff members more favorably than the individual with whom you are having difficulties. Favoritism can open up a Pandora's box of problems.
- *Try the direct approach.* Talking with the staff member may or may not help, but it is worth a try. However, you need to meet with the staff member on equal terms, putting aside your position of authority. Even if you agree only that there is a personality conflict and to try to stay out of each other's way, just clearing the air may help.

If you are sure that you have been as fair and as accommodating to the other party as possible, but your employee continues to act with hostility, what can you do? As the individual's manager, you have the option of disciplining or even terminating the staff member. However, you must be sure that you aren't disciplining someone just for being difficult to work with. Especially if the employee in question doesn't like you, you can expect that your decision to terminate will be challenged vigorously in court. Liking everyone you work with is not a job requirement. Being able to work with everyone, however, is. A better solution is to transfer the employee to a different department.

Anger Management

Don't let yourself become angry, even if the other person's conduct justifies it. Stay calm. Let your staff member vent any feelings. Once the individual is done, he or she may be more prepared to listen to you and your side of the disagreement.

Pause once the person is through. Use body language to communicate to the other party, "I hear you and I want to help." Mirror the individual's position and posture, if possible. Getting on the same physical level as the other person can build rapport: sit if that person is seated; stand if that person is standing. When it is your turn to respond, speak in a calm voice. The other party will match the level of your voice. If you truly have heard out the other party, you should know exactly the source of the anger.

When you finally speak up, make an empathetic statement. Say something like, "I can see why you feel that way," or, "If I believed that . . . , I'd probably feel the same way as you do." Don't sound patronizing. Resist the temptation, too, to accept responsibility on your organization's part or another employee's as a way to put an end to the confrontation. Capitulation will only create further difficulties.

Rather, ask questions. Your intent is to determine the nature of the problem. Sometimes, the comments made by the other party are only a smoke screen, or the other party isn't as correct about the situation as he or she thinks.

Does this mean that you never should let your feelings out? Not at all. Sometimes, controlled anger can make clear an issue's importance. I know a manager who doesn't get angry at any of his employees when they make a mistake. Rather, she focuses on the situation itself, shouting about the problem the mistake has caused, demonstrating how important the error is and thereby encouraging more care by her employees in the future.

Likewise, you can show anger at an individual. If you think that seeing you show anger will serve your relationship well, then express it in a controlled manner. Don't yell and scream—such behavior will only make you look overly emotional and unprofessional. Ideally, rather than lose your temper, express your feelings of anger: "I feel angry because. . . ."

Violence at Work

There is one occasion when personality conflicts between staff members or between you and one of your employees may justify immediate termination. That is when the angry employee threatens either a peer, you, or another member of your organization. If a staff member has a predisposition to aggressiveness and perceives the workplace as a hostile environment, experiencing stress from a disagreement can trigger violent behavior.

What can you do? You can become sensitive to the level of employee stress in your work team, recognize danger signs, and address issues of stress and anxiety before they become dangerous to you and coworkers. Report potential problems to the human resources department and to your organization's security department, if you have one.

If your organization has an Employee Assistance Program (EAP), then you may want to refer the angry or troubled employee for counseling. If the threat comes from outside the organization, security measures must be taken to prevent access to the organization's premises. If the company has a no-threat policy and threats are punishable by termination, then security needs to be advised that the guilty employee is no longer to be allowed within the company. If the antagonisms appear intractable, then you may also want to alert the police.

Team versus Team

Conflicts can arise not only between you and a member of your staff but between work units or departments. Such conflicts may arise over battles for limited resources. Sometimes, they are due to differences in viewpoint about how to approach the same situation. Sometimes, group leaders have a personal conflict, and the feeling permeates down into their team's membership. The teams become silos, hoarding information and refusing to cooperate with one another.

To get the teams to work effectively together, one or both leaders need to meet to discuss how a better relationship between the groups will benefit both. Think of this as a modern version of old-fashioned horse trading, in which skills, abilities, knowledge, and technology are exchanged to move both teams forward in their efforts. As a follow-up measure, invite members of the other team to sit in on your team session. Learn to keep each other abreast of progress. Develop channels of communication and keep them open.

If you want to encourage a competitive urge among members, focus your group's attention on competing with teams from other companies, not their own.

In short, you need to practice the same conflict resolution techniques to build stronger ties with internal teams as you use to resolve conflicts between staff members or conflicts between you and a direct report.

Peer against Peer

Conflicts between managers are much more common today than conflicts between a manager and an employee. Disagreements on business decisions or procedures can disintegrate into personal conflicts.

Ideally, everyone in your organization is pulling in the same direction, collaborating and cooperating to achieve the company's strategic goals. But in the real world, problems can arise from mixed messages, personality differences, and real and not-so-real (like political or turf) dilemmas. Your first goal should be to avoid such conflicts. But, should differences arise, your second objective should be to resolve the problem before it escalates and impairs your ability to work together.

Problems fall into four categories: communications, turf and territory, professionalism, and interpersonal issues. Conflicts can arise between you and another manager when messages are distorted by jammed communication channels or by a third person in your organization who distorts your comments, either consciously or unconsciously. Turf battles arise over areas of responsibility, as one manager, like a gang leader, rumbles to protect the boundaries of authority. When one manager treats another with little respect, then a match is lit that can make ashes out of a positive work relationship.

Different problems demand different solutions. Let's look at some remedies and problems they are most suited to address.

- *Exercise professional courtesy.* Brusque demands of a colleague can only be alienating. Worse, hostility can seep down into the two departments, and ultimately the employees behave rudely to one another.
- *Establish a common ground.* This bit of advice might seem manipulative, but rather than criticize your colleague, even if you feel justified, flatter the person. You should be able to find a reason to say something nice. Use flattery to smooth the waters between you and a rigid, negative, or otherwise unpleasant peer and lay the groundwork for a better relationship in the future.
- *Watch your mouth.* Don't say anything about a coworker that you wouldn't want to have repeated by another.
- *Ask for help.* You can even go so far as to admit your own shortcomings in the process. You can defuse a conflict by making the other party seem superior to you.
- *Make small talk work for you.* Build connections with your colleagues based on personal interests, not just professional needs. Your common interests are grounds for a more positive relationship in the future.
- *Use humor.* Humor can be a powerful weapon for building allies, particularly when it is used to show others that you don't take yourself too seriously. Besides, a shared laugh is comparable to a favorite song, book, movie, or Broadway show—it builds rapport.

- *Avoid hostility by reframing the conversation.* Your colleague is short-tempered and is always ready for a fight. You can let the individual's hostility trigger your own anger, or you can paraphrase hostile remarks to prove that you were listening to the complaint, add a sympathetic comment that does not take sides, and then continue the conversation.

- *Confront the issue privately.* If you must confront a coworker, do so in private—not only away from your mutual staff members but away from other members of senior management. Raised voices have no place in the hallways of an organization or even in a management meeting. One CEO chose to bring in an outsider when she realized that three of her senior executives had territorial issues that they lacked the professionalism to resolve themselves. The new manager was hired as referee, a role the CEO didn't have time to assume herself.

- *Know where boundaries start and end.* You may be above issues of turf, seeing territorial battles in your organization as petty and willing to let others operate in your turf without permission, but others may not be so open-minded. If your intrusion into another's territory is likely to trigger a conflict, respect the boundary and get off that turf immediately. If you need to go into another's area of responsibility to accomplish an objective, speak to that manager first. Either ask the manager to cooperate by doing the work for you, or ask permission to do the work yourself.

■ Did You Know . . . ?

Silos—the compartmentalization of business into relatively independent, freestanding operating units—are real, and they can be really bad. A study by the American Management Association found that 83 percent of the respondents said there were silos in their companies. Fully 97 percent of those with silos think they have a negative effect. More telling, 31 percent believe that silos have destructive consequences, creating turf wars and territorial battles, lack of cooperation, and power struggles. The primary cause, said the respondents, was the attitude of the unit manager. A noncollaborative corporate culture and tradition didn't help.

   The biggest offender was the research and development department. Marketing, finance, and purchasing were also named.

Intuitively, you may know how to resolve conflicts. But in today's leaner, meaner organizations, it is easy to forget. It may help to keep in mind that failure to address disagreements early, before they become conflicts, can decrease productivity and innovation and may impede the career advancement of the executive(s) involved.

■ Tips

- If you say something, and you find the person with whom you are talking becoming upset, then pause. The silence that follows should help the other person to regain control. You can then probe to find the source of the problem.

- We all have hot buttons—from personal to professional to political issues. If you accidentally press someone's hot button, you may be able to return to your previous relationship if you take remedial action immediately. Don't let the other party go away upset.

■ See Also

Kaye, Kenneth. *Workplace Wars and How to End Them: Turning Personal Conflicts into Productive Teamwork.* AMACOM, 1994.

Masters, Marick F. and Robert R. Albright. *The Complete Guide to Conflict Resolution in the Workplace.* AMACOM, 2001.

Mayer, Bernard. *The Dynamics of Conflict Resolution: A Practitioner's Guide.* Jossey-Bass, 2000.

Thiederman, Sondra. *Making Diversity Work: Seven Steps for Defeating Bias in the Workplace.* Dearborn Trade, 2003.

Weeks, Dudley. *The Eight Essential Steps to Conflict Resolution: Preserving Relationships at Work, at Home, and in the Community.* Putnam Publication Group, 1994.

■ **Self-Assessment**

How Do You Rate?

Which approach to conflict management do you usually take when faced with differences?

1. Are problems that concern you handled by others?
2. Are your ideas and comments ignored?
3. Do you feel your concerns aren't being met?

If you say yes to these three questions, you may often wimp out when faced with conflicts.

How would you respond to these three questions?

1. Is negotiating difficult for you?
2. Do you find it hard to make concessions to others?
3. Are you unable to say, "I'm sorry?"

If you say yes to these, you may be more inclined to fight than to compromise.

And finally . . .

1. Do you look for reasons behind a disagreement with another?
2. Do you ask questions to clear the air?
3. Do you make an effort to avoid a recurrence?

If you say yes to these three questions, you tend to seek out solutions to conflicts and resolve them by getting to their cause. Congratulations!

9

Disciplining and Terminating Employees

The topics of discipline and termination are uncomfortable. After all, you want to deal with your employees as responsible adults who want to work. Unfortunately, not every employee will turn out to be as responsible as you wish. Sometimes, too, you will be faced with an otherwise excellent employee who has difficulty adhering to one or more rules that must be enforced.

Rule infractions happen. Here are some examples of rule violations that you may have to deal with.

- John is one of your most productive employees, but he has become sloppy about safety measures. One day, as you walk through the plant, you notice that John is working in a hazardous zone without his protective glasses and gloves.
- Ethel, a supervisor, has been coming in late every other morning. Her team's work continues to be satisfactory, and she is meeting all her project deadlines, but you know she is setting a poor example for her employees.
- Anna, your administrative assistant, skipped out of the office for a two-hour lunch break, leaving behind some critical work.

Although each individual has broken a department or corporate rule, each instance must be examined individually before taking corrective discipline.

Most organizations have two counseling tracks: one for performance problems, another for rule violations. The existence of two tracks reflects the fact that rule violations are a more serious issue than a shortcoming in job performance. Besides, poor job performance is not necessarily a deliberate act of the employee and can often be redressed with either training or positive reinforcement.

Counseling for Misconduct

As a first step in rule violations, the employee is given a verbal warning. The written warning follows if the violation or other offense is repeated. The message should be clear: Upon another repetition of the incident, the employee will be suspended or terminated, depending on the nature of the offense.

Suspension is given in the event of repeated misconduct or a serious offense. Sometimes the employee is paid while away from work, sometimes not. The nature of the misconduct determines that. The staff member is expected to use the time away to think over what happened and come back with a new frame of mind. If the problem continues, then the employee is terminated.

No consideration is given to either a transfer or a demotion. The assumption is that the employee is at fault. Depending on the misconduct, for instance extreme violation of safety rules or theft, termination may actually be the first step and not the last step in disciplining a rule violator.

Besides varying according to the nature of the offense, disciplinary actions depend on:

- The effect that the offense has on the business, including coworkers.
- The employee's response to being called on the behavior.
- The possibility that the behavior will be repeated.
- Previous disciplinary actions against other employees for similar offenses.

For instance, a verbal or written reprimand would follow a first offense of the following kinds:

- Knowingly filling out a time sheet of another employee.
- Having one's time sheet filled out by another employee or altering a time sheet.
- Habitual tardiness without explanation.
- Chronic absenteeism.
- Disorderly conduct on corporate property.

- Immoral conduct or indecency on company property.
- Chronic early departure from the workplace.
- Contributing to poor housekeeping.
- Malicious gossip or spreading rumors.

A repetition of such misbehavior would lead to suspension, even termination.
Behaviors that call for immediate discharge include:

- Possession or consumption of nonprescribed narcotics on company property.
- Intoxication at work.
- Instigation of a fight on company property.
- Theft.
- Intentional harassment, including sexual harassment.
- Destruction of property.
- Insubordination.
- Misrepresentation of important facts in seeking employment.
- Violation of confidentiality or sharing of trade secrets outside the business.
- Extended unexcused absences.
- Gambling on corporate premises.

Consequently, you need to ask yourself some questions before taking action.

- Is this a first offense or an habitual occurrence? Has the individual been warned before?
- Is a safety issue involved? Has the employee or other workers or customers been put at risk?
- How is the employee's attitude in general? Have there been previous rule violations?
- Are there extenuating circumstances that need to be considered before making a decision?
- How have you responded in the past when other direct reports have committed the same infraction?
- Does your organization have a written policy that dictates action under the circumstances?
- How serious is the offense?
- Has the employee lost the company either business or profit?

The one-on-one counseling session in which the misbehavior is discussed is very similar to a counseling session about marginal employee performance.

Let's take a look at some examples of rule violations and discuss the best ways to deal with them.

John, the productive worker who has become sloppy about safety rules, needs to be reminded that he can't violate the rules. If you see him without protective clothing or safety goggles, you need to tell him to put the proper safety gear on immediately. If he repeats the offense, you need to warn him that continued violation of the safety rules will result in his suspension without pay. If John cannot be persuaded to comply within a reasonable (short) time, then you have to terminate him.

If a meeting with Ethel, the late arrival, reveals that she has had to take a family member to the hospital for chemotherapy treatments in the morning, then some flexibility may be called for. This is especially true if she seems apologetic and is even willing to work through lunch to compensate for lost work time.

As for Anna, the administrative assistant who failed to take the responsibilities of her job seriously, opting for a long lunch even though her work was not completed, you would have to consider her job record. Is this a first-time offense or a continuing problem? Although such rule infractions are rarely cause for dismissal, they can escalate into other instances of neglect or insubordination, which if allowed to go uncorrected can lead to termination. At least a talk is in order.

Obviously, administering discipline to employees is never a cut-and-dried procedure. But some action needs to be taken in each and every instance of a rule violation. Let me explain why.

Fair and Consistent Treatment

Unlike giving a negative performance review, the need for disciplinary action usually becomes more public than either you or the individual would like it to be. Most coworkers of the problem employee will be aware of the rule violation. Everyone can see, for example, when an employee arrives late or leaves early, when an employee who reports to you is insubordinate, or when a worker gets into a fight and threatens a coworker. In such instances, your employees are all interested to see how you respond, and there is bound to be a lot of talk. Consequently, you need to make certain that you respond in a fair and consistent manner. The discipline should be "consistent" in that the punishment should be appropriate for the offense, and it should be "fair" in that it should be similar to that given violators of the same rule, all other issues being the same. For instance, it would be inconsistent to give Fred a warning for arriving late three times in one week and dock Sarah's pay for leaving early twice.

Further, you need to act as soon after the infraction as possible to prevent any misconceptions that you are soft on rule violators. Of course, before issuing disciplinary measures, you should check to be sure that the individual knew and understood the work rule that was violated.

I shouldn't have to remind you that company policies, rules, and procedures should be communicated to all employees. Such communication is the best tool you have to avoid rule infractions and subsequent discipline. Employees cannot be expected to adhere to rules and guidelines unless they understand them.

Communication and Correction

The rules of the workplace should be given to each of your direct reports upon their employment. Rules that deal with security and safety, such as the requirements about protective clothing and securing the work area, should be prominently posted. Constant reminders help keep employees in compliance with the rules as well as avoid debate about what is acceptable.

When rule violations happen, remember that the purpose of discipline is not to punish but to correct the behavior. After all, the employees you are dealing with are adults. Corrective discipline gives them the opportunity to try again and to change unacceptable behavior. Rather than simply impose punishment, let the individual know that you don't expect a recurrence of the problem.

Those managers who practice punitive discipline seem to spend much of their workday looking for wrongdoings against which they can level punishment. Such a management style is unhealthy for the workplace, communicating a lack of trust in one's employees and a demand for blind obedience—which actually encourages willful disobedience of rules and regulations. Employees play a game with their managers when they work in such environments, deliberately breaking the rules to see if they can beat the system and get away with it.

So explain the reasons for the rules. Look upon disciplinary action as corrective in the initial stages. It should become punitive only when counseling fails to change the employee's behavior.

Internal Investigations

When an incident occurs and you weren't there to see what happened, you need to talk to those who did see it. This is particularly true if the defendant denies responsibility for what happened. Meet with witnesses as soon as possible after the incident. The questions asked should be open-ended and phrased to show no bias that might influence the answers. Larry, who works in a major appliance retailer, told me about an incident in which he was involved. A senior manager was investigating an employee's complaint against another manager. As a colleague, Larry was contacted. The senior VP asked him, "You don't think [Joe] is a bully with employees, do you?" A fair and objective question? Not at all.

Keep notes of witnesses' comments. These will be part of your documentation for your next meeting with the employee. During this investigative stage, you may want to put the employee on suspension to minimize tension as you look into the situation.

If you will be interviewing several individuals who were present or are familiar with the situation, ask each the same questions. Compare notes. If you are dealing with members of your own department, you should be familiar enough with their relationship with the employee to recognize lies told either to protect or to impugn the employee.

Once you have insights into what actually happened—the who, what, where, and how—you are better able to discuss the incident with the employee.

Bend Only So Far

Although your goal is to give a rule violator the opportunity to correct the behavior, sometimes you will have no choice but to dismiss an employee because of inexcusable behavior. Certainly, acts of gross negligence that cause accidents or illegal acts must be met with swift termination. As unpleasant as this may be, your staff must understand that certain behavior will not be tolerated. Any action short of termination is bound to be interpreted as weak by the offender's peers. They may even feel resentment at having to continue to work with someone who has committed a major offense.

Reasonable Rules

One way to avoid excessive rule violations is not to have too many rules. This may seem like an easy way out, but it's not. Rules do serve a purpose—they keep the workplace safe, cost efficient, and running smoothly. However, rules may become a burden rather than a help when they regulate too much of an individual's workday.

So, before establishing a rule, consider its intent. See if you can create a rule that meets your goal yet doesn't put unnecessary restrictions on your workers' approach to their jobs.

Probation

If the employee has made serious mistakes or misjudgments on the job, but you believe that the employee has the potential to turn around, you may want to put the individual on probation. A typical probation period lasts from one to three months. During this time, the worker's performance should be monitored strictly for any repetition of the problem.

At the end of the probation period, the employee's behavior should be assessed. An employee who violates the terms of the probation and is subsequently fired will be hard-pressed to prove unfair treatment to a judge or jury.

Probation is often used when an employee has shown some aberrant behavior, such as drug or alcohol abuse. The employee agrees to seek help, and an agreement is formulated to that effect. The probationary period also gives a company the chance to investigate further charges against an employee. A worker who fails to come up with a reasonable plan to improve or correct improper behavior will be fired at once. Likewise, if the investigation identifies a major violation of company rules, the employee will be terminated.

Suspension is a fairly drastic measure, one step short of termination for misconduct, and it can be tricky. Some employees enjoy the paid vacation it offers. Those suspended without pay return to work broke and angry. Their coworkers aren't that thrilled, either, because they had to do the individual's work during the suspension.

Certain behavior, like possession of an unapproved weapon at work, having a hand in the till, or endangering the health and safety of coworkers, demands immediate termination. The doctrine of "employee at will" theoretically gives you the freedom to fire workers whenever you wish. But unless you have a good reason for termination, you may be vulnerable to a lawsuit claiming the firing was unfair. Such legal cases usually charge that the termination was due to racial, age, or other bias (see Chapters 6 and 7). Consequently, documentation is as important in terminating employees for rule violations as it is in terminations for subpar job performance.

The Termination

The easiest firings are those produced by unexpected crises. For instance, one of your staff members, unprovoked, hauls off and belts another. Your marketing manager is revealed to be running a scam in which he is contracted with himself to produce marketing pieces. A purchasing manager is discovered to be taking kickbacks. These are easy terminations because the provocation is clear and the remedy obvious.

But such terminations are rare. More frequent are the situations in which an employee returns from suspension and commits an offense that would provoke a counseling session or verbal warning if the individual had an unblemished record. You would like to begin the disciplinary process again, but the system demands that the individual be terminated.

No matter how unfair the situation seems to you, or no matter how talented the employee, you must rid your organization of the individual. That's your responsibility to the firm.

If you are concerned that the employee may take the case to court, imagine yourself defending your action in front of a jury. The questions that an attorney is likely to ask include:

- Was the employee aware of the rule and that his behavior was in violation of that rule?
- How do you know that the employee knew?
- Was the employee confronted in a timely and specific manner about the rule violation?
- How often did you talk about it?
- Was the system of progressive discipline followed?
- Were the disciplinary actions appropriate to the offense?
- Is the rule applied consistently to all employees? What about discipline for violation of that rule—is that consistently applied?
- Is documentation complete? (For more about documentation, see Chapter 7.)

Look for anything that a third party could twist to suggest that the real reason for the termination is not the individual's behavior but rather a personal grudge or bias. Check out past performance assessments for previous rule violations.

Finally, determine if there are any mitigating circumstances. Ask yourself, "Could a neutral and unbiased jury come to the decision that you behaved unfairly?" Certainly, talk over your decision with your own manager and/or someone from your firm's human resources department before firing the individual.

The meeting with the employee shouldn't take more than 15 minutes. The goal is to convey the decision to terminate the employee. For the meeting, you should do the following:

- Prepare what you will say ahead of time. Bungled terminations usually result from a manager acting without thinking first.
- Be prepared to give an adequate reason for the discharge.
- Allow the employee to have a say.
- Make it clear that the decision is final.
- Suggest that the individual go to the human resources department with further questions.

Depending on the misbehavior, the response may vary from tears to shouts to threats of violence. Anger is the reaction that managers fear the most: "You can't do this to me! I'll get you for this!" Fortunately, anger is the least common response, and it can be defused by listening.

Of course, if you have reason to believe that an employee might become emotional or even violent, you may want to arrange to have a member of your company's employee assistance program or a security person nearby, depending on the reaction you expect.

Increasingly, companies escort out angry employees terminated for rule violations. Where sabotage is likely, they also restrict reentry into the workplace unless a representative from the security department is present. It may be unpleasant to tell the employee this, but such precautions could prevent the employee from exacting revenge on the organization.

If the employee appears to be in a reasonable, rational state of mind, treat the person in a professional manner. To do otherwise likely will embarrass the fired worker and unsettle coworkers, who may be demoralized by the bum's rush being given a former colleague. Further, such behavior may so anger the terminated employee that a charge is instituted against the company, with or without cause.

Immediately after the meeting, document what happened. Actually, documentation under these circumstances may be more important than documentation of a termination meeting due to continued poor performance. Assuming that the incident is serious, necessitating immediate termination, you will want to write up what happened, the information obtained in investigating the situation if you were not present when the misbehavior occurred or was discovered, and the reasons for choosing to terminate the employee rather than take other action, like suspension.

You need to share the reason for your action with the remaining staff members. Don't think you can get away with saying nothing. Be forthright but sparse in your explanation. For instance, you might say simply, "Michael was fired this morning after several infractions of the rules." Or, "Despite repeated warnings and attempts to schedule her work hours so she could meet family commitments, Sharon was fired because of chronic lateness."

Honesty may be the most prudent policy, but even if they are true, damaging comments could interfere with a former employee's chances for a new job. You might seem callous to the remaining workers, and if your words are vile enough, they could even trigger a defamation lawsuit on the part of the terminated worker. A defamation charge isn't a challenge to the employee's dismissal. Rather, it charges that you significantly damaged the employee's good name, reducing that person's chances of being hired by another company.

A defamation case usually depends on whether or not distribution of damaging information was intentional—whether you meant to hurt your former employee. To sue for defamation, a former employee must show that you made a false or damaging statement, told or wrote that statement to at least one other employee, were negligent or intentional in communicating the statement, and/or harmed the worker in some way (such as causing him to lose a position elsewhere) by communicating the statement. Some unflattering comments don't usually qualify as defamation. You do risk defamation when you falsely claim that the employee committed a crime, was incompetent at the job, used drugs or alcohol at work, or otherwise acted in some way unfit for the job.

But legal action shouldn't be a cause for worry if you follow the procedures outlined here. Nor should you let your compassion for people stand in the way of taking action when an employee repeatedly violates rules. Such compassion is misdirected. Rather, your attention should be focused on those staff members who, despite their many personal problems and difficulties, adhere to the company rules and policies. Don't let one bad apple spoil the rest of the barrel.

■ Quotable Quote

Coach Vince Lombardi put a manager's responsibility this way: "A player's got to know the basics of the game and how to play his position [employee training]. Next, you've got to keep him in line [discipline]."

■ Did you know . . . ?

If you have a system of employee discipline, you should have a system of appeals. The right of appeal is a way for employees who argue with a discipline decision to have their case heard—and to reassure juries that the employee had an opportunity to plead his argument. Some organizations provide employees with rights of appeal by setting up mediation teams, where employees and management listen to the facts of the case and make a judgment about its fairness and adherence to organization policies. Union contracts specify grievance procedures for employees to follow when they believe they have been disciplined without just cause. Civil service boards and arbitration hearings are other vehicles for employees to appeal disciplinary actions.

■ Tips

- Ambiguous rules do little. For rules to work, everyone affected by them should be able to understand exactly what they mean.

- It is *your* responsibility to see that employees know all the rules and policies they are expected to follow.

- Focus on the misbehavior, not the personality, of the rule violator.

■ See Also

Cava, Roberta. *Difficult People: How to Deal with Impossible Clients, Bosses, and Employees.* Firefly Books, 1997.

Crowe, Sandra A. *Since Strangling Isn't an Option—Dealing with Difficult People—Common Problems and Uncommon Solutions.* Perigee, 1999.

Weiss, Donald H. *Fair, Square & Legal: Safe Hiring, Managing and Firing Practices to Keep You & Your Company Out of Court.* AMACOM, 1999.

10

Learn to Listen

Savvy managers listen as much as, if not more than, they speak. They listen not only because they want to show that they are interested in others' ideas but also because they know they will learn more by listening than they ever will by talking. Good listeners welcome new information and new ideas.

Asked if they are good listeners, many managers will automatically say, "Yes. I've always been a good listener. My employees know that they can come to me and tell me exactly what's on their minds. I always hear them out and never interrupt them."

Passive versus Active Listening

Unfortunately, if you identify with these managers, you are probably a passive listener; that is, you are available and accessible to your employees. Certainly, availability is important, but as a manager, you need to go further. You need not only to provide others with the opportunity to speak but also to work on understanding, interpreting, and showing interest in what is being said. That is what is meant when we use the term *active listening*.

In Chapter 12, I point out that you shouldn't dominate conversations by interrupting others when they speak. Let me add here that, occasionally, interrupting a speaker is acceptable to make sure you understand what is being said. Clarifying your understanding is one aspect of active listening. Restating major points that a speaker is making is another.

Remember, too, the important thing is that the employee get the message across. So if a staff member needs help in articulating a problem or offering a solution, then you should be willing to give it. For instance, let's assume that one of your employees, Chris, has a concern about a plan you want implemented. She's nervous to share her concern with you, and consequently, she becomes tongue-tied and rambles. You can help Chris get back on track with a statement like, "Chris, you mentioned there were three things that were bothering you. I understand now about one and two. Could you tell me about the third problem?"

What Did Chris Propose?

Even if Chris has been very articulate about her worries, you might want to use a question to summarize what you believe. "So Chris, if we implement the plan, staff won't be able to do the work and we'll have to get outside help, thereby exceeding allocated expenses."

In doing this, you may be surprised to find that that isn't exactly what Chris meant. "No, I think we can still get it done within budget, but I think we shouldn't begin until we train members of the team to handle the new tasks. The training would only delay implementation by a month."

Chris will be pleased that you heard her out and accepted her idea. "So, Chris, how should we organize this training? If it will ensure successful completion of the project, it's worth the delay."

Being heard is important to everyone, and listening to people attentively and courteously shows that you respect and appreciate what they have to say. By giving Chris and other staff members your full attention, you will make them feel good about working for you.

Hear the Employee Out

What if you disagree or the individual is saying something that isn't new to you? Regardless, let the person finish. More important, listen to what is being said. Don't tune them out while thinking about your response. Don't assume that you know what's coming next—you could miss some important information. Instead, focus on what's being said. Smile. Nod. From time to time, make encouraging comments that show you are interested and are actively listening (e.g., "Right," "Yes," and "Sure"). If you are preparing a response instead of listening, you are not giving your full attention to the speaker.

At regular intervals, summarize the points being made. Review what you have understood so far. This ensures that everyone has the same understanding at the same time. "So, Chris, we've agreed that you will go on the Internet to check out training organizations that can come on-site and give our unit the training it needs, right?"

What if you aren't following what is being said? If you need repetition, further explanation, or extra information, don't hesitate to ask for it. Whether you are speaking with a subordinate or with a supervisor, ask the person to clarify their comment. "Can I just check this out with you? It seems like you're saying. . . ," or, "I'm not clear on this. Can you go over it again for me?" or, "Let me make sure I understand. You want me to add several thousand dollars to the budget to help us finance new programs, despite the tight financial constraints we're operating under. Is that right?" Take responsibility for finding out the things you need to know, and listen to the answers you are given. If you think your message might have been misunderstand, you might tell the other party, "I can't have explained myself clearly. What I wondered was. . . ."

If you question and clarify what the other party has said, your effort at clear, two-way communication should be respected. If you don't raise questions despite confusion, you might either lose a good idea or make a serious management mistake. Either one will cost you.

Bad Listening Habits

Why is listening such a problem for most people? We assume that listening, like speaking, is a skill that we master as we grow up. But active listening takes the same effort as developing and refining our speaking skills.

Often, as we grow up, we actually develop bad listening habits, ignoring what others are saying because we:

- *Consider the subject dull or too complicated.* We tune out a speaker because we feel the subject will be boring or, even worse, fear that we will be unable to understand what the person is saying.
- *React, not to the speaker's words, but to the speaker's appearance or mannerisms.* Consequently, we don't hear the good ideas.
- *Overreact.* Our enthusiasm or anger can color what we hear.
- *Listen only for facts.* We need to give all our attention to a speaker to understand the full message.

- *Fake attention.* Many people are so happy with their ability to "act interested," that they use the skill when they actually should be paying attention.
- *Tolerate or create distractions.* Doodling, interrupting, and turning the pages of a book or a magazine are all distracting actions that should not be done or tolerated.
- *Daydream.* We need to teach ourselves not to allow our minds to wander— to remain focused on the subject at hand.
- *Disagree.* When we disagree with a speaker, we get so involved in formulating our response that we don't always hear all of the speaker's points.

How Are Your Listening Skills?

If you think you have one or all of these problems, it's time to make some notes on just how good or bad your listening is. Begin by keeping paper and pen handy and making a list of specific listening errors you catch yourself making.

Each time you note a specific listening error you've made, try to recall what you were doing at the time that caused the error. As you remember and visualize the cause, categorize the error under one of the above habits. By keeping a careful record, you may discover the listening mistakes you make most often. Work, then, to avoid these. Fortunately, we can break our bad listening habits, but before we can do that, we need to be aware that they exist.

Turning Over a New Leaf

Studies have shown that typically we remember about 30 percent of what we hear. The effective listener will try to improve on this percentage through the following techniques.

Focus on What Is Being Said

We think about four times faster than we talk. That is a lot of thinking time. You can take advantage of it. Rather than think about what you will say next, ask yourself what further information would be helpful in understanding a speaker's message.

If you are in a meeting, take notes if you can do so without distracting yourself from what is being said. (There will be more about note taking in this chapter because it can be a major aid for a busy manager.)

It's very easy to let our thoughts distract us from what is being said. In today's lean, high-stress organizations, our minds are preoccupied with numerous concerns. They have no time to be interrupted by someone talking to them. Consequently, they don't listen and so lose out on valuable insights and information.

If you want to be a good listener, you need to make a serious commitment towards becoming one. Don't be one of those people who are poor listeners simply because they have no intention of listening well. They're too wrapped up in their own concerns to hear anyone else.

Prompt Further Information

We often assume that an entire message has been communicated when a speaker stops talking. Not so. The speaker may have much more information to share. Any statement can be followed up by at least one more statement of explanation or example. Therefore, your response, whenever possible, should be a question that elicits further information.

This question should be neutral, nonjudgmental, and nonaccusing; it should seek only to keep the conversation flowing along the theme already established by the speaker. You don't have to ask a specific question. Repeat what the speaker just said with a questioning tone. For instance, if the speaker is defending himself against a customer's complaint, telling you, "I shouldn't be blamed for a systems error," you might say, "You feel that you are being blamed," or, "You think the problem is due to a systems problem." Such a response naturally leads to further information—and maybe awareness of an operating problem.

Also, if you are concerned about upsetting a staff member further by anything you say, rephrasing what the employee has said will enable you to carry on the conversation without further igniting the situation.

Probe with Open-Ended Questions

Don't ask questions that can only be answered with a yes or a no. Closed questions won't explore either the speaker's feelings or the facts for errors and insights.

Beware of Your Personal Biases

As we listen to what people are saying, their words pass through our personal frame of reference built over the years from life experiences. Some remarks can trigger emotions that impede our ability to understand the message from the speaker's perspective. Consequently, an important step toward becoming an effective listener is for you to recognize how perceptual filters may influence your understanding. This insight will reduce the danger that emotional reactions might cloud your thinking.

Restate What Has Been Said

Many books suggest that we paraphrase, but that doesn't mean that you should parrot the speaker. Rather, you should repeat what you heard *in your words.* Say, "Let me be sure I understand clearly what you want me to do. First . . . second . . . third . . . ," or, "Are you saying that . . . ?" or, "The main points you've covered so far are. . . . Have I left out anything you said?" This is reflective listening.

The difference between parroting a speaker and reflective listening goes beyond demonstrating to the speaker that you have truly heard and understood. By paraphrasing the individual's views, you are giving the person a chance to reflect on what was said, and maybe even to have a change of mind after hearing it again. Some handy paraphrasing responses are:

- "If I understand you correctly, you're saying. . . ."
- "You really mean that. . . ."
- "As you see it. . . ."
- "Let me see if I get where you're coming from on that—you think that. . . ."
- "So, to sum up then, you feel. . . ."

Reflective listening shouldn't be used in each and every conversation you have with employees, peers, customers, or your own manager. It works best when you and the other party are in disagreement over an issue and want to talk things over, when you or someone else has a conflict to resolve, or when someone wants feedback on an idea.

Overlook "Hot-Button" Words

Sometimes, an individual will use profanity or call you a name in anger. If you allow yourself to get hung up on the individual's word choice, you may miss the primary message. Hear the customer or employee out.

Avoid Me-Too Interceptions

Your staff member comes in to tell you about a problem with a customer. "Jameson is a real crank. I can't do anything to please him. Do you know that yesterday. . . ." Before your worker completes the story, you jump in, "If you want to talk about annoying customers, I remember this old customer we had when I first came to work here. He. . . ." Before you know it, you are talking about yourself rather than allowing your employee to express frustration about a *current* client.

Yes, you should look for opportunities to share common experiences, but timing is key. Don't grab the ball in a conversational interception. Hear out your employee—even if you have heard a similar complaint before.

Be Flexible

You are talking about Topic A when the employee makes a remark that seems off the topic—in fact, puts you squarely on Topic Z. The comment may seem irrelevant, but it may be a clue to what's really on the employee's mind. To find out more about what your employee is thinking, shift gears from Topic A to Topic Z. You can always go back to Topic A after you've finished with Topic Z.

Respond to the Feelings, Then Focus on the Facts

Too often, managers do the reverse just to avoid an emotional outburst with an upset employee or customer. Let me tell you a story.

Frances, who is a creative designer in an ad agency, had sat through a meeting with her supervisor, an account manager, the firm's vice president, and the client representative. Every idea for a new marketing campaign that she presented was vetoed. Although she was told that the work was good, the group said it did not capture the client's needs. At the end of the meeting, Frances was furious and, fuming, she went into the account manager's office.

"I can't believe what just happened," she told Bill. "I put in a lot of overtime to come up with those designs. They represent my best work. How could they simply disregard it?" she asked him. "Calm down, calm down," he said. "Go back to your office and prepare some new designs." He, then, turned back to the material on his desk.

"But you don't understand," said Frances. "I don't know. . . ." Bill was preoccupied with other tasks and wasn't even listening.

As Frances left, she slammed the door.

Later that afternoon, Bill was speaking to Frances's team leader. "How are her new designs coming?" he asked. "They aren't," Leslie answered. "She has no idea what the group meant when it said her designs weren't suitable. She's just sitting at her desk staring into space. What advice did you give her?" Leslie asked.

That's when it came to Bill. He hadn't given her any advice. He didn't want to cope with her anger or frustration and, consequently, hadn't done anything more than tell her to "calm down" and get to work. He should have allowed her to share her feelings, then discussed alternative designs that might satisfy the client.

Customer service representatives are familiar with the need to respond to feelings first when confronted with an irate customer. Let's assume a customer calls to complain about a late delivery. The rep says, "I'll have another delivery out of the warehouse in an hour. You should get it tomorrow." Right move? Wrong. The rep solved the customer's problem but failed to acknowledge the customer's justifiable anger.

Questions, comments, explanations, and even solutions come a lot easier after, not before, pent-up emotions are released.

Don't Assume

Too often, when someone is speaking, we assume that we already know what they are talking about and, consequently, don't have to listen. Worse, we don't listen for what we don't want to hear.

At a construction firm, a foreman told the regional manager that he was making irresponsible promises to customers. "There's no way that we can make these completion dates," he said. "Delivery of raw materials is also running behind schedule. And I've got too few men on my crew." "Don't worry," the regional manager reassured. "I'll look into it and see what I can do." But he did nothing.

As time went on, there were other such discussions. The regional manager knew that the foreman had received lots of flak from customers. Deliveries continued to be behind schedule and staff still was short. But, again, the regional manager did nothing.

Six months later, the foreman quit to join another construction firm, taking many of his former customers with him. "Why are you doing this?" the manager asked. Clearly, he hadn't heard the foreman's complaints. So he lost a top-notch worker.

"Where's Richard?"

To improve your listening skills, make a concerted effort to practice them and avoid the previously described listening mistakes. If you still find people reminding you about something that they say they had discussed previously with you, your problem may not be a problem with listening but instead, a problem with remembering what you hear. You might want to carry a little notebook and scribble notes about conversations in it. Listen to what is being said and note the key points in your own words. For instance, if one of your employees has asked to take a long weekend, and you have agreed, write down the fact in your notebook. Then transfer the note to your desk calendar so you don't wonder where Richard is on Thursday. As Confucius said, "The weakest ink lasts longer than the best memory."

You may also want to work to improve your memory. One of my colleagues observed just a few days ago that she is bombarded with so much information every day, she has a hard time keeping track. She is attentive and observant, and she is a good listener. But she often forgets small things. So she has taken to writing down the results of all phone calls and taking down her own minutes of meetings, and she reviews these notes frequently to increase her retention. She also makes a conscious effort to concentrate to ensure she remembers, even when she doesn't have her pad and pencil with her. She's even given herself a personal incentive to remember, thereby giving her more reason to keep in mind the myriad bytes of information that pass over her desk.

■ Quotable Quotes

"No one ever listened himself out of a job." —Calvin Coolidge

"Know how to listen, and you will profit even from those who talk badly."
—Plutarch

■ Tips

- Misunderstandings are caused by "wishful listening"—by hearing only what you want.

- Think about the message you are hearing, not the person who is saying it.

- If you promise to take action, do so. Put your promise in writing as soon as you can to avoid misunderstandings.

- Use silence as a tool to encourage hesitant speakers.

■ Did You Know . . . ?

You can tell how people think if you listen to their choice of phrase. Categories include the visual, which is indicated by phrases such as, "I see where you're coming from," and the auditory, indicated by phrases such as, "This sounds like a problem to me." A person who is influenced more by emotions will say, "I feel that we should move toward . . ." Not only does this technique give insight into how people think, it will also enable you to establish rapport with them. Listen, and then mirror their thinking preference.

■ See Also

Burley-Allen, Madelyn. *Listening: The Forgotten Skill.* John Wiley & Sons, 1995. Kratz, Abby Robinson. *Effective Listening Skills.* McGraw-Hill Trade, 1995.

11

How to Speak Assertively

Have you thought about how you communicate and what your communication style says about you? Let's assume that you plan to have dinner with an old friend, but at the last minute, your manager asks you to work on a rush job. Your friend will be in town only one evening. Would you typically:

1. Say nothing to your manager about your plans and simply agree to work late to finish the job?
2. Refuse your manager in no uncertain terms, berating him for his lack of planning?
3. Explain you won't be able to work late this evening because you have made special plans, but you could arrive early the next morning to complete the work?

Here's another hypothetical situation. Let's assume that one of your employees has made a serious error. You believe it should be brought to her attention. Would you typically:

1. Tell her, but in an apologetic and embarrassed manner, even offering to do the work in the future to prevent a recurrence of the problem?
2. Angrily reprimand the employee, accusing her of making a dumb mistake and demanding that she correct it immediately?
3. Discuss the mistake with the employee, attempting to determine the cause and identify ways to avoid its recurrence?

The three responses in both of the above examples characterize very different communication styles and behaviors. In both situations, the first response illustrates a passive communication and management style, the second an aggressive communication and management style, and the third an assertive communication and management style.

Of the three styles, it should be pretty evident which is most productive for you as a manager. An assertive response will help you achieve your goals—to make your point or communicate your need—without putting down or otherwise alienating the other party. To understand why the assertive style is right for you, let's look at all three styles in detail.

Passive, Aggressive, and Assertive Managers

Managers who use a passive communication style allow others to control them. They accept all criticism as valid and feel guilty, even apologetic, when they have to criticize others. They will take the line of least resistance and say or do nothing, concealing their feelings or desires. For instance, they will let an employee get away with murder rather than discuss shortcomings in work performance. They may even take on the employee's responsibilities rather than discuss the shortcomings. A passive style can lower staff respect for the manager.

When it comes to communicating with their own manager or customers, they may fail to represent their unit well, make a weak case for its needs, or accept criticisms without clarification. When this happens, they lose further staff respect and their own self-esteem. They may feel exploited, but those with whom they speak usually have done nothing to exploit them.

Aggressive managers, on the other hand, make their feelings known—often to the point of disregarding others' feelings. They may be domineering and insensitive, hence leaving others feeling resentful, angry, and put down.

Although employees may not openly defy aggressive managers, they will drag their feet. While tough language may gain the manager the edge over the short term, over the longer term, it will alienate employees, colleagues, and even their own boss. Managers who make demands of their own manager in a hostile manner only build distrust and resentment.

Assertive managers gain others' respect and do not frustrate or irritate others, because they express themselves in an honest, straightforward manner. They may stand up for their rights, but they do it in ways that don't violate others' rights. Assertive communications is self-enhancing but not at the expense of others. Assertive managers are open, honest, and up-front, because they believe that all people have an equal right to express themselves honestly. This openness and honesty encourages respect and cooperation from employees, managers, and others.

Here is the same sentence from all three styles.

1. *Assertive.* This is what I think.
2. *Aggressive.* This is what I think—you're dumb to think otherwise.
3. *Passive.* Whatever I think is probably not important to you.

Obstacles to Communicating Assertively

You might be thinking, "I can be assertive when I need to be." But shifting from one communication style to another only confuses others. Better to learn to communicate in an assertive manner all the time. How can you do this? To begin with, you need to identify why you sometimes don't communicate or behave in an assertive manner. There are three common obstacles to assertiveness.

1. Low self-esteem
2. Inability to handle conflict
3. Poor communication

Low Self-Esteem

If you see yourself as inadequate, limited in your skills and abilities, and unable to handle your new responsibilities, you may suffer from a poor self-concept or mental picture of yourself. Consequently, you may pass up an opportunity to take on a high-visibility project or to make a presentation to senior management from fear of doing a poor job. In the past, you may have done a poor job on a project or became tongue-tied in speaking before an audience, and the mental images of those occasions discourage you from trying again.

Alternatively, you might sit through a planning meeting in which your ideas are ignored. Later, you get into an argument with the facilitator, blaming that person for not giving you sufficient time to express your thoughts. You don't know what caused you to lose your temper, but likely your aggression stemmed from the fact that your ideas—and, in your mind, you—were ignored. The situation might have triggered memories from childhood when kids at school taunted you. You were put down then, and you feel as if you were put down during the meeting.

Both instances led to negative self-talk, an inner voice that compared the current situation to a past experience in which you did not meet expectations, damaging your positive self-esteem. To address this problem and behave more assertively in the future—to take on that project or make that presentation or leave the group meeting without feeling ignored—you need to silence your negative inner voice. Don't let the voice be a self-fulfilling prophecy, contributing to either a passive or aggressive response. Decrease how often you discuss your weaknesses with others and refrain from dwelling on negative thoughts. Instead, identify some positive self-statements and emphasize those. Maybe you aren't the most organized person, but if you can tell yourself that, "I can organize my work easily," in time you will be both saying and doing it. Write your positive thoughts on 3″ × 6″ cards or sticky notes and place them in your office where you will see them during the day. Share your goal to become more positive about yourself with friends and ask them to support you by discouraging you from dwelling on your shortcomings.

Inability to Handle Conflict

If you have been able to resolve conflict successfully throughout your life, you probably have developed a positive attitude toward it. When faced with a difference of opinion, you can be assertive rather than either wishy-washy or aggressive. Rather than become defensive or angry or, alternatively, give in to avoid the disagreement, you have learned to express your feelings by focusing on the issue, focusing on points of agreement as a foundation for discussion of points of argument, and emphasizing solutions rather than determining blame.

Poor Communication Skills

You may be very articulate but still lack the specific skills to respond to criticism or aggressive put-downs, praise, or other emotional situations. You need to learn how to express your feelings. "I statements" enable you to focus on the problem or situation without accusing or blaming the other person. For instance, you might say to an employee who interrupts you at meetings, "I'd like to finish describing my idea without interruption," instead of, "You always interrupt me," or, alternatively, letting the individual cut you off and take over the discussion. The point is to express what you feel, think, or need.

- "I feel angry when. . . ."

- "I think this because. . . ."
- "I need this done today because. . . ."

You don't create the likelihood of a conflict, because you aren't blaming anyone for a situation. Rather, you are making clear, concise, simple statements that reflect your wants, needs, or feelings. "I get angry when you break your promises," rather than, "You make me angry when you break your promises," or, "I believe the best policy is to. . . . ," instead of, "The only sensible thing is to. . . ." Let's say you want feedback on a new software program. If you say, "This is a good system," or, "This is the best system on the market," you close the door to feedback, but if you say, "I like this system," you allow your staff members either to agree or to disagree.

To provide constructive criticism, you might say, "Elsie, I've noticed that your typing has a lot of errors lately," raising a performance problem, rather than, "Elsie, you have become a bad typist lately." The latter statement blames Elsie personally and does not justify the comment. Factual descriptions are assertive, whereas judgments may be aggressive. More examples of aggressive communication include, "If you don't change your attitude, you'll be in real trouble," and "If you continue to arrive after 9:00 AM, I will have to give you two days' probation."

Likewise, make requests clear and direct. Ask, "Will you please . . . ?" rather than "Would you mind . . . ?" or, "Why don't you . . . ?" Where there is doubt or uncertainty about how you and a peer might proceed, you might ask rather than demand, "Can we work together to find a solution to this?"

Body Language

Your delivery is as important as the words you use. Body language is the tone and pitch of your words and the facial and body gestures that are part of your communications. Because body language conveys over 90 percent of any message, you need to exhibit assertive nonverbal behavior.

Let's say that your manager has assigned a peer to work on a report that is actually your responsibility. You can say, "I am angry that you asked Larry to work on the Needles report. I'd like you to tell me the next time you need a report because it is my responsibility." So far so good—you have assertively shared your feelings.

Now let's consider your voice, posture, and body gestures as you made your statement. Your voice should be level—controlled, firm, *and* relaxed. You don't want to frighten your manager. Toward that end, keep your head erect and relaxed, maintain eye contact, and don't point a finger. If you think you are too upset, hold back talking to your manager until you are more at ease with the situation. But if the situation does upset you, don't ignore your emotions. That's a passive response— and you want to avoid passivity as much as you want to avoid aggression.

Praise and Put-Downs

Let's look at two situations, in particular, that can create awkwardness. The first might not seem difficult, but for some people it is: responding to praise. Your manager tells you, "You did a great job on that report." Some people might say in response, "The report? I really didn't have time to prepare," or, "Oh, it was nothing," which has the effect of impolitely throwing back the praise at the manager.

These are nonassertive or passive responses. Alternatively, some managers might say, "Do I get a raise?" or, "I did a better job than anyone else on staff," or just make a "Humph!" sound of acknowledgement. No matter how justified it may be, it's unlikely that the manager would want to offer praise in the future, because the compliment had either no effect or a negative effect.

Let's assume that your manager says you've done a terrific job in running a customer focus group. You might say assertively, "Thank you so much. I was prepared for all eventualities." Perhaps you might answer, "Thanks." Sometimes, all that is needed are the words *Thank you* or a smile.

Put-downs are more difficult to handle, but they can be managed assertively too. Let's assume that you have been assigned to research a potential corporate ally. In the past, the task has been given to a peer, but your manager has decided to give you this opportunity. Tim, your peer, is resentful and asks in an accusing tone, "Do you really think you can handle this task? A mistake could cost the company a lot of money."

Rather than get angry, you might tell your colleague, "I'm sure I'll do a good job." You might want to follow up to better understand what prompted your coworker's comment: "I see that you are upset. Do you have a problem with the boss asking me to do the research?"

When your colleague admits that he is upset with your being assigned a task he normally does, you can then respond to the real reason behind the put-down.

Let's assume that your peer seems to accept the idea that your manager wants to increase your responsibilities in several areas. However, when you submit your analysis before the group, he tells everyone, "Well, you actually did a good job." In other words, he put you down—but in a subtle fashion.

Your peer indirectly attacked you, showing indirect aggression. You can ignore the remark and open the door to its repetition at other group meetings (passive response), or you can stop by your peer's office later in the day and say, "I didn't understand what you meant by that remark at our meeting today. What are you really saying?" Thus, you put your peer on the spot by insisting he explain. If a problem lies between you, it should surface so you can address it. (See Chapter 8 on conflict management.)

There's another form of put-down: the nonverbal kind. Instead of words, the individual communicates through a pout, a smirk, or an exasperated sigh.

You have asked your employee to finish an inventory report before 5:00 PM. Rather than say anything, she frowns and gives an exasperated sigh. Yes, she knew that the inventory report would be due by the end of the day. The deadline shouldn't come as a surprise to her. You can ignore the body language, or you can ask, assertively, for clarification. For example, you might ask, "Alice, I don't understand. Is there a problem?"

It turns out that Alice was invited to dinner. It was a last-minute offer from some friends, and she wants to go. You can tell her, "I need the report in time for a 9:30 meeting. Will you be in early tomorrow and get the report to me in time?"

She tells you that she will have it on your desk by 9:15. The problem is solved. At least, this problem is handled. But you may want to ask Alice, "I wonder if I should have given you the information you needed to complete the report sooner in the day. Do you know if there is a way to get that information?"

Alice might have a solution—which would put an end to her having to put in overtime and to any more exasperated sighs about inventory reports.

"That's a good idea, Alice. When you sighed, I really didn't know what to think. Let's talk about the situation tomorrow, after my meeting."

Avoiding Manipulation

Sometimes, individuals will attempt to manipulate you. Manipulation can bring on either passive or aggressive response patterns. Let me share three assertiveness techniques that you can use to retain control of the conversation.

Negative Inquiry

This gets people to open up and give you information you might not otherwise have. Let me describe a situation in which negative inquiry might be effective. You didn't get the bonus you think you earned. Rather than whine or yell at your manager, you might ask simply, "Jay, I was wondering why I didn't get a bonus this year." Let's assume that your manager responds simply, "I didn't think you deserved it." He's holding back information, and you know it. You could let this response add to your frustration, or you could remain calm and ask another question like, "What did I do that you think I should not have done?" Jay might then tell you that you didn't do any one thing but your performance was "just average," that you still haven't mastered all the skills and abilities you need as a manager. "You make all the mistakes a new manager makes." Which might prompt you to ask Jay, "What specifically have I been doing wrong?" Now you are on a roll—if you can find out the problem, you can remedy it and get that bonus next year.

For instance, Jay might mention that your paperwork tends to be a bit late. "Am I taking too much time?" you might ask, then pause. Jay could respond, "No, just longer than someone with more experience might take." You might continue to ask questions about your job performance, identifying examples of average work. At the end of the conversation, you might ask Jay, "If I correct all these problems you've mentioned, will I have a chance to receive a bonus next year?" He, in turn, might reply, "Very probably."

What did you do? First, you asked questions that focused on the problem but did not criticize the manager or yourself personally. Consequently, you were able to remain calm. More importantly, you determined what was bothering your manager. Negative inquiry encourages others to say what they really want.

Broken Record

In Chapter 12, I will show how this technique can keep you from letting a colleague manipulate you. It's another assertive communication technique and is especially helpful to those managers who have trouble saying no.

Let's say you have a persistent salesperson in your office. He seems unable to accept the fact that you don't want to buy what he's selling—1,000 stuffed animals with your firm's name on them to use at a trade show.

The salesperson might ask, "You want your booth to get lots of attention, don't you?"

You might respond, "I understand, *but* I'm not interested."

"But these stuffed animals are found to generate follow-up calls."

Your reply: "I understand, but I'm not interested."

Exasperated, the salesperson might say, "You don't understand or you would want to buy these. Let me ask you, who is your firm's biggest competitor?"

Rather than reply to the question, you would repeat, "I understand, but I'm not interested."

At this point the salesperson might taunt you with, "Your competitors would be interested in using these materials."

Your reply: "I understand, but I'm not interested."

The salesperson would likely give up at this point. If not, you would continue with the broken record technique until this persistent person takes the lot of beanie business boosters elsewhere.

Fogging

This technique is somewhat like the broken record, in that it requires persistence on your part. The technique enables you to respond to someone's critical comment. This technique is especially useful in dealing with criticism from a peer. It's another solution to an indirect verbal put-down, but it also works very well with someone who wants to manipulate you, someone like Diane who liked to make P.T., her young colleague, uneasy about his work.

P.T. told me that Diane one day said, "I see that you've turned out your usual sloppy paperwork."

Rather than become defensive, P.T. turned to Diane and replied, "You're right. My paperwork could be a little neater."

"The same comment about your paperwork could be made about your appearance. You're dressed in your usual sloppy manner."

Again, rather than let her manipulate him into losing his temper, he replied, "That's right. I'm dressed in my usual way."

She continued, "How do you expect to be respected by looking like that?"

P.T. answered, "My clothes sense isn't exactly my strong point." Diane gave it one last try: "Strong point? I don't think you have any."

P.T. told her, "I do have a lot of faults."

Diane walked away, aware that she couldn't rattle P.T. Which may explain why she later involved him in a key crossfunctional project and recommended P.T., whom she continued to call "the kid," for the Golden Eagle Award for his contribution to the team's efforts.

Developing an Assertive Image

Developing an assertive style isn't easy. Constant practice is necessary. The following eight steps should help, however.

1. *Listen to yourself.* Are you speaking in an assertive manner? Are you too passive or too aggressive?
2. *Keep a record of your assertiveness.* Record each day those situations in which you found yourself responding assertively, those in which you blew it, and those you avoided altogether so that you would not have to act assertively.
3. *Reflect on a particular situation.* Review how you handled a specific situation—for example, seeing an employee come in late after numerous warnings. Did you ignore the behavior once again, did you lose your temper, or did you call the employee into your office and speak calmly to determine the cause of the tardiness?
4. *Review your replies.* Think about what you specifically said. While you might generally have communicated in an assertive manner, did you lose it during your conversation and slip briefly into a passive or aggressive style? If so, what do you think prompted the lapse?
5. *Consider alternative responses.* Ask yourself how you could have handled the situation better. Could you have dealt with it more to your advantage?
6. *Imagine yourself handling the situation in a new way.* Try out new responses to situations. Be assertive, but be as natural as you can. At this point, it may be helpful to model yourself after someone who has handled a similar situation well.
7. *Do it.* Be aware of the feedback you receive, both verbal and nonverbal. Did you accomplish your goals?
8. *Be aware of feedback.* Continue to adapt your behavior to achieve your desired interpersonal goals. Ask colleagues and peers, "How am I doing?"

The best managers are open and direct communicators, able to express their feelings, needs, and wants to others. Managers tend to get results when they unambiguously communicate their goals and objectives. Energy is often wasted defending and attacking, when in reality, goal-oriented behavior usually works best.

Those who have this assertiveness knack are comfortable with themselves, and others are likely to be comfortable with them—at least, they aren't likely to feel threatened by them. They won't try put-downs, verbal attacks, or exploitation. Rather, they communicate in a straightforward manner. A healthy self-respect grows between assertive managers and their staff. Openness begets trust and builds confidence.

■ Tips

• If you agree with praise, don't be afraid to say so. "Thank you. I was pleased with the work myself." If you don't feel the praise was justified, don't argue—just thank the person.

• Make a refusal brief and clear but not abrupt. "I would rather not. . . ."

• Don't make excuses. They will just backfire on you. Besides, making excuses is nonassertive behavior.

• Keep in mind that a request isn't a command. If a request is being made, then you have the right to say no.

■ See Also

Burley-Allen, Madelyn. *Managing Assertively: How to Improve Your People Skills.* John Wiley & Sons, 1995.
Davidson, Jeff. *The Complete Idiot's Guide to Assertiveness.* Alpha Books, 1997.

12

Communicating Up, Down, and Sideways

As a manager, half of your job is communications related. Whether you are giving directions to your workers, updating your manager about the department's current operations and needs, or discussing with your peers how you can more effectively work together, an effective communication style may make all the difference.

You might take your communication skills for granted and feel that you don't need any special training. After all, you have been able to talk since you were a baby. But there are dos and don'ts to ensure effective communications. Communication is a process that must take place for a message to go from the sender to the recipient. The emphasis is usually on the last step, and managers are taught to get feedback from the recipient to ensure that the message has been received and understood.

In Chapter 10, you read about the listening filters, such as different perceptions, emotions, and poor timing, that can impede the communication process. But communication problems aren't always due to listening shortcomings. Sometimes, the sender doesn't convey the message clearly.

Let me share with you three experiences of new managers.

In the first case, John had told his employees what seemed like a hundred times that he didn't want them to take their lunch break at the same time, yet day after day at 12:30, the office would be empty.

Marge felt she was ready for a promotion, and she went into her manager's office to explain why she felt she deserved it. But, as she later told some friends, "I never got to raise the issue. I think my boss deliberately avoided the discussion."

Easy going, it takes a lot to get Michael upset, so I was surprised when, furious with his assistant, he called me to complain about her. Because he had only told me the week before about how wonderful she was, I was shocked to learn that he was thinking of putting her on probation. Once he calmed down, he told me that he'd had a report due to a prospective client that morning, and his assistant hadn't even started work on it. "I told her last week that I would need it today," he fumed, "and now she claims I never said a word to her."

All three situations have one thing in common: the managers blamed their communications problems on the other party. While many times, the person spoken to may not have been listening, the fact remained that getting the message across was the managers' responsibility—and they failed.

What Went Wrong

None of these managers had made an effort to be understood or checked to be sure that they were heard. If they had been addressing their entire department about a serious matter or making a request of their manager, they might have taken the time to plan what they said. But they saw no reason to treat as equally important these instructions or queries. They needed to learn to communicate clearly and with impact at all times, regardless of when, why, or with whom they were speaking.

All managers should know certain basics.

- *Be direct when the situation demands it.* Say what you mean clearly. Do not garble your message behind phrases that obscure or soften its impact.
- *When making a request or giving a directive, be polite but decisive.* You can thank your employees for doing extra work without being apologetic. (See Chapter 11 for examples of passive communication.)
- *Take a moment to think before speaking.* What do you really want to say? What emotions do you want to express? Which ones do you not want to express? How can you communicate through your use of language?
- *Be certain the time is appropriate for communicating.* Praise is usually welcome at any time, but avoid criticizing the work of an employee who has one foot out the door, leaving for a three-day weekend. Better to save your observations for when the employee will be less distracted.

- *Make sure you have all the information before making a statement.*
  You can either delay the discussion or ask questions first to help you col-
  lect the necessary information.

How do these rules apply to the situations earlier in this chapter? Let's look
at what happened with John. Remember, he complained that he had repeatedly
asked his staff not to take lunch at the same time, yet at 12:30, once again, he had
found the office empty.

John's mistake was that he hadn't been clear about his instructions. Because,
he hadn't explained his directive, the staff didn't understood why it was so important that someone always be available during lunch. He should have met with
his staff and asked them to make a schedule that ensured the office was covered
at all times. If some employees wanted to lunch together, he could have suggested that times be rotated, so that all could share the responsibility for answering the phone and also have opportunities to join their coworkers for lunch
periodically.

By stating exactly what had to be done, giving a reasonable explanation, and
working out a solution, John would have made his instructions clear. His previous directive was not clear, so the problem continued. When I explained what
he had done wrong, John was able to eliminate the problem. He only had to go
two steps further: explain the reason for his request, and suggest a way for the
employees to comply.

The problem was solved. Had it not been, John might have acted more au-
thoritatively, imposing a schedule on the staff.

Now let's look at what happened to Marge.

Upward Communications

While some managers find it tough to get messages across to employees, some
find it even more difficult to make an impact when communicating upward—
that is, when talking to a manager or higher executive. Again, the best way to get
the message across is to be fully prepared.

There are basically two kinds of upward communications: conversations by
you to your superiors and those from your superiors to you. The specifics vary,
but generally they involve some exchange of information, like your manager giving you instructions or your providing information to a member of senior management. Occasionally, too, you may present an idea or request additional resources
to complete a project.

Preparation is key to all of these situations, but particularly when you are asked for a project update or other information. Under those circumstances, if you don't know the answer, promise to get back to the requestor soon. Then research the facts and present the information as soon as you are ready—but not before.

You can't anticipate what your manager wants to talk about when he drops by your office or walks over as you are standing by the printer. Under such circumstances, be concise and offer what you know. If your manager wants more details, get them. Depending on your manager's preferred style of communication, you can e-mail them or deliver them in person.

On the other hand, if you are called into your manager's office, ask about the nature of the meeting beforehand. Once you know the subject, gather all the information you can find on it. Anticipate what questions will be asked and make sure you can answer them. Do you have documents that your manager might want to review? If so, bring them along.

Let's assume that you have an idea or a request of your manager, like Marge's request for a promotion. Choose a time when you know your manager is free or even make an appointment. Once again, come prepared. For instance, Marge would have done better had she brought documentation on her accomplishments over the past two years. It wouldn't have hurt, either, if she had alerted her boss to the purpose of her meeting. Even if she didn't get what she wanted, her boss would have been aware of her aspirations and might have prepared a compromise offer—maybe a bonus.

Marge should also have practiced beforehand the most economical way to present her case. Wordiness can lose a listener's attention. Further, Marge should have prepared her case in a manner so that she didn't play all her cards at once. She could have pointed to some of her past accomplishments. If her manager hesitated, she could have gone into greater detail, stressing how her efforts had significantly helped her manager. Copies of her past performance assessments would have also been handy, had they supported her contention.

Let's look at a similar situation. In this instance, you want to speak to your manager about an idea you have for reducing a redundancy in your unit's workflow. How should you best go about it? After all, it is a good idea.

Before meeting with your manager, consider your idea from his perspective. How would it help address problems? You want to play up these benefits. Document the specific advantages of your idea. Provide convincing supporting data if you can.

Even then, you may encounter resistance. If you expect opposition, prepare in advance. Before an objection is raised, raise it yourself, then systematically and objectively disprove it, speaking calmly and objectively like a bystander, not as a defender.

What happens if the idea is rejected? Find out why. It may be possible to overcome the objection by making adjustments to the initial idea. If you get what you want, include a reassurance that the person will like the final results. Leave your manager with positive feelings about you.

Some objections are common, like concerns about cost and risk. If the idea was tried before and it didn't work, you might be reminded. Resources may be short. If you know your manager well, you may be able to anticipate specific objections. If you didn't anticipate the objection, listen carefully. If you aren't clear about the objection, ask for more information. Don't argue or become defensive. Attack the questions raised, not the questioner.

Show how you might be able to handle the objection. If resistance to your idea continues, solicit the objector's plan for overcoming his or her own concern. "How do you think we can overcome this problem?" Close ranks to find a way to overcome shortcomings in your idea. If you see yourself losing, leave the door open. Ask, "I'd like to think through your concerns to see what I can come up with. May I come back?"

Communicating Sideways

Now let's look at Michael's problem. It wasn't as simple as he'd thought. Once he calmed down, he discovered that his assistant had known about the report but had been unable to work on it because she was busy doing work given to her by Sid, the other manager she assisted. She had told Sid that Michael's work had priority, but he had insisted. Michael's work dealt not only with a potential prospect but also had been assigned to Linda before Sid's, so Michael felt justified in talking to Sid about it. Before he did, he spoke to me, and I gave him some advice. From what Michael had told me, Sid could be manipulative, getting people to agree to do something they didn't want to do. He would often make the same request in three different ways, use emotional blackmail to make a peer feel guilty (e.g., "I let Linda work on your assignment last week. I felt you owed me."), wear the other party down with repeated requests, or take an aggressive approach.

I told Michael about a technique called the broken record. After telling Sid that he should not have interfered with Linda's work, Michael made it clear that he did not want a repetition of the situation. In the future, Sid should discuss Linda's workload with Michael before speaking with her.

Sid apologized, but he tried to get out of Michael's demand that they work together to coordinate Linda's assignments. I told Michael that he had to remain firm. Each time that Sid came up with a reason why it would not work, he should respond no and then repeat his demand that they discuss Linda's assignments weekly to ensure that each got equal time. For instance, "No, I don't think it will take too much time for us to do this," or, "No, I want us to oversee Linda's workload, not put her in the awkward position of having to choose which job to do first," or, "No, I don't think we are unable to appreciate the importance of the other's work. We can make sound judgments about her time."

So long as Michael said no calmly and pleasantly, without showing anger or feeling upset, Sid had no reason to take issue with his response—other than that it would keep him from monopolizing Linda's time.

Sid is someone with whom Michael wants to remain friends, but he also knows that Sid is one of those colleagues with whom you sometimes have to talk tough. You have to be clear on the position you plan to take in any discussion and stick to it. Even if the other party tries to redirect the conversation, by mentally hanging on to your position statement, you can control the discussion and steer things back on course.

Saying No

Sometimes, saying no is easier than at other times. For instance, you might not want to say no to your own manager or to a customer. Under those circumstances, you should say no but follow up your response with an alternative. For instance, in talking to a senior executive with an unrealistic deadline, you might say, "No, I can't promise we can do the work by then, but how would it be if we completed it before the end of the week?" Equally difficult is saying no to someone with whom you want to remain on good terms—which includes your employees. You can take the sting out of the word no by giving a good reason for your reply. If you explain why you must say no, the individual will know that you are not just being difficult or uncooperative—you are refusing the request, not rejecting the individual making it.

While Michael was able to resolve his problem with Linda and Sid, I have to add that he was somewhat at fault for what happened. He gave Linda instructions about how the work should be done. He also told her when he wanted it completed. In explaining the task, he focused on what she didn't know about the project, not what she did. He didn't underestimate her capability and thereby suggest she lacked the capability to do the work. He showed her past reports done by her predecessor, and he explained the bigger picture—why having no typographical errors was imperative and why the document should look good as well as read well. What Michael didn't do was to tell Linda to contact him if she ran into any problems. Further, he didn't drop by to see how she was getting along on the assignment. He knew that the job would take several days, so he should have checked on the progress periodically. If he had done that, he would have known what had happened with Sid and would not have had to postpone the meeting with the prospective client.

A Memorable Presentation

The upside of the story is that Michael made a terrific presentation and got the client for his firm. He was also assigned Linda as his full-time assistant.

In your position, too, you may have to make presentations, so let me share with you some tips on how to put together a memorable one. At the very least, before you begin preparing your speech, ask yourself the following questions:

- What exactly am I supposed to speak on? Will my audience expect me to provide facts and figures or just an overview?
- How long am I supposed to speak? If you are making a speech to a client as part of a bigger corporate presentation, you may need only 10 to 15 minutes. On the other hand, if you are making a keynote address to an audience, you may have to fill an hour or more.
- What attitudes does the audience hold about the topic? Is it informed or not on the subject? Does it have a bias? Will the members of the audience have work to do after the presentation, or do they need more information?

So, to give an effective speech, you need to know the specifics of the topic, the time frame, and your audience. Once you have that information, you are ready to develop your speech. The speech itself can describe how to do something, update the audience's information, describe a typical experience with X, set limits and clarify issues, argue the pros or cons of an issue, or solve a problem. The approach should be appropriate to the subject. Whatever the purpose, you can develop the presentation by relating your approach to your audience.

Consider asking a question, telling a story that makes the subject come alive, conducting a minisurvey of your audience, or posing a quiz or an exercise to get audience interest. Your approach should communicate that you understand your audience's needs.

If you decide to use visuals, make sure that they are clear, accurate, and easy to follow. Be as up-to-date with technology in your delivery as you can. If possible, use a laptop to deliver a PowerPoint-based presentation rather than depend on a flip-chart or overhead transparencies. If statistics support your point well, use them in your speech. Provide handouts, and take the time to explain them to your audience.

Keep the speech itself simple. Expert speakers believe that the same rules that apply to writing apply to speaking: "Tell 'em what you plan to say to them, tell 'em what you said you were going to tell 'em, and tell 'em what you told 'em."

When the time comes to deliver the speech, take a deep breath, pause, and smile to the audience. Consider members of the audience as friends, not opponents. Don't come with a written speech. Rather, prepare notes and refer to them as you speak. If you are using visuals, practice using them to ensure your thoughts are in sync with your slides.

Let's assume the worst scenario: The laptop won't work, the handouts aren't done as promised, and you have a cold. So life isn't a bed of roses. Don't apologize to your audience. Get to the speech and go on. When you are speaking, you must do the best you can with what you have. Present yourself as resourceful and competent. Apologizing only makes others think you are unprepared.

If you get anxious about speaking, try to identify the cause of your nervousness and deal with it. Most people are anxious about speaking, so there is no point in denying your tension, at least not to yourself. If you're nervous about the size of the audience, look for a friendly face, or try to get the audience on your side from the start by telling an amusing story. If you have the usual generalized nervousness common to most speakers, the best cure is to practice in less threatening situations. If you expect to do a lot of speaking for your firm in the future, you might want to practice by volunteering to lead a discussion group in a civic organization or chair a staff meeting.

Communication Problems

You may have to deal with other situations that demand strong communication skills. For instance, I have offered advice about how to say no to a request, but how do you communicate bad news to someone—whether an employee, supervisor, or peer?

Damage done in the delivery can be far worse than the message. You don't want to sound uncaring when you tell an employee that he can't take a day off to see his son play softball. Nor do you want to say yes and then come back an hour later with some reason why you can't let the employee off. Where the news is really bad—like upcoming layoffs—you may want to prepare your employees. Start by saying, "I'm going to have to give you some bad news." Such an outright statement lets people prepare emotionally for the upset. Follow that up with the bad news and the why behind it, if explaining the reason will help the listeners to understand better.

When delivering bad news, show up at the meeting with the numbers and results in black and white, if you can. This tactic will distance you from the situation, minimizing personal resentment against you. If there is any kernel of good in the bad news, mention it. If a project has been killed, suggest that perhaps information or insights can be salvaged from the experience. If there will be downsizing, tell the group that there are no plans for further downsizing—if that is the reality.

Another situation that some new managers find difficult is to ask questions in a manner that prompts the information they need to do their jobs better. In your job, you will be asking questions to help you make decisions, questions to confirm facts, and questions designed to evoke reconsideration of actions (like in one of those planning sessions we discussed in Chapter 1).

For the purpose of inquiry, start by asking open-ended questions to gather facts. Postpone closed—yes or no—questions until confirming facts. Make certain you ask your questions in a logical sequence. Start by defining the trouble, then identify possible causes. Next, identify the true cause of the trouble before asking questions to gather ideas from the employee, colleague, or customer about how to solve it.

Don't come to a conclusion until you've gathered all the information you need to make a well-considered decision.

Confirmation questions are the yes or no questions mentioned earlier. Is it true that you weren't here at 9:00 AM when Mr. Crawford called? Were you rude to Rene at lunch? Have you completed the report for me?

When you want people to think about what they're doing, you should ask a rhetorical question such as, "Why do you work as hard as you do?" or, "What does quality really mean?" or, "Have you ever wondered why customers choose to buy from us and not our competitors?"

Questions can be powerful—not just in the information they provide, but in their impact on the flow of a conversation. For instance, when discussion meanders, you can get back on track with a question. When you're at a loss for words, you can ask a question. Questions, then, buy you time to think. Questions also will help whenever you're under attack. You might ask an employee who disagrees with your suggestion, "Why do you believe my idea won't work?" If a colleague gets upset about a remark you made in a group meeting, you might ask,

"What have I said to make you feel that way?" Questions can also help when a customer complains: "Please tell me exactly what went wrong?" or, "What will it take to get you back as a customer?"

Let's look at another kind of situation you may encounter in your position. You are busy and have been rushing around the office, preoccupied with how you will get a tough job completed before the day is over. You pass one of your employees in the hallway. The individual says, "Hello." Preoccupied, you walk by without saying a word. So what, you think. I have important things to think about. Now put yourself in that employee's shoes. You see your boss and offer a greeting, yet your manager walks by without a word. How do you feel? Without cause, you begin to wonder if you have done or said anything to offend your manager. Perhaps you may label your manager as rude and indifferent. In future interpersonal communications, that impression may exist, rightly or wrongly.

I'm not suggesting that a smile and a brief hello will earn you a congeniality award at the end of the year, but I am suggesting that they can leave people with the impression that you are someone they would like to work with. I'll go even further: the ability to engage others in small talk can achieve big gains. If you enter a meeting, ask Claire, one of your colleagues whose son just went into the Marines, how he did in boot camp and then listen to her prideful stories. On Monday, if you and one of your employees arrive at the same time, inquire how he spent his weekend. People love to talk about themselves and their families and friends, so give them the opportunity to do so. You will be amazed at the rapport that grows from these brief conversations, rapport that you can save up and use when you need a helping hand with your work or career.

You Called?

So far, we have discussed how to communicate one-on-one and how to make memorable presentations. But did you know that about 30 percent of your one-on-one communications are via telephone? Let's look at how you can maximize your telephone conversations.

I'm talking about live conversations. So, just as you might make an appointment to talk in person with a customer, you should make an appointment for a telephone conversation with that same customer if you expect to be on the phone for awhile. For your lengthier calls, prepare a list to ensure that you cover all the points you intend.

Let's assume that you are talking and you suddenly are disconnected. If you called, then it is your responsibility to redial. If someone walks into your office while you are on the phone, motion them out of the doorway, or into a seat, but don't interrupt your phone conversation.

When you mistakenly take a phone call for which you are not prepared, spend a few minutes on the phone as a courtesy and then reschedule it for a later date.

What should you do if you pick up your phone and find an extremely angry coworker or client on the line? Quietly listen. If you try to explain the situation and find the individual is still upset, you might want to suggest that you need more information and then set up a phone meeting. If the anger disintegrates into abusiveness, don't respond. Just calmly say, "For the moment, I don't think we have all the facts to resolve this. I will call you tomorrow after I have done more research." End the conversation. Call back the next day—by then, the individual will be able to speak calmly.

I hope I have convinced you just how important your communication ability is to your position.

■ The SEER Technique

If you want to be heard when you reply to a question, try the SEER technique. This technique ensures that your replies are clear, concise, and memorable. Begin with a one-sentence **S**ummary in which you describe your position. Next, **E**laborate on that answer with details like who, when, where, why, how, and how much. Follow this up with an **E**xample to go from the abstract or conceptual to the concrete. End with a **R**estatement of your Summary. Try this technique—it works.

■ Tips

- Be clear in your mind what you want to say before you open your mouth.

- Come prepared with a list of questions for meetings in which you expect to get a major project assignment from your manager. Try to cover the who, what, where, what, and why—particularly the why.

■ Flow Chart Your Communication

This technique is designed to determine if you are guilty of regularly interrupting individuals. By making tally marks on a plain, white piece of paper and counting these after five or ten minutes, you can determine the frequency with which you cut others off. You might even create a form that tallies interruptions by both you and the other person. Divide a piece of paper into two parts, one half interruptions by you, the other half interruptions by the other party. You can draw two circles on each side, to represent you and the other party. As the conversation goes on, note those times you interrupt the individual and also the number of times you are interrupted. Once the meeting is done, review the findings. The more interruptions you record on your side of the paper, the more evidence you have of a problem in communicating. You may also want to record awkward periods of silence because they, too, represent communication problems.

■ See Also

Carnegie, Dale. *How to Win Friends and Influence People*. Pocket Books, 1990.
Mills, Harry. *Artful Persuasion: How to Command Attention, Change Minds, and Influence People*. AMACOM, 2000.
Munter, Mary. *Guide to Managerial Communication*. Prentice Hall, 2002.
Patterson, Kerry and Joseph Grenny, Ron McMillan et al. *Crucial Conversations: Tools for Talking When Stakes Are High*. McGraw-Hill, 2002.
Stone, Douglas and Bruce Patton, Sheila Heen and Roger Fisher. *Difficult Conversations: How to Discuss What Matters Most*. Penguin, 2000.
Walters, Dottie and Lilly Walters. *Speak and Grow Rich*. Prentice-Hall Press, 1997.

13

How to Speak without Words: Body Language

Any discussion of communication skills must include attention to body language—your voice, gestures, and visual presence—and the impact it has on the communication process.

Knowing how to use body language is a useful communication skill. So is knowing how to read it. Body language is important regardless of whether you are speaking or listening.

Let's assume that you are portraying a manager in a movie. How would you be perceived by those watching the video if you spoke in a whiny voice; a raspy, harsh tone; or a high-pitched, rapid, quivering voice? Certainly, you wouldn't come across as someone credible, capable, thoughtful, or caring—all characteristics of an outstanding manager.

If you stooped over, you would seem to lack self-confidence, even if you don't. When you toy with the papers on your desk, an employee might think you weren't interested in his idea, regardless of what you say about being interested. If you cross your hands and feet, your body language may be telling the employee that you aren't interested in anyone's ideas but your own. Verbal communication accounts for only about 7 percent of the meaning others will extract from your words. More important is the remaining 93 percent accounted for by intonation, inflection, pitch, emphasis, speed, volume, body posture, gestures, and use of personal space.

Crosscultural Communication

Body language is particularly important when attempting communication across cultural and language barriers. To native-born Americans, the spoken word is by far the most important communication tool. In other cultures, however, the way words are spoken—along with the gestures, posture, and facial expressions—is of greater significance. Consequently, Americans encounter communication problems when working abroad.

People who have worked in foreign cultures have told me numerous times about how important body language is to communications. For instance, an Asian executive who lowers his eyes when he says yes to a proposal actually means no. He is simply reluctant to destroy the positive relationship with the other party by saying no.

The interesting thing about body language is that we are often totally unaware of how we react to it. We may, for instance, form a negative judgment about people because they slouch, won't look us in the eye, or talk with their hands. Contrary to our positive messages to our employees about how important they are to our organization, we may send another message with our voice, facial and body gestures, and posture. Likewise, your body language may influence their opinion of your leadership and management skills.

How Do You Sound?

Do you speak with a high-pitched voice? If so, you may be perceived as nervous or lacking confidence. People with low-pitched voices sound more confident and competent. Compare your reaction to two people, each with a different pitch. What impression did each leave you with? Wouldn't you rather report to the individual with the deeper, stronger voice?

Now tape your own voice. How do you sound? Does your pitch need to be lowered? If so, you may want to turn to a voice coach, a self-help tape, or book to tell you how to change. If you want to make it to the boardroom, practice the lower, hushed tones most often heard there.

On that tape, check also your vocal variety, speed, and volume. Ask yourself if you are speaking in a monotone. Learn to modulate your voice for greater effect. How about the speed with which you speak? Nerves can cause some people to hurry their words. If you do that on occasion, learn to pace your words to add credibility to your remarks. A slow rate of speech implies well-chosen words and underscores the importance of the message.

Needless to say, sometimes you will want to speak faster to convey excitement or enthusiasm. A faster rate also creates interest and will gain you more attention. Listeners will have to work harder at hearing what you are saying, but the faster pace will keep their minds from wandering.

If you think that you may have lost some of your audience, you may want to ask questions of the group to ensure that your message got through. Don't try to regain their attention by speaking in a piercingly loud voice.

Loudness has come to be associated with unruliness and even vulgarity. Too soft a voice isn't good either, being perceived as a sign of shyness, nervousness, and even incompetence. The ideal is somewhere between these two extremes.

Understanding and Using Gestures

Tone and pitch aren't the only body language to be alert to. Those with whom you are talking can tell if you are interested, engaged, in the right mood, patient, bored, annoyed, dismissive, and so forth by facial and body movements.

For instance, learn how to smile so it shows more than at your mouth. You know how novelists will describe a character's smile as extending to the eyes. When you smile, it should show in the rest of your face—the lines around the eyes, the pupils, the forehead, and the cheeks. When you fake a smile, those with whom you are talking usually know it. Just think of some people who have smiled at you, yet you knew they weren't sincere. Their words and expressions didn't match, or their smile seemed to last too long—genuine smiles only last a second or so.

Stand in front of a mirror and pretend that your reflection is either one of your employees or your manager. Are you looking everywhere at the reflection but at the eyes? An evasive gaze suggests dishonesty or disrespect. Practice, instead, to look others in the eyes (or bridge of the nose) when you speak to them or they speak to you. Accompany all handshakes with smiling eyes. A direct gaze and broad smile create a positive image. A jaw that is set or a frown that extends from eyes to mouth communicates resistance, displeasure, or disapproval. It isn't just the facial expression. When your eyebrows are lowered, your voice drops and you will sound gruff. Try it.

Watch your laugh as well as your smile. As strange as it may seem, we laugh when we feel uncomfortable or embarrassed. Washington observers say that the inappropriate smiling contributed to former Vice President Dan Quayle's reputation as inexperienced. Laura, a marketing manager at an oil firm, was known for laughing when she had to communicate bad news to her employees. Most people laugh when they are happy or amused, and sometimes when they are relieved at the end of a difficult situation, but Laura laughed as she delivered bad news to her staff or had to say no to an employee's request.

Her staff learned to read Laura's behavior and tensed up whenever she laughed, instead of feeling upbeat and happy. Her laugh also reflected on her professionalism. They came to think that someone who wasn't in control of her emotions would also not be in control of work situations.

So learn to laugh on purpose. That is, let your laugh be a sign of interest, genuine amusement, or happiness.

The Impression You Create

A business executive I know once told me that how people stand on an issue is often determined by where they stand—on an organization chart. Likewise, I would say that how people stand on a subject they are discussing with others may be determined literally by how they stand—that is, their posture may contradict what the mouth is saying. For instance, if you face your audience with your hands on your hips, you are showing confidence, determination, and the ability to take control of the project you are describing to your staff. Whether standing or seated, good posture—head up, shoulders back—indicates that you are in control and have confidence in yourself. Such posture should encourage similar confidence in you by your staff members. Good posture is also a sign of respect for those with whom you are interacting. A slouch or slumped shoulders can convey indifference or withdrawal.

There are two basic groups of body postures: open/closed and forward/back. The open/closed is the most obvious. If you sit with arms folded and legs crossed and your body turned away as you listen to a staff member's presentation, you may be silently saying that you don't agree or maybe even that you hate his proposal. If you sit with your hands open, your feet firmly planted on the ground and your body open, you may be telling your staff member that you are very much interested in what you are hearing.

The forward/back postures indicate whether listeners are actively or passively reacting to communications. So if you lean back and look up at the ceiling, doodle on a pad, or maybe clean your glasses, you are passively listening or actually ignoring the speaker. On the other hand, if you lean forward and point toward the speaker, you are saying that you very much like what you are hearing.

The body language you want to use when listening to staff is the responsive mode, in which you are accepting what you hear, or the reflective mode, in which you show interest but aren't yet ready to accept the idea. The body posture labeled the fugitive mode is very much what it sounds like—you aren't interested in what is being said, are bored to death, and would like to get the hell out of the room. The combative mode is also one to avoid: yes, you lean forward, but your body posture isn't open at all—in fact, you look angry and ready for a confrontation.

If you want to encourage communications with your staff, particularly to get them to share profit-making and cost-cutting ideas with you, you need to watch what your body says. You want to suggest in voice, facial and body gestures, and posture that you are receptive to hearing their suggestions.

Watch your mannerisms, too. Don't play with the keys in your pocket or the pen in your hand when you talk. Other annoying habits that can detract from an image of authority and from your message include scratching your head, jerking at your tie or scarf, strumming your fingers, twirling your letter opener, or spanning your fingers.

Getting the Real Message—Or Not?

Just as our voice, face and body gestures, and posture communicate our sense of self-confidence and interest in what others are saying, so others' behavior may tell us about whether they agree, are comfortable, like us, and so forth. Nonverbal behavior is important to understanding others as well as interacting positively with them.

But before I share this information, let me offer one caveat: if you doubt the veracity of a speaker's words, you may want to probe gently further. We've all read books and heard presentations about what various gestures mean: that arms folded across the chest indicate a closed, defensive attitude; that leaning forward means interest; that shrugged shoulders mean indifference; that narrow eyes and a set jaw mean defiance; that a smile and nod mean agreement; and the like. But not every vocal intonation, facial or body gesture, or posture means what the textbooks tell us. Yes, they all offer clues, but our interpretation may be inaccurate.

Think about your own body language. You've had a tough day, but let's say you have concluded important talks with a customer and it looks like you will get the business. You're tired, so you walk into your office with your head down, eyes on the floor, and maybe slumped shoulders. You may be pleased with the outcome of the meeting, but those who see you might wrongly assume that the session went poorly and that the deal is off.

Fortunately, your assistant asks you, "How did things go?"

"Great," you reply, "But I need to take a break."

The point is, you can't make an accurate interpretation from one or two gestures. You have to see the gesture in context and as exhibited by an individual. Certainly, if you think you are getting mixed messages from verbal and body communications, then it is wise to ask a question or two.

Let's assume, for example, that one of your staff members looks tense but is talking calmly, coolly, and objectively about a situation. It might be wise for you to say, "It looks like you're tense or concerned about the delivery to the warehouse." That comment will encourage the person to share their concerns.

Your questions should be asked in a quiet voice, without judgment. Give your staff member the opportunity to correct any misunderstanding or, on the other hand, verify your interpretation. The response to your query may even be subject to question. Is the speaker's vocal pitch, intensity, or pace different from his usual way of speaking? The response may be neutral—"Everything's OK"—but the nonverbals may give additional clues. You may have to probe further. Chat with the person on a neutral subject to determine what's normal, before you try to interpret how the individual reacts to an unpleasant issue.

Keep in mind, too, that people may give false nonverbal clues. For instance, Larry is a merchandising manager at a major retail chain. He likes to tell jokes—lots of jokes—and almost all are bad, either offensive or unfunny. Yet Carol, his administrative assistant, smiles and laughs at each and every one of his jokes—even the blue, sexist ones. Does she think he's funny? Ask the other assistants with whom she lunches. She would like to sue the man for sexual harassment, but "Times are tough, and I need the job," she tells her pals.

Unconscious body language, however, can tell us a lot about what a person is feeling or thinking. Often, managers ask me how they can tell if an employee is lying. I suggest they check out their staff members' body language.

Is He Telling the Truth?

Lies may sound convincing, but you can often identify them by the non-verbal behavior of the speaker. When an employee lowers her eyes and tells you, "I completed the assignment this morning," you may have cause for suspicion that the work isn't yet done. When another employee sighs, heaves his shoulders, shoots you a dark look, and says, "Of course, I don't mind working late," he would rather not.

Here are some signals to look for when you believe someone is not telling the truth. No single gesture by itself will tell you, but several together should make you question any verbal message.

- There is an incongruency between what is said and how it is said. For instance, a job candidate tells you that she doesn't care that she is working in one of your department's smaller cubicles, but her low voice and pained look tell you otherwise.
- The employee fails to maintain strong eye contact and, instead, looks at the floor or the ceiling—anywhere but at your face.
- The employee repeats the same comment several times to overcome any doubt you might have. The more often the message is repeated, the more doubtful its truth.
- The employee replies in a higher-pitched voice, especially one that is also louder than normal. This is an involuntary, often fearful, response.
- The speaker's eyes shift, often to the left, and blink.
- The speaker's eyes become smaller. Tiny pupils are sometimes an involuntary response by the body to a deliberate falsehood.
- The speaker swallows harder and more obviously, another involuntary physical response to having told a lie.
- The speaker's face is flushed. Perhaps the worker is perspiring. That is the body's truth machine at work.
- The individual covers his or her mouth in an attempt to muffle the information because it is a lie.

When you suspect that an employee is lying, you should maintain eye contact and neutral body language, remain silent, and wait for a response. Sometimes, your reaction to the employee's words may be enough to prompt jabbering until sufficient information comes out to enable you to probe for the truth. Speak up. Respond, "I don't feel that you are being honest with me. What is the real situation?" Again, wait. The employee is likely to admit to the falsehood.

Give People Their Space

Besides learning how to use voice, body, gestures, and posture, you should understand proxemics, the study of spatial relationships and our use and appreciation of space, which is also part of how body language impacts interpersonal communications.

The term *proxemics* was coined by researcher E. T. Hall in 1963, when he investigated our use of personal space in contrast with fixed and semifixed space. A fixed space might be an office, whereas a semifixed feature might be furniture. Informal space is the distance between us and another party. What is comfortable informal space depends on the situation. For instance, guests at your own home are likely to stand closer to you than colleagues in your office, plant, or store. When we intrude into another person's informal space, we can arouse defensive or hostile reactions. We can get that same kind of response if we invade someone's personal fixed space, like entering someone's office or semifixed space, like sitting in someone's chair. As adults, we are better able to control our outrage when someone sits in our chair than a child who comes into class and finds another youngster in her chair. The very elderly can also be sensitive about their personal turf. Try to move an elderly resident in a nursing home to another table in the dining room, and you will see what I mean.

In your office, while your boss might smile if he sees you sitting at his desk, even if you are sitting there to write a note to him, you might see a fleeting irritation. Likewise, if you borrow a chair from a peer's cubicle without asking, your colleague may not say anything but may see your action as trespassing.

The distance between you and another can convey a desire for intimacy, declare a lack of interest, or indicate a desire to increase or decrease domination over the person. Spatial changes give a tone to a communication, accent it, and at times even counteract the spoken word.

Let's assume that you are sitting at your desk and a staff member enters your office. Rather than stand on the other side of your desk or sit in the chair in front of your desk (think subordinate positions), she stands very near your chair. Although it's your office and your desk, all symbols of your authority, she is standing, which is a symbol of control. Such dominant body language might make you feel defensive and likely would influence the subsequent conversation on a subconscious level. The further a staff member stands from your desk, the less authoritative the body language and, perhaps, the more convivial the communication because you don't feel threatened. One manager told me about his boss who immediately tells employees to take a chair when they enter his office.

In the case of competitive colleagues, you can see proxemics at work at group meetings, one-on-one sessions, and even office gatherings. Dale, Howard, Robert, and Tony all report to Sally. When Sally calls meetings, Dale claims the chair immediately opposite her, because sitting opposite the boss is a power position. Howard, Robert, and Tony each head for the chairs nearest to Sally.

Tony once told me about an argument that he had with Robert in Robert's office. Tony had a proposal for Robert's approval and went to his office to review its key points. He sat across the desk from Robert—so far, so good—but then he put the proposal before Robert, which was a bad move. As Robert listened to Tony's explanation of the proposal, he began to shift items on his desk until the proposal was moved to Tony's side of the desk. In essence, Robert was reasserting his dominance over the desk and, indirectly, reminding Tony that he had not yet accepted the proposal.

As Tony got up, he picked up the proposal and, this time, handed it to Robert, who took the document and put it in his briefcase, another dominant gesture.

I don't need to tell you how Dale, Howard, Robert, and even my friend Tony hover around Sally at social occasions at their office, each demonstrating their desire to be heir apparent. There is talk that Sally plans to make one of her four middle-level managers the supervisor of the other three. No one knows yet who will get the position—Sally hasn't given any clues. She would seem to be better at controlling her body language than her direct reports.

Voice, facial and body gestures, posture, and distance—all are forms of body language. They can strengthen your communication or damage it. Just as you develop and master verbal communications and listening skills, you need to master body language.

■ Did You Know . . . ?

Britons and Americans tend to leave more personal space around them than other nationalities and are more likely to move away if they feel that their space is being invaded. People who live in rural areas also seem to prefer to stand further apart than city dwellers.

■ Tips

- When standing near people, leave a personal space of about a yard.

- To show that what you are hearing interests you, tilt your head slightly and make friendly eye contact.

- Take that pen or pencil out of your mouth. A throwback to the need to be nursed, it demonstrates that you are feeling fearful or uncomfortable.

■ See Also

Griffin, Jack and Tom Power. *How to Say It at Work: Putting Yourself Across with Power Words, Phrases, Body Language and Communication Secrets.* Prentice-Hall, 1998.

Richmond, Virginia P. and James C. McGroskey. *Nonverbal Behavior in Interpersonal Relations.* Pearson Allyn & Bacon, 2003.

Wainwright, Gordon. *Teach Yourself Body Language.* McGraw-Hill, 2003.

14

Written Communication: Print and Electronic Messages

In today's fast changing workplace, overlooking the value of the written word is easy to do. But because the world is moving so rapidly, clear and effective writing is more important than ever. No matter how well planned a project or how smart a new idea, neither is likely to become reality until it is written down and passed on to the people who will determine whether it is viable.

Rather than slow down a business transaction, a written message ensures that there are no misunderstandings. Writing slows things down only if the message is poorly worded. So you need to be able to send effective print and electronic messages.

How good are your writing skills? Here are some mistakes that many writers make.

- *They write to impress, not express.* Your primary purpose should be to communicate your ideas. Fancy words and long sentences might have impressed your English professor, but they aren't likely to do more than annoy in the business world. Use short, familiar words that sound sincere and conversational; avoid formal or academic phrases.
- *They put everything in a single sentence.* Such sentences are also throwbacks to college papers. Longer sentences are harder to follow and are

almost always less precise. To see if your sentences are too long, count the number of words with three or more syllables in an average sentence. Now multiply the total by .4. The result will identify what has come to be called the fog factor, that is, the number of years of education needed to understand your writing. Language experts Robert Gunning and Douglas Mueller have found that the higher the level, the more difficult the message is to understand. Perhaps you're writing for a highly sophisticated audience, so a fog factor of 16, the college graduation level, would be acceptable. But most of the time, it's better to write at a level no higher than that of a high school graduate—a 12.

- *They differentiate themselves from their audience.* Instead, they should personalize their writing. When you write, use the personal pronouns *I, me, you, we,* and *us.* "It has come to my attention that . . . ," is likely to divert readers from the important message. Instead, be specific and say, "I learned . . . ," or, "Marketing tells me . . . ," or, "Government studies remind us. . . ."
- *They use the passive voice instead of the active voice.* The passive voice forces you to use more words and lessens the impact of your writing.
- *They are wordy.* Their writing is filled with needless words or phrases. Phrases such as *there is* mean nothing and, more importantly, add nothing to a sentence except length. A poor example: "There is contained in the enclosed. . . ." Better: "The enclosed pamphlet contains an important message. . . ."
- *They use phony phrases, overused openings, and clichéd closings.* Don't propose a *paradigm* that's really a *model.* Don't write, "Per our conversation." Instead write, "As we discussed. . . ." "If you have any questions, don't hesitate to call," can be made reader friendly: "If you have any questions. . . ."

Organize Your Thoughts

If clarity is a problem, then the secret to improving your communication may be to spend more time planning what you will say before putting it down on paper. Jot down a few words, phrases, or other notes to help organize your thinking. Outlining is also helpful, particularly if you are writing a lengthy memo.

In outlining, break the document down into a lead sentence; separate paragraphs, each for a different thought; introductory sentences for each paragraph to position it within the main document and allow for scanning; and a closing or summary statement at the end. Once you start writing, keep in mind this important point: managers don't have time to write a long document unless the content demands it, and their readers don't have time to read a long document unless the content requires it.

Know Your Audience

Before you begin to write, there's another issue to consider: who is your reader? If you can identify with your reader, you are more likely to use the right tone and the right level of information—neither too simple nor too sophisticated. Gauging your readers' knowledge of the topic will help you to avoid either patronizing or baffling them. If in doubt, explain any potentially difficult terms.

Because your intention is to build a bridge to the reader with your words, imagine you are sitting across the table from them. Under such circumstances, you would address the reader directly as *you* and refer to yourself as *I*. Do so in your written communication. Taking this idea of connecting with the reader further, read what you've written—does it sound conversational or stilted?

I mentioned the importance of using the active voice. The active voice, makes it clear who is speaking and, therefore, makes you seem warmer and more approachable. This isn't to say that the passive voice should never be used. While its constant use will slow comprehension and stop the reader from becoming interested in the message, it can be useful when you want to avoid placing blame on the reader, useful when that reader is the customer. It is also useful to avoid assuming blame yourself.

Before sending off your document, check that you have removed any element that might turn off the reader. Reread the document with these questions in mind.

- Did I use everyday language, not officialese?
- Did I avoid jargon or abbreviations that the reader wouldn't know?
- Does the message make sense?
- Could anything in this message seem offensive—whether intentionally or not?
- Did I use spell check?
- Is the grammar correct?

These rules apply to every document you write—e-mail or snail mail. Let's look now at some specific business communications.

Write It Right

Meeting Minutes

If you write the minutes for a meeting, you want to be sure that you record what was said in a fair and balanced way. Jot down notes during the session as you go along and write up the minutes as soon as possible. Write in the simple past tense: "Tom Brown said that. . . ." and, "Michael recommended that we. . . ." If you are unclear about what has been said or decided, ask for clarification. If an area of discussion becomes particularly sensitive, check with the group about how it should be recorded in the minutes, if at all.

There are several ways of presenting minutes, and your organization may have its own procedures. Certain elements should always be included, however. They are: the names of those present, where and when the meeting took place, the main issues discussed and decisions made, details of what action is to be taken and by whom, and the date of the next meeting (if appropriate).

Project Proposals and Reports

Presenting your ideas persuasively in writing is how to make them a reality—and gain organizational visibility.

The best reports are accurate, brief, and clear. If the report is for a specific person, always take into consideration what that person finds useful. Some people want details, while others prefer highlights and will ask for more information only if it is needed. If you expect that the report you're writing will be read by many people, provide a summary of results at the beginning. This way you can please as many people as possible. A reader can study the summary and selectively read the detail. Use graphs, charts, and diagrams where appropriate. Many people prefer to study a visual rather than peruse text or tables.

When you sit down to write a report, there are six steps to follow.

1. *Define the problem.* It may be obvious to you, but it may not be obvious to those who are reading your report for the first time. Before a single word of a report is put down, this thought needs to be completed: "The purpose of this report is. . . ."
2. *Develop a work plan.* Likely, your proposal will need a work schedule—the estimated time to complete the project and the specific tasks with it.
3. *Gather relevant data.* Complete and accurate findings are the basis for all well-received reports.

4. *Process your findings.* Once you have your data, you need to analyze the findings and draw tentative conclusions.

5. *Develop conclusions.* Always remember that conclusions are derived exclusively from findings. If you fail to link the two, the report's credibility will be shattered.

6. *Generate recommendations.* The final step is to offer recommendations based on the conclusions. Arrange your ideas by priority and sequence, making them consistent with the problem statement, providing options whenever appropriate, and expressing them in a manner most likely to secure their acceptance.

If you have some doubts about the finished document, you may want to show it to a colleague to review the accuracy of findings, the logical consistency of the conclusions and recommendations, and the tone and readability of the document. You want to be sure that the finished report does what you intend—to persuade, inform, report, request, or analyze. Was your goal for the reader to take action or simply to review the information? Is the document accomplishing that goal?

One final thought. Your proposal or report is more likely to get approved if it is easy on the eye. You should use double spacing and wide margins, include plenty of headings to help break up the text, use lists or bullet points where appropriate, and place graphics as near to the referring text as possible.

Correspondence

A well-written letter can boost business and leave the reader with a positive impression, whereas a poorly written one can cause confusion and damage your relationship. If your letters typically go unanswered, or if recipients phone to ask what you mean, your letters may not be clear. Letters may have many purposes: to request information, appeal for support, reply to a complaint, and answer questions raised by another letter.

A letter that requests information will be clear about what you want, by when you want it, and, most importantly, spell out any benefits to the reader of responding. Finally, it will end with a thank you.

If you are appealing for support from the reader, you want to establish rapport early in the letter. The letter should make clear why it is in the reader's interests to continue to read it, and it should counter any worries they might have about assisting you.

If you receive a letter of complaint, your response should be prompt and well considered. Your intention should be to defuse the situation. If your organization is at fault, apologize early in the letter. If the complaint is unfounded, say so—but politely. If something within your authority would make the customer happy, regardless of who was at fault, you may want to conclude with such an offer. Often, disgruntled customers only want to know that their complaint has been acknowledged. The effort to make them happy will delight them, and delighted customers are repeat customers.

So far, we have been talking about communications in print. Let's focus on electronic communications.

Electronic Communications

Writing skills are as important in electronic as in paper communication.

Minutes, memos, and reports—increasingly, all these documents are sent electronically. When it comes to e-mail, you need to address two questions: how can I send better messages, and how can I better manage the e-mail I receive?

Not everyone is skilled at writing e-mail or knows when e-mail is needed. Some managers send e-mail just because they have the technical capability to do so. Thus, they waste both their time and the time of those who receive their messages. People who were compulsive memo writers continue to write—they've just found a new medium.

The e-mail we receive shows that not everyone is skilled at writing digital messages. Some managers' e-memos are indecipherable notes, phrases joined together with dashes that require a phone call for interpretation. Other messages ramble and are excessively long—the equivalent of several pages of paper. Writers often don't realize that electronic communications are still communications, and they don't take that extra moment to review and organize their thoughts before keying them onto the screen and pressing the send button.

Often, too, senders of e-mail seem to assume that the recipients are mind readers or else are so familiar with everything happening, that they can take a sentence out of context and understand its relationship to the bigger picture.

Also, a preponderance of e-mail messages is sent under the subject heading "FYI," which can make reviewing your morning e-mail frustrating, particularly if you receive many messages during the day. Instead, use a precise subject that tells readers exactly what the e-mail is about.

Here are some rules to follow when sending e-mail.

- Keep messages clear but concise.
- To help recipients prioritize e-mail, highlight at the top of the message whether your e-mail requires any type of action—for instance, "Performance Standards, for Your Review and Approval."
- Make certain that your information is accurate. Because e-mail can be printed, archived, forwarded, and even broadcast, it becomes a permanent document with your name attached to it. Contrary to what the delete key says, e-mail is never permanently deleted and can be retrieved.
- Don't send an e-mail if you are angry or emotional. Cool off, then review your response. You may find you want to send a more tactful message.
- Reread each e-mail for spelling errors and correct grammar. E-mail shouldn't go out with misspellings, incomplete sentences, or grammatical errors any more than snail mail should.
- Be discriminating when attaching lengthy attachments. They take time to download as well as time to read.
- Consider the volume of e-mail a recipient receives before including them in a broadcast list.
- Be careful about identifying some e-mail as "urgent." Use this warning sparingly. Otherwise, you may find yourself in the same predicament as the boy who cried wolf too often.
- If you have not had any correspondence with someone, introduce yourself with your first e-mail by identifying your company, area of interest, background, etc.
- If you e-mail someone only occasionally, use a greeting and a closing. If you are in constant and consistent e-contact with someone, not every message needs a greeting. However, a brief sign-off, like a simple "Thanks," is polite.
- Add contact information at the bottom of your e-mail messages in each and every message you send. Include your name, title, e-mail address, company, phone and fax numbers, and company Web site address.

How should you manage the e-mail you receive?

It's very easy to get caught up in your e-mail, checking almost every few minutes to see if you have another message. But that is a terrible waste of time. Better to check your e-mail about twice a day, more often only if you receive time-sensitive information. If you aren't able to check your e-mail for a period of time, be sure to leave an outgoing message indicating the date when you will be reading and responding to your messages.

Separate attachments from e-mail and electronically file them. Don't allow e-mail to accumulate to the point that your server cannot handle another message.

 **Did You Know . . . ?**

Nearly 80 percent of people read their e-mail as soon as it arrives. They either don't want to or don't know how to disable the function on their computer that tells them as soon as they have new mail.

■ How Do You Rate?

Answer yes or no to each of these questions.

- Is your message immediately obvious?

- Does the average sentence length exceed 25 words?

- Does your writing contain lots of exclamation marks?

- Do your sentences or paragraphs start with the same word?

- Do you use capital letters for words that don't need them?

- Do you use words or expressions more than once—words like actually, basically, really, generally, or very?

- Are there often spelling mistakes in documents you send?

- Do you try to be funny in correspondence with customers, vendors, or colleagues?

- Do you use jargon in your writing, regardless of the reader's expertise in your field?

- Do you feel uneasy about your punctuation?

How many times did you answer yes? Seven to ten yes answers suggest that your writing may be difficult to follow and you need to work on your written communications. Four to seven yes responses suggest that you are halfway there but spending a little more time on your written communications would be worthwhile. Three or fewer yes responses, and your writing should be easy to follow; the effort you make to send precise, brief communications is likely appreciated by those who receive them.

■ Tips

- A printed version of a memo can be more effective than an electronic one when used to mark a shift in policy.

- The spell check feature is the first line of defense against errors but not the last. You are. Spell check is a useful tool, but it's no substitute for a careful review by you. After all, if you choose the wrong word but spell it correctly, the spell check won't spot the error. And it certainly won't tell you if you misspelled someone's name, a place, or a product.

- Use humor sparingly in your business communications, if at all. When you're face to face, someone can tell you are joking. Not so when you joke on paper. You could offend someone unintentionally.

■ See Also

Axson, David A. *Best Practices in Planning and Management Reporting.* John Wiley Sons, 2003.

Flynn, Nancy and Randolph Kahn, Esq. *E-mail Rules: A Business Guide to Managing Policies, Security, and Legal Issues for E-mail and Digital Communication.* AMACOM, 2003.

Kostner, Jaclyn. *Bionic E-teamwork.* Dearborn Trade, 2001.

15

Creating Followers: Building Teamwork

This chapter is about your responsibilities as your unit's leader. Too many new managers assume that they don't have to worry about *leadership,* because they think that term is only used in talking about CEOs and presidents. Not so. If you're responsible for the performance of a group, then you're both a manager and a leader.

That you are a manager means that you already have achieved a certain level of professionalism in your field. To continue to succeed as a manager and beyond, you must begin to develop your leadership potential. You don't have a choice in this matter. You're a leader because that's what the people who work for you expect you to be. They look to you for purpose and direction.

As a manager, you handle things like scheduling problems and how to allocate resources to the work. Your planning perspective is tactical (see Chapter 1). As a leader, you will be concerned with your unit's purpose and its direction. You also will build a sense of teamwork within your unit. The *Oxford English Dictionary* defines a *manager* as "a person controlling or administering a business" and a *leader* as "a person who causes others to go with him, by guiding and showing the way; guides by persuasion and argument."

There is much interest today in this thing called leadership. In dynamic environments, where change is rapid and there are few points of reference, leadership is needed.

This Thing Called Teamwork

Within this book, you will discover many of the skills you will need to be an effective leader, such as the skills of delegation and empowerment (Chapter 5) and communication (Chapters 10, 11, 12, and 13). But in this chapter you will learn about a skill critical to leading your staff—called *followership*—and how you can use this quality to transform your group into a top-notch team.

In Chapter 17 on meeting management, I use the term *team* to refer to groups that meet over time to complete a project (e.g., crossfunctional teams) or staff that come together in meetings for either a single purpose or to review ongoing operations. In this chapter, the term is used solely to describe a staff of employees that operate together to achieve a common goal. They achieve that objective through *teamwork* and exhibit a *team spirit* like that of a football, baseball, or volleyball team. Your employees have measurable goals and a visible purpose around which they unite. They also have a leader—you.

Every work unit has the potential to think and act like a team, but whether or not that happens depends upon you and how you lead your group—your followership (or leadership) capability. As John Adair, a British leadership guru, has observed, "Leaders must be ratified in the hearts and the minds of those who work for them."

Team Thinking

Many departments do not operate as teams—that is, they do not *practice teamwork*. Members may talk to each other at the printer or over lunch, and their work efforts may be designed to meet the overarching objectives of the department, but these employees work on a day-to-day basis largely as individuals. Such situations are unfortunate, for studies indicate that teamwork and team spirit are critical to increased organizational productivity and profitability. In addition, working together as a team, employees have more fun.

Teamwork satisfies a need for socialization. Working together also helps people grow as they learn from each other and develop important skills. Working together toward a common goal, they gain a sense of purpose that is motivating and fulfilling. When people work together in an atmosphere of trust and accountability, they put aside turf issues and politics and focus on the tasks to be done. This is why their efforts have significant results.

What is so different operationally between a team and a dedicated staff of workers? Where a sense of teamwork exists, employees look out for one another.

They know about each other's work and can answer questions when their coworkers are out. On the other hand, if this sense of teamwork is missing and an employee is absent, nothing is done in that person's area until they return.

In a team, coworkers also look to each other for advice and to their leader to show them the way when things are difficult. In a department, competition among employees often precludes the possibility of asking for help. Teams have an *esprit* that shows a sense of bonding and camaraderie. As a team is created, employees begin using the pronoun *we* more than *I.*

Such team spirit isn't built overnight. Employees begin as a disparate group of people who just happen to work together in the same department. They will continue to operate as such, doing their jobs as they are instructed, focusing their attention on getting through each day, until you, as their manager, pull them together into a team. How do you do this?

As the leader of your staff, you:

- Encourage cooperation, rather than competition, among team members.
- Involve the entire team in making decisions related to team projects. Give subgroups within the team autonomy in designing their projects.
- Not only delegate to employees but also empower employees, sharing decision-making responsibility with them (see Chapter 5).
- Set up a system for measuring team performance as well as individual performance.
- Show that you value the work of every team member. You will have people with different levels of skills. Acknowledge that each contributes to the team's success.
- Let the group know that each of them benefits from coworkers' successes, because these achievements make the team that much stronger. You celebrate individual successes as team successes, too, because everyone has contributed in one way or another. A lesson of war is that soldiers do not fight for abstract causes; they fight for the person in the foxhole next to them. That example gets to the heart of why teams work; they support one another for the greater good of everyone.

A critical element of making this transformation from staff to team is creating a work culture where collaboration and cooperation exist. Such a workplace is characterized by:

- *Open communication.* When teamwork is present, team members, because they trust each other, are open and honest in their communications.

- *A willing acceptance of assignments.* Team members don't haggle over who does what. They willingly accept assignments given them by their leader and by their coworkers. Motivated by peer pressure, they work hard to get their jobs done right the first time and to meet deadlines.
- *Understood and accepted goals.* Often, the team sets its own objectives and goals. Other times, goals come from their leader or senior management. However the goals are set, the team works collaboratively to achieve them. Because their leader has explained why these goals need to be achieved, team members assist one another to make them a reality.
- *Results orientation.* Teams focus on their objectives, and their efforts are designed to achieve them. Periodically, under direction of a leader, the team assesses its progress. That knowledge serves to direct future team effort.
- *Shared trust.* In a healthy team, members essentially trust one another. Despite occasional conflict, members get along well and enjoy each other's company.

Many work environments in which teamwork is practiced involve team members in decision making, practicing participative management. Members set group goals relating either to their operation or the corporation as a whole. Hammering out the goals collectively not only utilizes the wisdom of the entire group but also secures ownership to the goals. As you've probably learned by now, the more your workers contribute to decisions, the more likely they are to work to support them.

Goals are more easily met, too. When goals are set as a group, all members are clear on who is responsible for what. There is no overlap in responsibility or unassigned responsibility, as sometimes happens in more traditionally run departments. You may be thinking to yourself, "All this sounds great for my staff members and even for the organization as a whole. What about the hard work I put in to become a manager? Will I be losing my newly gained authority if I involve my staff in planning and decision making?" Not at all. Sharing both does not mean that you abdicate control over the group. Consider your responsibilities as team leader.

From Group Manager to Team Leader

As a team leader, your major responsibility is to model the behaviors and attitudes that you want to see within the team. What does this mean? For one, you need to share information with your team, just as you expect members to exchange information with one another. Further, you need to show respect for each member and the unique contribution that person makes to the team effort.

When you first form a team, expect that your staff will have some doubts about your willingness to model the behaviors described above. You have to devote time and attention to building an atmosphere of mutual support, encouragement, communication, and approval. Encourage your people to have fun, too. Laughter brings people together, and it's a great stress buster.

Followership

When I talk about your role as leader, I have no single leadership style in mind. I grew up watching lots of Westerns and war movies. Consequently, at one time, I based my understanding about what made a great leader on the roles played by John Wayne. But that autocratic, directive leadership style is only one of several you can use.

The tell-and-sell approach (think John Wayne) has the leader making all the decisions. It is based on Theory X, a concept developed by Douglas McGregor, late professor of industrial management at the Massachusetts Institute of Technology. McGregor offered two frameworks for management thinking. Theory X assumes that employees don't like to work and consequently have to be directed and even coerced to put in a day's work for a day's pay. Theory Y sees employees as adults who, under the right leadership, learn not only to accept responsibility but to seek it out, as their manager demonstrates that their personal goals are consistent with those of the organization.

Participative, relations-oriented leadership is in harmony with the assumptions of Theory Y. The leader acts as a source of information and exercises minimum control, depending upon employees' sense of responsibility and good judgment to get things done.

Both styles can be used to build team spirit and teamwork. Likewise, a third style called democratic or consultative leadership, can be used. In this style, the leader discusses options with, consults with, and draws ideas from employees before making a decision. I have come to call this the Jean-Luc Picard style, after the character from *Star Trek: The Next Generation.* If you are a fan of the show, you may recall how Picard hears various opinions and then makes a decision, telling his command group, "Make it so."

All three styles of leadership support team building. You might use the authoritative style where you need lots of control over the work, whereas you might use the participative style where the process and procedures are flexible and the work demands creativity and initiative. The participative style is more in tune with today's employees than the directive style, but if—as a new manager—you aren't comfortable with that style yet, you may want to opt for the democratic, Picard style until you have established a solid rapport with your employees.

Whatever style you choose, it's important for followership that you communicate the importance of teamwork to your staff.

Let's assume that your company has had to lay off 3 of your 12 employees. The work that had to be done before the staff cutback still has to be done. Working as a team won't necessarily help with any single employee's career advancement, but cooperation and collaboration with one another will make it easier to get the work, once done by 12, done by 9 employees. That's the WIIFM (What's in It for Me?) in teamwork. For instance, in this situation, while teamwork won't necessarily help any single employee's career, it will ensure that the department's work is done. Teamwork enables a staff to handle external pressures, like an economic downturn that leads to staff cutbacks, as well as internal pressures, like an unrealistic project deadline.

Leadership Role

As your team's leader, you will be watched to be sure that you live up to your employees' idea of a leader, so you need to know what employees look for in a leader. Let's look at the attributes one by one. Employees want their leaders to do the following:

- *Clarify direction.* A leader provides the team with a sense of purpose. This can be a weighty responsibility for a new manager but, as a leader, you must take charge of yourself and of those who report to you. Responsibility for others emerges from setting goals as well as following through on those goals. Most importantly, responsibility means a willingness to be accountable for the actions of others under your charge as well as for your own actions.
- *Be masters of their skill.* You are a manager now because your expertise was the launching pad for your promotion. As a leader, your employees want you to maintain your professional presence—and more. They also want you to acknowledge that you don't have all the answers and, consequently, that you force yourself to stretch and learn new skills.

- *Focus, focus, focus.* Clear focus keeps the unit pointed in the right direction and gives followers an unmistakable sense of direction.
- *Listen.* When you listen, you not only know what's going on around you, but you enable followers to share ideas, even when those ideas may conflict with your viewpoint. You let your followers know that you want them to be involved in the decision-making process. Listening opens the door to genuine communication as well as improved focus.
- *Coach the team.* Demonstrate a desire to teach others. Not only do you acknowledge your need to learn more, you also offer opportunities to your staff members to grow.
- *Be patient.* Being patient, because some people learn more slowly than others, demonstrates respect for people, which is integral to creating a sense of trust, a fundamental of teamwork.
- *Be passionate.* Great leaders are enthusiastic and committed to achieving their goals. Everyone has the ability to be a great leader, but the real ones express their purpose, goal, or objective relentlessly.
- *Perform.* Tom Peters has said that he, "would rather have a B strategy with an A execution than an A strategy with a B execution." He's talking about superb execution, the ability to get a job done in an A+ fashion. Great leaders strive for this level of performance.
- *Use vision as a guide for behavior on a day-to-day basis.* You need to communicate your unit's vision each and every day. Walk around and engage people in discussions of what they're doing and why to help them link their everyday actions to that vision. Before that, however, with input from your employees, you have to create a vision that is compelling enough that your team will identify with it on a deep, personal level—without compromising their values.
- *Create resonance.* Richard Boyatzis, author of *Primal Leadership: Harnessing the Power of Emotional Intelligence,* describes resonance as a "positive energy that motivates people to perform at their best."
- *Earn your employees' respect.* People obey a leader they fear but follow a leader they trust and respect.
- *Show courage.* Employees want a leader with the courage to act for the group's benefit with minimum regard for the leader's own well-being and self-interest.
- *Exhibit mutual trust.* The most significant adhesive binding team members together is mutual trust. In light of recent financial scandals, at no

time has this been as important as the present. Trust translates into belief in a person—the team's leader. In everyday conversations, when your employees speak of trust in you, they are also thinking about these characteristics.

- *Honesty.* Your employees are confident in your fairness—in the rewards you provide, the assignments that you give, and the opportunities for training you hand out.
- *Reliability.* Employees expect their manager to carry through on promises. Your employees are no different. If you say that you'll do something, they want to know they can count on your word. Can they?
- *Fairness.* If your employees disagree with you, they want to feel they can express their beliefs without being punished. They can trust you to listen to their ideas without disapproval, either now or in the future.
- *Truthful.* Your employees want to count on you to express feelings freely, to say what you mean and mean what you say. There are no games being played on either side.

Trust is a value, and like many values it is best understood by considering the behaviors associated with it. Consider the following:

- *Consistency and predictability.* Unpredictable behavior breeds anxiety and mistrust.
- *A congenial, supportive atmosphere.* Your employees want to feel free to express themselves freely. Withheld feelings make for mistrust.

The important point for you, as a leader, to remember is that trust builds trust and mistrust begets mistrust. The more you give of trust, the more you get back and vice versa. Thus, it's essential for you to use techniques that are certain to build, increase, and maintain trust. There is nothing vague or mysterious about creating trust. Like many values, it transfers into behaviors. Exercising these behaviors produce trust.

As a New Manager/Leader . . .

Have you gone around to find out what you don't know? Your first priority as a leader/manager, especially if you happen to be taking over a new situation, is to find out about policies, problems, and opportunities. Not only will you get a better perspective on your position, but the responses to your questions will teach you a great deal about the people with whom you have spoken.

■ **Tips**

- Create a positive atmosphere free from rigidity.

- Don't dissuade team members from speaking out.

- As team leader, communicate strategic aims clearly and review and update them regularly.

- Use time with team members not only to teach but also to learn about opportunities to improve operations. A leader finds ways to make the most of team members' insights and ideas.

The Good, the Bad, and the Ugly

With a thank you to Clint Eastwood, let me share with you what is good about a good leader and what's bad about a bad leader. The "ugly" is made up of two situations that bad leaders can create.

The good from good leaders:

- The team works as a team, not just as a group of individuals.
- The team's members work to achieve a common objective.
- Team members support each other.
- The team is prepared to put in extra effort when required.
- Team members aim for excellence, not just for doing their jobs.
- Task assignments are clear.

The bad from bad team leaders:

- The group is unclear about what it has to do.
- The group is not motivated, so tasks take longer than they should or may not even get completed.
- The individuals don't work as a team and consequently don't perform as well as a real team.
- The group won't be able to sustain a workload under pressure.

The ugly from a bad team leader:

- Time and resources may be wasted, and the job may not be done properly.
- Turnover will be high, as employees leave rather than stay in such an environment.

■ See Also

Gubman, Ed. *The Engaging Leader.* Dearborn Trade, 2003.

Maxwell, John C. *The 17 Essential Qualities of a Team Player: Becoming the Kind of Person Every Team Wants.* Thomas Nelson, 2002.

Quick, Thomas L. *Successful Team Building.* AMACOM, 1992.

Schwarz, Roger. *The Skilled Facilitator.* Jossey-Bass, 2002.

Tracy, Diane and William J. Morin. *Truth, Trust, and the Bottom Line: 7 Steps to Trust-Based Management.* Dearborn Trade, 2001.

16

Solving Problems, Making Decisions

Problem solving and decision making are not the only activities of a manager, but they are extremely important ones. Much of your success as a manager will depend on your ability to make the right decisions. Often, those decisions will be related to choosing the best of several good resolutions to problems; other times, those decisions will involve a judgment call between two or more alternative courses, both with downsides.

Because decision making is the final step in problem solving, decision making is often treated solely as it relates to problem solving. But more insights into both decision-making and problem solving can be gained by looking at them as two distinct competencies.

Let's begin with the ability to make good decisions.

The Nature of Decisions

As a manager, you will be making several different kinds of decisions. For example, you will be making considered decisions, choices made after careful consideration of a variety of possible solutions. For instance, a considered decision might involve the purchase of new office equipment or the addition of a product to your current line. As you can tell, they aren't the kind of decisions that you will have to make every day. Besides a lot of personal thought, they may require the involvement of others—from your employees and peers to your manager and other members of senior management. You may have reached a conclusion but ask colleagues or staff to act as devil's advocates and poke holes in your decision. You want them not only to consider the choice but also scrutinize it in terms of any implementation problems that might arise and the internal and external environment. Peter Drucker, the management guru, has said that this process of "dissent" adds to the likelihood of someone making the right decision.

Clearly, this process is time intensive—it takes time to find alternatives, to seek other viewpoints, to get dissent if any, and to determine implementation issues. But time spent in these activities generally minimizes trouble in executing the decision and maximizes the probability of success.

Operational decisions represent another category of quandaries you will encounter in your job. These decisions are made to avoid and address problems. For instance, you might have to sign a purchase request for office supplies like stationery and pens or for raw materials like electronic components, pipes, screws, and nails, or you might distribute work assignments when an employee is absent. Such decisions tend to become routine over time. While they are vital to the flow of business and may have immediate impact, they should become very much a part of the job. As a new manager, these decisions were likely tough to make, but as you become more familiar with the work, they should become easier and easier.

You also have to learn to make what are sometimes called ten-second decisions. These aren't snap decisions—those are decisions you can make without any thought. Examples of snap decisions include:

- "Should I call a customer or write him a letter?"
- "Should I meet with my team this afternoon or wait until tomorrow?"
- "Should I eat lunch at my desk or go out?"

Ten-second decisions seem as insignificant as snap decisions, but they could have ramifications, and you need to give those some thought before making them. For instance, an employee has asked you if he could take tomorrow off. "You don't have to tell me now—just before the end of my shift." You think: He has done some outstanding work, but he has no vacation time left. If you say yes, you could be setting an unwise precedent. What should you do? Perhaps a distributor asks if her outlet can be placed ahead of another for delivery tomorrow. Should you do as requested, or could accommodating this single client alienate many more—even lose you an account?

Faced with a ten-second decision, you need to learn to think at least ten seconds before making a decision. You know that the individual asking the question wants an answer soon, but you may want to postpone the decision until you can think more about the matter. Too often, the ten-second decisions we make set precedents or are actually operational questions that demand further analysis.

We also have to think about our motivations when we make a ten-second decision. Let's go back to that employee's request for a day off. Do we think that granting this will increase the individual's motivation, or are we trying to buy his friendship by saying yes. Taking that further, if we say yes, we should ask ourselves if a day off would achieve either result.

Replying no to the request would probably put the decision into the final category, a swallow-hard decision. These may be personally uncomfortable, because they may negatively impact interpersonal relationships either with our employees or our boss. Although these decisions may make us uneasy, they are necessary. They are the kind that you, as a manager, are being paid to make. Many times, the decisions we make will be unpopular.

Unpopular Decisions

As a manager, you may have to make a decision that won't be well received. But keep in mind that a manager who refuses to make unpopular decisions when needed undermines her own managerial role in many ways, depending on the nature of the decision. It may affect operations, it may affect the respect in which you are held, it may make you seem more a yes-person than a team leader. A decision to let quality standards slip rather than get tough with one or two workers, for instance, may make you seem like a nice person, but it will undermine corporate performance. It is doubtful that the remainder of the staff will end up thinking well of you. Those who see how you let standards slip won't be impressed by your management performance.

Some newer managers may get tough on poor performers or make other unpopular decisions, but they may hold others responsible for the decision, trying to disassociate themselves from it. Such avoidance can cause workers to question their managers' capability, if not their word. It's important to recognize that, as a manager, you will have to make unpopular decisions. No matter how unpopular it is, as a representative of your company, it is *your* decision. Accept responsibility for it. The respect you earn will outlive any temporary unpopularity.

Managerial Indecisiveness

Fear of making an unpopular decision is one reason that many managers hold off making a decision. They think if they wait long enough, circumstances will change, making no decision necessary. Other reasons for indecisiveness include:

- Fear of making a wrong decision or a mistake
- Fear of the unknown
- Fear of taking responsibility

These issues are emotional, and they can be overwhelming. Those who suffer from indecisiveness may excuse their behavior by saying, "I wasn't sure what to do, so I decided to wait," or, "I need more information," or, "I thought the boss would make that decision." Indecisive managers may think that they are explaining away their indecisiveness, but those who work with them soon get wise. Regardless of the consequences, now that you are a manager, if you have to make a decision, then make it. You will make mistakes as everyone does, but you can learn from these. Making no decision is usually worse than any decision you could make—both for the issue under consideration and for your relationship with your employees, colleagues, and manager.

None of this is to suggest that there is no risk associated with decisions. Most involve an element of risk, some more than others. Should risk be a concern, you can reduce it by testing a decision. For example, if a new product has a problem—service difficulties or customer complaints—you can look at some possible solutions and simulate the financial outcomes of each, from holding a customer focus group to redesigning the product from scratch. You can also review past precedents. Sometimes, past experience will direct you to the right decision, but other times you may want to set your own course. A previously correct decision may be wrong as times change. If following precedent feels wrong, then it is probably time to innovate.

As you make one decision after another, you will find it easier and easier to make them. You will have staff members and colleagues with which to consult, individuals outside your organization to whom you can also turn, and past experience to rely on. You may turn to one of the problem-solving or decision-making techniques that I'll discuss later in this chapter, but you may also rely on hunches or intuition—gut feelings.

Experience on the job—solving problems and making decisions—will build your own internal databank of knowledge that will allow you to trust your feelings. Even if you don't make a decision totally based on intuition, your feelings can help provide you with the basis to start the process. Most experienced managers use a combination of objective analytical tools and intuition for decision making, especially if the cost of a mistake can be high.

Besides, should you need official sanction for a decision, it is better if you can point to evidence to support it. With some decisions, you may need to prepare a report detailing your recommendation and how you reached it. Such a report might have to indicate the nature of the decision but also why the decision is required, who will be involved in implementation, and when the implementation will take place.

Where a decision is made to address a major problem, particularly one impacting the organization as a whole, such a report will be a necessity to impress management to move on your recommendation.

Problem Sensing

Problem solving can take up a lot of time. So it makes sense for you to resolve problems before they develop, let alone grow to impact the bottom line. I've come to call this preventive management. As you walk through your workplace, you should be looking for recurring problems—gaps between what should be and what is. Rather than ignore them, you need to stop and talk to those nearby to determine if the situation is chronic. If it is, you may have a problem in its early stages, and you may want to identify its cause now rather than wait until it becomes more serious, impacting production or job performance.

Let's assume that one of your employees comes to you with a problem. Let's further assume that this problem is relatively small. You could take over and solve it, but this may be an opportunity, instead, to teach your employees to bring solutions to you instead of only problems. Your employees may not do this because they think it is your call. So you have to learn to pull back intentionally and encourage your workers to think through a problem and come up with answers. Getting employees who have never demonstrated initiative to do so can take several steps.

When an employee first brings a problem to you, you might come up with the solution. The next time she brings the same problem or a related one, you might ask for a suggestion. If she has none, you might remind her of what was done before and ask if that suggests something. Next time the person comes to you, you might suggest she go back and think about the problem and bring at least one solution to you. In coaching your employees in problem solving, encourage them to go beyond one or two tries at a solution. Allowing them to give up too soon will only encourage them to hand the problem over to you instead of trying another solution. (For more about coaching employees, see Chapter 6.)

Not every problem is within an employee's ability to address. On occasion, you may even have to bring together your entire staff to work on a problem or, where the problem impacts the entire organization, representatives from different parts of the organization.

Problem Solving

Before discussing problem solving in detail, let me go over some basics.

As you know, a problem is a situation that is a deviation from standard—something that needs correcting, a disruption in normal operations, or just a plain mess that needs cleaning up. Sometimes a problem, while an uncertainty or a difficulty, can represent an opportunity once a solution is found.

Analyzing a situation is called problem solving. Arriving at workable solution is decision making.

Alternative solutions to a problem may be arrived at in many different ways, including by hit or miss or through the blind hog method. (The saying goes that even a blind hog can find an acorn now and then.) But the likelihood of finding a workable solution is greatest when you follow this seven-step process.

1. Define or identify the problem.
2. Get the facts.
3. Interpret the facts.
4. Develop alternative solutions.
5. Select the best practical solution. The decision-making step in problem solving.
6. Implement the solution.
7. Evaluate the effectiveness of the solution.

As we look at each step in detail, keep in mind that you need not form a group or involve your staff in this process. While involvement of your staff may bring insights into the nature of the problem or assist in implementation of the solution, the same process can be used by you, alone, to come up with a solution.

Definition of the Problem

The most difficult step in problem solving and decision making is to identify the *real* problem. Frequently, the symptoms of a problem are mistaken for its cause. Take, for instance, turnover. As you read in Chapter 4, turnover is a symptom of such problems as poor supervision, boring work assignments, improper hiring criteria, and inadequate salaries. If your work unit had high turnover, and you focused exclusively on that, you would not put an end to the problem. You would be addressing a symptom rather than the root cause.

Get the Facts

The second step in problem solving and decision making is to gather all the factual information needed to make a careful assessment of the situation. Sources of factual information include financial records, drawings, policies and procedures, reports, and actual observation. A frequently overlooked source of facts is the employee or group of employees involved in the situation. Being closest to the actual operation or process, employees often have ideas about what should be done to eliminate a problem. So you should consult with employees when you look for the reason behind a problem.

Let's take our problem of turnover, for instance. Exit interviews with departing employees may provide insights into the problem. A group meeting about the workplace might also identify ways in which it might be improved.

How much information does a supervisor need to identify the reason behind a problem? This question can't be answered in the abstract. The situation determines how much information will be enough. I remember the period after September 11. Two weeks later, a CEO told *The Wall Street Journal* that he had not made a decision since then. He was uncertain what would happen next. When I mentioned this to another CEO, he observed that a decision maker never thinks that all the facts are available to make a decision, no matter the circumstances. Today's fast-changing world has only made incomplete information more of a problem. But to wait for all the facts to come in before making a decision, he told me, is to make a decision—not to do anything. Managers have to make a decision. After all, if it is the wrong decision, they can always make another decision.

Interpret the Facts

This step actually starts as information is collected. Facts are fitted together, and their relationships are considered. Questions are asked. Why did this breakdown occur? Is it a design flaw? What is the magnitude of the problem if we don't address it? The nature of the problem, of course, will determine the questions asked. The important point here is that a manager needs to probe and then dig even further. The good news is that most problems leave paper trails, and careful analysis of printouts, market research findings, and other data, depending on the nature of the problem, can cast a light on a dilemma or suggest further research. In time, the facts will begin to create a picture, like the pieces of a jigsaw puzzle.

During this process, you may encounter opinions, attitudes, and perceptions. They may be clues to the source of the problem or, alternatively, they can derail you from the real source.

Although problem solving is a seven-step process, know that, whether working on your own or with your staff, there will be a great temptation to move immediately to identifying solutions.

Develop Alternative Solutions

The next step in problem solving is to come up with some alternative approaches to resolving the problem. You may come up with alternatives based on your past experience or that of your peers. You might call your staff together to work together on potential solutions. If the problem involves many parts of your organization, you may want to form a crossfunctional team, with representatives from throughout your company, to brainstorm solutions.

In this stage, you don't want to stop at a single idea or to analyze the feasibility of any idea that is suggested. Just because some alternative has never been tried in the past should not prevent its consideration in the current situation.

How many alternatives should you have? The answer is "enough." In some cases, this may be three or four; in other cases, it may be as many as five or six. Generally, the nature of the problem and its complexity will influence the number of alternatives you need to identify. One alternative that should be included is: do nothing. Not all problems disappear without action, but some do, so managers should ask themselves, "Would the condition disappear on its own?"

Select the Best Solution

This is the decision-making phase in the problem solving process. Initially, a weeding out approach is used; that is, the alternatives are reviewed, and those that clearly do not seem suitable are thrown out. The rest are then reviewed carefully. Each will be analyzed in terms of its direct as well as indirect impact on the problem including costs, delivery, employee morale, potential resistance, and the like. Each alternative will have positive and negative consequences, and analysis should identify both for each alternative. For instance, you don't want to put in place a solution that would produce a problem worse than the one it was supposed to solve. If the consequences of a solution are more costly than the problem, then you want to continue the search for another solution—a practical one. Many solutions didn't work because managers forgot that they wanted a practical solution.

Once a solution has been selected, your responsibility is to do all you can to make it succeed.

If you work as a group, and you have several good solutions, you may want to try multivoting to make your final selection. Here's how it works. You review the ideas, link ideas where possible, and then ask members to vote. Each time, the list should be cut in half. In a short time, your list should contain a workable number of alternatives for further study and final decision making.

If you have only a few ideas, you can vote to determine if you have consensus on one. Keep in mind that consensus doesn't require everyone to be in agreement, just that the chosen idea be one that everyone can live with.

Implement the Solution

You want to implement the proposed solution as quickly as possible to put an end to the problem. Don't forget, however, to inform those who will be affected about its implementation. You may even need to train those whom you expect to make the change happen. To put a solution to work without advance preparation of affected employees is to court disaster. Communication is essential. The solution will meet less resistance and will be more successful when everyone concerned knows why, how, when, where, what, and who will be influenced by it. (See Chapter 18 on change management.) Often, it is not the change that upsets people—it is the way it is pushed through.

Evaluate the Effectiveness of the Solution

Once you've implemented the solution, you need to monitor it to see if it is producing the positive results you expected. Too often, the best answers on paper don't work exactly as they are supposed to. Are costs down? Is service quality up? Are you making promised delivery dates? You may have to make small adjustments, select another alternative, or even begin from scratch if the selected solution is not doing the job it was supposed to do.

■ Problem Solving and Decision Making: Tools and Techniques

A number of tools and techniques can enable you to better identify the cause of a problem, select the best decision, *and* monitor results. As you solve problems, it is as important to be sure that you have the real cause of a problem (don't make the assumption that you know the cause) as it is to come up with a workable solution and test it.

Brainstorming. This technique can be used to identify problems, solutions, or the consequences of alternative solutions. Basically, it is an idea-generating technique in which group members throw out their ideas as they think of them so that each has the opportunity to build on the ideas of the others. It is especially useful for creating a breakthrough whenever you are presented with a new, unusual, or different situation that is not amenable to a traditional solution.

There are few rules to brainstorming. The most important is that, during the process, ideas are not evaluated. Only after the brainstorming is over are the ideas evaluated and the list of suggestions narrowed to one or two good ones.

Pareto analysis. This technique recognizes that many things may be creating problems but only a few of these may be key to the situation. Your intent should be to identify and address those critical few to resolve the situation. Measurable data are necessary for such analysis, so the initial step may be to gather information on quality, cost, or productivity. Then analysis determines which elements are having the most impact—whether it is people being put on hold, warehousing problems that are creating customer service complaints, or missed delivery dates. The process assumes that 20 percent of the factors impact 80 percent of the issue; the next step, then, is to identify action plans to address that 20 percent of the elements.

Scatter diagrams. These diagrams study the relationship between two factors—problem and situation—to see how often they occur at the same time. The more scattered the timelines of problems, the less likely the two factors are related to each other. You might compare a number of potential factors—from using a certain product, using a particular piece of equipment, or the behavior of an employee—to identify the likely cause of the problem.

Workflow diagrams. These show the flow of materials, people, or information within an organization. Detailed workflow charts help to identify at what point a problem affects the system, usually because work has to be redone.

Cause and effect diagrams. The group first determines the nature of the problem. It then identifies likely causes of the problem, ultimately reaching agreement on the major causes. The members then try to visually connect all the causes back to the general problem, drawing lines to show relationships between causes. More lines are drawn as additional causes are traced to these problems. In searching for causes, the team ultimately comes to the root cause of the problem, the one they need to address before they can address the others.

Because the final diagram often resembles a fishbone, the technique is also called fishbone analysis.

Variance analysis. All the steps needed to produce a product or complete a process are identified and studied to determine where problems are likely to occur and their consequences.

Managerial Mistakes

As I went through the steps involved in problem solving, including decision making, I identified some red flags, which I'll highlight here. These are common—and costly—mistakes new managers can make.

- *Make unnecessary decisions.* On occasion, the nature of a problem will be such that no action should be taken. Because decisions entail risk, it might be better to let sleeping dogs lie. This is a management judgment on your part, and you have to be prepared to make it.

- *Fight a recurring problem with the same solution.* Often, the manager focuses on symptoms rather than the root cause of the problem. Consequently, the solution doesn't work—or works for only a brief period.

- *Does not evaluate benefits in terms of costs.* Where there's no analysis of the costs ($) associated with a solution, the most far-fetched kinds of decisions are likely to be considered and selected. The result should always be evaluated in terms of its costs—tangible as well as intangible.

- *Delay a decision.* You've heard of paralysis by analysis; it's a condition caused by managers procrastinating when a decision is needed. Unlike cheese, decisions don't necessarily improve with age. Even if the decision is not the right one, it is better made in a timely fashion so the manager has the time to correct the mistake before it does too much damage. Further, making a decision—any decision—rather than brooding about it allows a manager to pay attention to other problems—or potential problems.

Did You Know . . . ?

Americans are guiltier of paralysis by analysis than any other nationality. The British have a reputation for inadequate analysis, whereas other Europeans fall between the two extremes. The Japanese are thorough analysts but move quickly once a decision is made.

■ Tips

- Challenge all assumptions.

- New ideas are as valuable as any others but should not be adopted just because they are new.

- Don't let personal feelings about the source of an idea influence your selection.

- Before you undertake decision making, be sure you have identified the criteria on which to base your decision.

■ See Also

Higgins, James M. *202 Creative Problem Solving Techniques.* New Management Publications Company, 1994.

Kaner, Sam, Lenny Lind and Catherine Toldi, et al. *Facilitator's Guide to Participatory Decision-Making.* New Society Publications, 1996.

Markus, Donalee, Lindsey Markus and Pat Taylor. *Retrain Your Business Brain.* Dearborn Trade, 2003.

Williams, Paul B. *Getting a Project Done on Time.* AMACOM, 1996.

Zeitz, Paul. *The Art and Craft of Problem Solving.* John Wiley & Sons, 1999.

17

Managing Meetings

Meetings can serve many different purposes. Informational meetings share news with staff. Educational meetings teach employees something new. Discussion meetings provide a forum for employees to give their opinions, brainstorm together, and find solutions to problems and ideas for new projects and ventures. Planning meetings focus staff attention on critical goals and energize employees.

Whatever their intent, the key to success is how well the meetings are managed.

The Bad Side of Meetings

Too many of the meetings we attend don't accomplish what they set out to do. They seem to fit the jokes made about meetings. "A meeting is a place where people take minutes and waste hours," or, "A committee is a group of people who individually can do nothing and who jointly decide that nothing can be done," or the old rubric, "A camel is a horse designed by a committee." Further, they swallow up valuable time and energy. Today, meetings take up as much as 30 percent of our work week. Senior management can spend almost 50 percent of their week in meetings.

Too often, meetings are held unnecessarily. There is no point in calling a meeting if you can accomplish the same goal on your own. If you need information from another person, you can get that information via telephone, on e-mail, or over lunch. It's even possible to talk to a group in a virtual environment. Meetings make sense when you believe that several people in the same room can come up with a new solution to a recurring problem or when you want the individuals' support to implement a new policy or procedure or otherwise change operations.

A Well-Organized Meeting

The best-run meetings are brief and focused. Such meetings happen by design—that means that they have a clearly defined mission, operating ground rules, and a well-organized agenda.

Mission

A shared understanding of the meeting's purpose is critical. Attendees need to know why they are meeting. You might have an operating meeting that is held every second week, or perhaps you lead a crossfunctional team. Regardless of the purpose of the gathering, attendees have to know what it is.

Ground Rules

These are the guidelines by which the meeting is run. Among the questions that such ground rules should address are:

- Where and when will meetings be held?
- How will the need for emergency meetings be handled?
- How long will meetings last?
- How will decisions be reached?
- How will the team work with other groups within the organization?
- Who will be responsible for preparation of meeting minutes?
- Who will handle communication with senior management, if need be?
- How will the team handle conflicts and disagreements among its members?
- Will the team evaluate each session after the fact to help improve subsequent sessions?

As head of the meeting, it's your task to lead the group in setting the ground rules. To stimulate discussion, you might raise some questions. For instance, you might ask, "What was a major problem with the last meeting you attended? What could we do to avoid that problem this time?" or, "How can we be sure that we stay focused on the agenda?" or, "What will enable us to manage the discussions without overcontrolling the flow of ideas or information?"

When attendees help write the meeting guidelines, they buy in more to the end result. Members who don't follow the ground rules are likely to feel group displeasure, which for many is worse punishment than any one-on-one criticism from you.

Here are some sample ground rules.

- All meetings will begin and end on schedule.
- The position of chair will be rotated.
- Discussion time will be limited to that set on the agenda.
- Meetings will be held every second Tuesday, from 9:15 to 11:00 AM, in the conference room.
- Three days prior to the meeting, members will receive a copy of the agenda and any handouts. Members will be expected to read these before the meeting. Those who have not read supporting documents will not be allowed to participate in related discussions.
- The focus will be on issues, not personalities.
- Only one member will talk at a time.
- Decisions will be made by consensus.
- The group will evaluate each meeting to determine progress toward its objective and the quality of the meeting itself.

Part of your responsibility as meeting chair is to ensure that these rules are followed. If a member violates a rule, you may want to interrupt the session to remind the individual. Alternatively, you may want to speak to the person after the session.

You are responsible for the group following some rules. For instance, if the rules state that all meetings will start on time, you need to start all meetings on time—you shouldn't wait for late arrivals, no matter who they are. To be sure that the session ends on schedule, you and the meeting participants should prepare the agenda so it includes sufficient time for discussing each topic. If a topic goes over the allotted time, you may want to ask the group if it would like to pick up on the subject at its next meeting or continue on the current topic and postpone another agenda item.

So guidelines give meetings the structure they need to ensure greater productivity.

Agenda

Preparation of the agenda is, ideally, the group's responsibility, although initially you may have to put one together. If you've been invited to participate in a meeting and haven't received an agenda, you should ask for one before making a commitment to be there.

A well-organized agenda specifies not only the date and place for the meeting, the starting and ending times, and the subject matter to be covered, but also the amount of time to be spent on each topic. When you allocate time to topics, you explicitly weight their relative importance. This ensures enough time—no more and no less—is spent on each subject.

The agenda should also note if guests are expected. It should describe who they are and their roles during the meeting, whether they will be there solely to hear and contribute to the discussion, or if they have been invited to make a presentation to the group.

If the participants need to be informed about a topic to discuss it intelligently, provide the information they need in advance of the meeting. To ensure that material gets read, include summaries at the start of lengthier documents to explain their worth. Flag or highlight key parts of documents. If possible, see that white space and headlines are liberally used in the documents. Also, use double spaced or one-and-one-half spaced typing to make handouts easy on the eyes.

These preparations are as important, if not more so, for electronic meetings and videoconferencing. Companies have found that virtual meetings can be cost-saving and time-saving alternatives to bringing together managers from diverse parts of the world to speak together. As telecommunications and intranet systems become more powerful, you can expect to participate or even put together a telephone conference call or online videoconference in the future. In that event, here are some further rules to follow.

- Be selective with information and avoid overload. Plan to cover fewer topics to provide sufficient time to cope with the complexity of the technology.
- Take into account global time differences when setting up meetings with participants from different regions of the world.
- Be sure that all attendees have handouts they will need for the meeting. If members find they need additional handouts, you can fax or e-mail them. Have fax numbers and e-mail addresses handy.
- In a telephone conference call, repeat your name when you first introduce yourself. Speak up clearly.

- If you are part of a videoconference, remember that those not in the room can see you and be mindful of body language and facial expressions.

The Mission's Implications

The purpose of any meeting you lead plays a major factor in your selection of participants. Needless to say, if it is a staff meeting, all your employees will attend. If a crossfunctional group is involved in developing a new product or resolving an organizational problem, then you might want participants with relevant expertise.

Generally, in selecting individuals to participate in crossfunctional projects, you should look for people with both knowledge in their functional areas and strong interpersonal skills, although you should be realistic enough to set aside people skills if the project has a strong technical bias. If the project calls for a major shift in organizational direction, you will be better off with people who are unafraid of change than individuals with caretaker mentalities.

Needless to say, you want individuals who are interested enough in the project to give sufficient time to it. If a prospective member doesn't see participation as a worthwhile challenge, then another candidate is better for consideration. Look also for diversity in putting together your team. Limiting the group to people with interests similar to each other or your own would limit the final result as well.

You should also look for creative thinkers for your meeting, although you don't want only hotshot ideators. You should have more traditional problem solvers on board as well. The best teams are made up of both types of individuals. Creative innovators will give you an idea out of the box but may not have the patience to hang in there during implementation. The more-traditional problem solvers are more likely to find ways to make those breakthrough ideas work.

Further, bringing highly creative individuals who only think out of the box into a project whose goal is continuous improvement will only frustrate the creative persons, because their approach to problem solving goes far beyond the goal of the project.

As meeting leader, you will have to take this group through four stages.

1. *Forming.* The group finalizes its mission and agrees on acceptable team behavior.
2. *Storming.* During this phase, conflicts may arise. As ideas are shared and action plans are developed, proprietary feelings will grow. Being aware

of the potential for such problems, you should attempt to exert greater control during this phase.

3. *Norming.* The group is ready to get down to business. During this phase, participants will begin to take on informal roles as well as assignments. For instance, one member may emerge as an organizational leader, skilled at determining what needs to get done and when and able to get everyone pulling in the right direction. Another member might emerge as a writer/reporter, not only keeping the group's minutes but also taking on a major role in the writing of the final group report. Still another member might become an information gatherer, searching for facts and other information to help the team during its problem-sensing stage.

4. *Performing.* The group finally gets down to the task. Research is shared and decisions are made. If the group is a crossfunctional team, they may disband once the project is done. If the meeting is made up of staff, ongoing sessions will be held to support their operating and planning needs.

Meeting Facilitation

During meetings, your key responsibility is to facilitate discussion. You should create an environment where ideas are viewed fairly, no matter who contributes them, and where the group's energies are positively, productively focused. For instance, let's assume one participant not only criticizes another participant's idea but also the participant. Your task is to remind the member that the remark was uncalled for. You may also have to apologize to the individual who was attacked by a colleague: "Claire, I'm sorry that remark was made. It was totally uncalled for, and we welcome your ideas."

Confront disagreements. How you confront disagreements will depend on the degree of conflict and the stage of the team's mission. But it is imperative that you act immediately when conflict arises. For instance, Helen is sitting quietly in her chair, obviously upset. You might say, "Helen, you seem upset by what you have just heard. Could you share your concerns with the rest of us?"

When someone is monopolizing the discussion, you need to step in to draw out contributions from the rest of the group. Give the individual time to have a say, then interrupt and ask for others' opinions. While you don't want to put any one member on the spot, you might want to ask Jack what he thought about the previous comments or the discussion so far.

You may have some people whom you know have ideas but are reluctant to speak up. Under such circumstances, as meeting leader, you may want to encourage more active participation. For instance, you might ask one of these individuals, "What do you think of Joe's idea?" Better yet, you might ask, while looking at a specific member who hasn't spoken up yet, "Who has another suggestion about how we should proceed?"

If a member seems confused about another participant's comment, you may want to ask the speaker to clarify his remark. "Let me see if I understand your position. Are you suggesting that . . . ?" "What am I hearing is. . . . Am I right?" "Let me restate your last point to see if I understand." You might also want to paraphrase someone's comment if it seems to have angered another member. Putting the remark in your own words may help the upset participant realize that they were overreacting to the initial statement.

Periodically, in your role of meeting leader, you might want to stop the discussion to review conclusions reached so far. Not only will doing this ensure that participants stay on course, but it also allows the group to catch its collective breath if the discussion was heated.

There will come a point when the group will be ready to make a decision. You may want to call for a vote to see if you are correct that all discussion is over. If the group feels further discussion is needed, then allow that. If the group seems as if it can't get over this hump, then you may want to ask, "What do we want the end result to be? What are we trying to accomplish here?" Focus the discussion on critical issues. As the chair of the meeting, you should always be moving the team toward completion of its mission—which is often deciding which idea of several should be pursued.

The Decision-Making Process

As the person in charge, you want to improve the quality of the group's decision making.

Too often, the decision-making process isn't carefully managed. Someone suggests an idea, then another member suggests something, and someone else suggests still another idea. The group continues to move on until they tire out and just choose the final idea under consideration.

Sometimes, too, participants in a meeting labor to come up with the best way to achieve their mission, yet the ultimate decision is made by one person, usually the chair. If you are a good listener and have culled the right information on which to make the decision, this approach may be effective. But recognize that some attendees will be upset, especially if they were led to believe that they would have a voice in the final decision.

Decision by majority rule would seem a better way, but frequently, decisions made by majority rule are only halfheartedly implemented. Why? Minority members are resentful if they feel their points weren't considered. Many come away from such groups also believing that the final decision was a popularity contest, with the winner not the best idea but the idea from the most popular participant.

Finally, there is decision by consensus. This can be a highly effective approach, but it also can be time consuming when *consensus* is misinterpreted to mean *unanimity*. Consensus means that all members of the group can live with the final decision, whether it is their first choice or not. If some members can't accept the decision, they should be given an opportunity to express their concerns, or even to offer an alternative course. If they fail to persuade the group to rethink its decision, then they should accept it as final.

Most groups don't get so locked up in politicking that no decision is reached. If communications have been sufficiently open and the climate has been supportive, everyone should leave feeling that their side of the issue was given fair consideration.

So your role as chair of meetings is easier if you practice good communication skills (described in Chapters 10 to 14). As you can see, effective communication may be the answer to improved decision making. Communication up-front about how the final decision will be reached, communication during the meetings to ensure that all ideas have had a fair hearing, and communication about the shortcomings and strengths of each idea before a final decision—however it is made—ensures the process goes smoothly.

Meetings That Motivate

At the end of the meeting, participants should leave with an action plan, eager to, as Jean-Luc Picard in *Star Trek: The Next Generation* frequently says, "Make it so." That upbeat attitude stems from the participation that your leadership allowed. You told participants how happy you were to have their participation in the meeting. Further, you made clear to the group the impact that it would have. Maybe you had to point to a problem, but you also told the participants about the good work they have been doing—you didn't suggest that the meeting was an antidote to something wrong. And you expressed your confidence in the attendees' ability to get over this issue and show management how well it could perform.

■   **Did You Know . . . ?**

You aren't limited to brainstorming to stimulate creative thinking during a meeting. Other techniques include:

Brainwriting. Like brainstorming, brainwriting is based on free association. On a sheet of paper is written a single word or phrase that is related to the problem. The paper is passed from one member to another, and each participant adds a word or phrase. In ten minutes, the group should have added many words or phrases to the paper. As a group, the members then draw lines to connect related ideas. Groups of ideas are circled to form islands of thought. Linking the islands generally triggers workable solutions to the problem.

Rewriting problem statements. Write on a flipchart the problem that the group has been assembled to solve. Encourage participants to rewrite that problem—the wilder, the better. The freewheeling atmosphere will generate lots of different problem statements, one of which may provide new insights into the nature of the problem—and a better solution than ones that failed in the past.

   For instance, let's assume that complaints have been received due to delays in shipments from the warehouse. You could state the problem as, "Customers are angry about late deliveries," but you could also describe it as one of the following: "How to minimize customer complaints," "How to ensure customers have accurate information about date of product delivery," and "How to keep customers informed about the status of delayed orders."

Questioning assumptions. Some assumptions are erroneous. Raising issues that would seem already to have been considered and resolved may uncover faulty assumptions.

Ask *what if?* and *why?* questions. These can trigger lots of ideas, as can repeatedly asking *Why* during a discussion. Don't forget who, what, where, and how questions, either.

   These techniques can all generate interesting ideas. However, they only work if participants believe that they will be heard.

■ Tips

- With so much on their minds, people have a hard time recalling commitments made at meetings. So send an e-mail a few days after a session to remind members how important their assignment is to the group's efforts.

- Schedule your meetings to begin at odd times, like at the quarter or half hour. A meeting that starts at 10:15, for instance, may be easier to get to on time, particularly if the meeting before ends at 10:00.

■ See Also

Craven, Robin E., Lynn Johnson Golabowski, et al. *The Idiot's Guide to Meetings and Events.* Alpha Books, 2001.

Doyle, Michael and David Straus. *How to Make Meetings Work.* Erkley Publications Group, 1993.

18

Managing Change

Over 2,500 years ago, the Greek philosopher Heraclitus commented that the only constant is change. Today, change is only different in that there is more of it. There are technological changes like new equipment and processes. Non-technological changes include new government regulations and market changes. Changes internal to the organization include budget adjustments, new methods and policies, and reorganizations.

For your organization to make the most of its opportunities or defend itself against threats, it must be adaptable. For you to operate successfully in such a work environment, you, too, must adapt rapidly. Even more important, you need to recognize the need for change within your own operation and initiate it. This is where your ability as a leader is crucial.

You need to be a driver of change. This means that you must ensure not only that changes either you or senior management demand are made, but also that ideas from staff members are implemented if they will improve operations. After all, there is no single right or better way. Change management is about identifying and implementing a better way to do a job, then identifying and implementing a still better one, and so forth.

In this respect, the goal of change management is continuous improvement.

This is not so say that making change won't be a tremendous challenge, because the natural response to change is resistance. Some people equate change to stepping off a steep cliff into a deep chasm.

The Four Stages of Change

Faced with change, most people go through four stages.

At first, they refuse to acknowledge the need for change. This is the denial stage. During the second stage, resistance, they will resist efforts to implement the change by dragging their feet. It doesn't matter where the idea came from.

Todd is an employee in Grace's list department. He came up with a way to update lists more easily. Enthusiastic about the idea, Grace sold management on it. Eager to get started, Grace and Todd were surprised at the response of Todd's peers.

"What's wrong with the way things are done?" Linda asked.

"Yeah, Todd," asked Anna. "I think we do a pretty good job here. What makes you an expert?"

"I believe Todd thinks he is better than we are," said Hank.

Todd had to take some hazing, but in time the group admitted that Todd's idea would save them work. The group went from the resistance stage to what is called the exploration phase. During this stage, most employees accept the idea.

During the resistance stage, you will find about half of your employees willing to go along with the change. During the third stage, exploration, you should gain the support of another quarter of your group. The remaining quarter may never accept the need for change; indeed, they may oppose it so dramatically that you have no choice but to transfer or even terminate them.

During the fourth and final stage, acceptance, staff members see the change as the new status quo.

Resistance to Change

To overcome resistance to change, you need to understand what prompts people to resist it. There are four reasons for opposition.

1. *Fear of the unknown.* With little or no information about the reason for the change, your employees will imagine the worst. Instead of being energized for action, they will be tentative at best, paralyzed from fear at worst. They may believe that the change is unnecessary or will make things worse.

2. *Lack of involvement.* Employees rarely embrace change when they are not involved in planning it. They may even feel manipulated, if the changes were kept secret during the planning stage.

3. *Worry about job security.* After the change, more staff may be needed, or fewer employees may be enough. So further job insecurity is introduced into an already insecure workplace.

4. *Lack of confidence in management.* They aren't certain that the change will succeed, either because they suspect that management will not sustain interest in the change or because needed resources won't be forthcoming. Past efforts didn't live up to promises, and they expect the same to happen again.

The surest way to overcome these objections is to incorporate them into your announcement.

To identify how the news will strike your employees, consider how it impacted you. What was your first reaction when you heard about the change? Was it fear or elation? Was it confusion or understanding? Were you looking forward to the change, or were you worried about its effect on the status quo? Your employees are likely to feel the same way you did. You need to ensure that they understand not only the nature of the change but its ramifications on their work.

Communicating the News

As soon as the plans are made public, meet with your staff to answer employee questions and undo any misconceptions. Don't just tell your employees the reason behind the change—make a compelling case for it. Many experts attribute the failure of change initiatives to a lack of sense of urgency about the need to change. There is often too much emphasis on the who, what, and where and too little on the why.

Observe the members of your group as you discuss the change. How are they reacting? Don't assume that silence is a positive response. It can be a sign of uncertainty, passive resistance, or even active opposition to the idea.

Incorporate anticipated objections from your staff members based on your own reaction to the news. Mention one objection, and then disprove it; mention another, and then disprove it; and so on. If an employee brings up an issue you failed to cover, give that person the floor. Listen intently. Try to understand not only the objection but also the motivation behind it. Ask questions if you aren't clear about the problem voiced.

Don't become defensive or attack the questioner. Rather, compliment the employee for identifying either the reason for the proposed change or a potential snag in the plan. For instance, "You're right—we have a short time frame in which to bring the new system on." Then, throw the objection back to the employee, encouraging them to suggest a solution. If the schedule is tight and it will be tough to meet, you might ask the worker, "What steps will be the most time intensive?" or, "Do you have some ideas about how we might save time?" With conviction, respond to their comment. "If we can finish A within the first week, we should have more time to concentrate on B, and then complete C and the entire project within the time frame."

Before you close the meeting, confirm that you've satisfied all the individuals: "I believe I've handled all the questions. Are there any others?"

In concluding your presentation, don't forget to indicate your confidence that your workers can make the change a reality.

After announcing the change in a group meeting, you may want to speak one-on-one with those staff members who seem most resistant. If you can identify the main source of resistance—perhaps rational opposition, personal fear, or an emotional response to the idea of change—you may want to address that very concern during your conversation.

For instance, in talking with a worker who sees the change as unnecessary or misunderstands the nature of the plan, you may want to explain the change in greater detail. Project what would happen if the change is not implemented, then invite the individual to participate in making it happen.

If the individual is frightened, concerned about how the change might impact their career, you might want to point out how it could improve corporate prospects for the future, suggest how the change could offer opportunities for increased employability (via the development of new skills), and otherwise provide reassurances on a personal level for the employee.

Emotional responses, due to mistrusting the motives behind the change and a lack of involvement, may be countered with examples of why the current policies, procedures, or work methodology no longer are the most effective.

The Transition

Be mindful that you will be watched carefully by your staff members to gauge your own view of the change. If they see you continue to support the plan, they are more likely to be supportive as well. Not all, however, will be sold.

You may still have to answer further questions. If rumors arise, address them. Make it easy for employees to ask questions by being accessible. Develop an attitude that resistance is neither good nor bad. In fact, questions can offer opportunities to improve the change's implementation.

If job security will not be influenced—and you know that for sure—reassure your employees. If bad news is associated with the change, let them know that, too. Honest, open communication isn't only about good news.

As companies that restructured during the early 1990s quickly learned, employee job performance was more severely impacted if employees didn't know the state of their future employment than if they did. If some of your workers will no longer have jobs as a result of the change, and you can forewarn them, do so. Together, you may find a way for them to stay with the organization. If that's impossible, you may be able to assist them to find a new job when they are let go.

Practice Participative Management

While senior management may mandate change, generally its implementation will be up to you and your staff. If so, involve your employees in the decision making. Try to get as many of them involved as possible. This will encourage buy-in to the change.

Even after all these efforts, you may still find some people are opposed to the change. They will need special attention. If their opposition is very strong, consider one-on-one meetings with each in which you point up why staff support is important. During such meetings, it may help if you adapt your communication style, communicating with each person the way he or she needs to be communicated with; that is, each of us has a dominant communication style, and often we can win people over to our way of thinking if we adapt our communications to their style.

There are four dominant communication styles: (1) activator, (2) analyzer, (3) affiliator, and (4) conceptualizer. We all practice each of these, but we generally have one dominant style. The analyzer style places a high value on facts, figures, data, and rational thinking. On the other hand, a conceptualizer is known for placing a high value on ideas. The activator is someone who is focused on the present and isn't interested in talk of future opportunities. This person has lots of drive and gets things done but often seems impulsive, acting before thinking. The fourth and final communication style, affiliation, places a high value on personal relationships and interpersonal contacts. Someone who is primarily an affiliator is warm and understanding but may also be defensive or thin-skinned, very emotional or moody, and easily swayed.

So, for analyzers, you might say, "Let me walk you through this proposal, step by step. . . ." or, "Let's look at this in a logical, systematic way. . . ." To an affiliator, you might offer, "Let's get reacquainted again, before we get down to business. . . ." or, "Why don't we talk about it over lunch. . . ." or, "It would be helpful to get you involved in this from the very first stage."

In persuading a conceptualizer, you might open the discussion by saying, "I have a unique approach for you—something that has never been tried before. . . ." or, "This will pay off in the long term. . . ." or, "Let me begin by giving you an overview of the key concepts involved." Activators are best approached with, "We can get on it right away. . . ." or, along the same lines, "Suppose I skip the details and just hit the highlights," or you might try, "We tried to select the most practical approach. . . . What do you think?"

If ringleaders of the opposition emerge, confront them and seek to alter their attitude. If they won't give their support and, worse, if you discover that they are behind pernicious rumors about the change or otherwise negatively impacting the staff's morale, you may want to transfer them to another department or even consider termination.

Living with the Change

Throughout the transition, you can expect implementation problems. Mistakes are part of the learning process, after all. But they may arouse resistance to the change all over again. Tell your employees that the only failure you're concerned about is the failure to try anything at all. You should explain that solving some problems may generate other problems, which will cause further problems. That is just the nature of change. "All we can do is to address each problem calmly as it occurs."

You may also want to organize your change effort to begin where you are less likely to encounter problems. Build on one success after another until you have completed the change effort.

Plan Your Change Process

Detailed, step-by-step plans are essential for change projects. Many change programs fall by the wayside simply because insufficient thought was given to the plan and likely problems. Make sure that you give due consideration to all of the most likely problems, such as technical bugs, delays caused by suppliers, or unanticipated costs—don't wait to formulate plans for such contingencies halfway through the change effort.

Although you may think you have a clear idea of the end result, put in writing what you hope to accomplish from the change—not sweeping generalizations but easy-to-understand, easy-to-measure, task-related statements.

Write down the start and completion dates for the entire project, as well as milestone dates for completing each stage. Now define the various areas of responsibility and who will be held accountable for each part, what resources you will need, and how you will make assignments. If you need support from other parts of your organization, include that information in the plan.

To make sure that the plan is complete, ask yourself the following questions:

- Why is the change being introduced?
- What results do we expect?
- How will we achieve those results?
- What resources—people, money, and time—will we have to commit to the plan?
- How will we monitor results as we go along?
- What can go wrong with Plan A? If a problem occurs, do we have a Plan B?

You may be in charge of the project. On the other hand, you may want to choose one of your staff members to oversee the work. If you decide to do the latter, don't rely solely on past performance appraisals in making your selection. Past work isn't necessarily a good assessment of an individual's change capacity—the ability to plan, lead, manage, and implement a change. Technical competency may be a consideration, but so may dedication to the idea. Look for someone who has played a key role in a change effort in the past—someone who has demonstrated an innovative spirit.

If the change involves the entire organization, and you must work with peers, maintain a professional attitude. Don't get in a flap about what other managers are or aren't doing. Focus on completing your responsibilities effectively and efficiently. Don't share your fears about other managers' efforts with peers or, worse, employees. During periods of organizationwide change, stress is high. Take positive action to manage your stress (see Chapter 21), and don't contribute to others' feelings of anxiety.

If the change initiative is limited to you and your staff, make an effort to celebrate their accomplishments as you experience success. Reinforce the positive behaviors that led to the success. Initiating a major change is an uphill battle, and employees can become depressed in the midst of the effort unless they see progress. If there is real concern among employees—even you may have doubts about the change—consider a pilot program to test the idea. If the pilot effort is successful, you can expand the change to the entire department.

Reward and recognize those behind the success.

Final Steps

To make the change the new status quo, you and your staff may need to master new skills and abilities. Until your employees feel comfortable about their ability to do their work, they may still feel threatened by the change.

As soon as you know about a change, ask yourself, "What skills and abilities will my staff need? Which of these do they already possess? Where are the gaps?" Estimate how much time you will need to close these gaps and incorporate this into the change plan. Explain the need for a learning curve to senior management so that it doesn't have unrealistic expectations.

If the change affects the entire department, then group training is the perfect means for closing information gaps and building new competencies. Hold such sessions in any environment that encourages a free exchange of questions and ideas. Skill training, however, should be done on-site, in the workplace.

Be sure that staff members receive feedback as they master new skills and abilities. Don't expect perfection—be patient about mistakes. Support the training with your own coaching, focusing not on the errors but rather on what your staff members are doing right. Help your employees identify any problems they are encountering, why these are causing them difficulty, and how they can overcome shortcomings.

Selecting Essential Changes

Once you have completed the project, it is time to look to other opportunities to improve operations in your unit. Don't let your enthusiasm prompt you to initiate other change efforts before this one is completed. It is unwise to start another change program before the previous one has had a chance to prove itself. But once it is a success, propose to your staff that you meet once a month to identify problem areas and initiate smaller improvements. Use past successful change efforts as a stimulus to harness enthusiasm for the successful implementation of other ideas.

In some departments, employees send a flood of ideas to their manager. These ideas enable the unit's work to be done less expensively, more efficiently, and more profitably. In other companies, the bottoms of suggestion boxes are coated with dust. What's the difference? It's not in the quality of the employees but in the quality of the managers to whom they report. Some managers know how to encourage employees to share their ideas better than others.

Take Don, for example. The vice president of his organization's IT division, Don is responsible for both the firm's management systems and its Web site.

Marketing had asked Don to have the Web site redesigned to reflect the firm's new line of products. Marketing needed it done by the end of May, to co-incide with a marketing campaign that would include the firm's Web site address for online orders. Don gave his team the instructions, but he asked his people to complete the work by May 15—it was May 3.

The team got to work immediately, but only a day or so into the work, Don stopped by to ask the team to put aside the work for marketing and redo the de-sign of the homepage. The group had just completed that work and were begin-ning work once again on marketing's request when Don was back. He had this great idea for redoing the search function on the site. He wanted work to begin on it immediately.

Needless to say, the team missed the May 15 deadline and came very close to missing the May 31 deadline. The team worked late into the night to finish the design in time. But the chaos that Don created nearly did in the effort—almost sinking the marketing division's ad campaign.

Don was complimented on the fine job his team had done. On his way back to his office, he stopped by the creative department. Did he want to thank and congratulate the team? No. He had another idea he wanted the team to begin working on immediately, a major revamping of the site's contact pages. Ellen of-fered a suggestion, but Don cut her off, "Sure, Ellen, we might try that some time, but I'd like you to focus on this for now. And," he paused as he left, "I want you to know that marketing likes the design for its new pages. I wish you had com-pleted it sooner so I could have fine-tuned it. But we can do that after the cam-paign." He walked away.

I don't need to tell you the team's response as they saw Don walking jaun-tily away. No one would argue that Don is not a hard worker, but at the same time they would point to his tendency to make change for change's sake, without any purpose other than gaining senior management's attention for himself. His cre-ative team has numerous ideas for making the site more attractive to customers, but Don has never shut up long enough to hear them. Ellen will try sometimes to get his attention, but she is the only one of the team of seven who still makes an effort. The others do as they are told, burnt out from change overload.

You might say that Don is a change master, and he is, in that he makes change happen. But change management is more than that, as I mentioned. It is building a culture that encourages employees to achieve change through their own efforts and be eager to generate more change.

Don needs to learn to listen to his employees' suggestions. Because he has done so much to discourage input in the past, he will need to make an effort to get employees to start sharing their ideas. Toward that, he should do the following:

- *Share his vision with his employees.* Employee ideas will increase in value when they're on the same wavelength as their manager's. His efforts to empower his workers will be taken more seriously if he lets them in on his hopes for tomorrow, and they will offer plans that will have value in light of that information.
- *Hold better-faster-different meetings.* He can ask staff members for ideas on ways to perform work better to improve quality, faster to save money and please customers, and differently to distinguish the company from the competition. At the meeting, he can also try a zero-based approach, which essentially asks the question, "If we did not have any systems, structures, policies, and procedures in place, how would we create them from scratch to support our vision?"
- *Stifle his mouth.* Don may have a keen mind and be quick to identify both opportunities and obstacles, but he needs to hold back on his feedback when brainstorming with his employees.
- *Thank employees.* He should do this even before he says what he plans to do with his workers' ideas. Ideally, he will convene a group to evaluate each employee's suggestion. Further, Don should respond quickly, even if it is to tell the submitter that the group needs a little more time to decide what to do.
- *Reject ideas gently and tactfully.* He should say something like, "Thank you for your idea on. . . . The only thing that keeps us from using it is. . . . If you think of a way to get around this constraint, let me know."
- *Involve staff members in crossfunctional teams.* The best innovators prove to be those who spend some time working in areas peripheral to theirs and listen to others' ideas on how their areas can be improved, then come up with ways to make change happen in their unit.
- *Delegate more responsibility.* The more meaningful the work that people do, the more significant their good ideas will be. They are also likely to come up with fresh ideas about the work when it is new to them.

▇ Tips

- If you have cause for concern about a proposed change, speak up. Bring facts and figures with you to support your concerns about the plan. Your concerns may not be new to the change group, and your solutions may be very welcome.

- Be prepared with answers to questions such as "Why us?", "Why now?" and, "Do we have a choice whether we do this?"

- Make plans but adjust them—radically if necessary—if circumstances change.

- Because change can indirectly affect people in other departments, discuss your plans with these people and work with them to assess the projected plan's effect on them and what you can do to provide for their needs, including amending the basic plan.

- Identify opportunities for change by asking customers and employees for ways to operate more efficiently and effectively. Ask customers not only what they think about your performance but also that of your competitors, then compare their opinions. Ask your employees, too, how you can improve your operations. Seeking input will raise morale and improve corporate performance.

These ideas will work for any manager who wants to continuously improve the operation, be a change driver, and make the work unit eager to take on the next opportunity for change. Try them! Challenge your people to think about tomorrow and the next day, not just yesterday and today.

▇ Did You Know . . . ?

Cultural differences affect our responses to change. For instance, the Japanese tend to monitor the need for change and change accordingly, whereas Continental Europeans are traditionally reactive. The British, once conservative, have become more proactive, as have Americans.

■ How Do You Rate?

If you find yourself going through the four stages mentioned in this chapter, you are no less receptive to change than the average person. To further analyze your attitude toward change, here are some statements. Do they reflect your attitude toward change or not?

- "I like to look for more efficient or effective ways of getting the work done."

- "I have an open mind to new ideas and possibilities."

- "I am known for anticipating and leading change within my department."

- "I seize opportunities to reward, celebrate, and encourage successful change."

- "I like to work closely with people who are eager to improve the organization's policies, procedures, and other shortcomings."

The more statements that reflect your behavior, the less change resistant you are.

■ Quotable Quote

"It isn't the changes that do you in, it's the transitions. . . . Change is situational: the new site, the new boss, the new team roles, the new policy. Transition is the psychological process people go through to come to terms with the new situation."—William Bridges

See Also

Baum, David. *Lightning in a Bottle: Proven Lessons for Leading Change.* Dearborn Trade, 2000.

Bishop, Charles. *Making Change Happen One Person at a Time.* AMACOM, 2001.

Ludeman, Kate and Eddie Erlandson. *Radical Change, Radical Results.* Dearborn Trade, 2003.

Kotter, John P. *Leading Change.* Harvard Business School Press, 1996.

Ristino, Robert J. *The Agile Manager's Guide to Managing Change.* Velocity Press, 2000.

19

Negotiation

As the leader of your team, you are responsible for representing it in negotiations. By *negotiations,* I am talking not only about the traditional negotiations you might use in dealing with vendors, customers, or potential allies but also about nontraditional negotiating situations—what I call horse trading—that you use to get critical resources from peers or senior management and to get support from your employees.

This kind of negotiation involves understanding the other party's needs and working out deals in which you both feel like winners. If you follow the advice in this chapter, you can win more points than you lose and do so without alienating the other person.

How do you make deals so that everyone can come out satisfied? Staff members, peers, managers, and customers each relate differently to you, and so they each require different guidelines. Let's look, first, at how you can negotiate to gain the cooperation of your work team.

Employee Negotiations

The key to winning over your employees is a little concept called WIIFM. The acronym stands for the words *What's In It For Me,* and it entails clearly communicating the benefits to employees in doing what you would like them to do.

Let's say that you are trying to convince your assistant to learn a new software program, because it would enable her to design better looking documents for client presentations. She argues that she has the time neither to learn the new package nor to apply what she learns because she already has a full workload. Don't demand that she learn the skill. As the old adage says, "You can lead a horse to water, but you can't make it drink." You can insist that your assistant take the training, but you can't make her learn or apply the information unless you threaten to terminate her. If your relationship is a good one, there really is no reason to force the issue and, thereby, alienate your staff member. Try, instead, to convince your assistant that her best interests lie in learning the new software package.

Begin by determining if your assistant has any reason other than those she told you for not learning the new software. Is she uncomfortable with learning something new? Has she been led to believe that she might be transferred to another part of the organization—to a job she doesn't want—if she masters her training?

Let's assume that, in speaking with her, you discover that she has some concern about her job security—after all, some employees have been transferred, and others have been asked to take on the work of employees who were laid off. But it appears that her biggest fear is that she won't be able to assume more administrative tasks if she masters new computer skills.

"Actually, Nancy, I think this new software program will save you a lot of time, freeing you to help me more with some of my own responsibilities." Because this is what Nancy wants, she should be more receptive to your offer. You can also address her other concern by reassuring her, "The systems personnel tell me that the training would mean that you would be out of the office for only a week. I can get a temp to help with the basics until you return. If you find you need help to catch up with other work, we can either keep the temp on longer to help you or get some assistance from another administrative assistant."

"If we could do that, then I would be able to complete the training," she answers. "Do you really think I'd have more time so I could do more than clerical work?" she asks. As you reaffirm your earlier statement, you know you have won her over. You have made clear to Nancy what is in it for her (WIIFM) in going along with your request.

Both you and she have won. Your assistant gets more opportunity to show her capabilities, and you get someone skilled in a software program that will enable you to make better client presentations, plus you may have freed yourself of some of your paperwork. That means you will have more time yourself to take on greater responsibilities. Of course, to make this deal win/win, you need to keep your promise, which is to give Nancy the opportunity to assume greater responsibilities.

The same approach can be used with your team as a whole. Let's assume that you meet with your staff to inform them about some operating changes. Before you meet with them, think how you will present the information. How can the changes make their jobs easier, more interesting, or more efficient? If there is a problem, be prepared to point out some of the good work your staff has been doing before discussing the problem. After telling them about the change and its benefits, express your confidence in your team's ability to show management how well it can perform. Become a cheerleader for your team.

If one of your staff members raises some questions, answer them to the best of your ability. You want to maintain their confidence and sustain morale by accepting your employees' concerns rather than denying them.

Many years ago, I attended a meeting led by an organization's VP of marketing. A major change in organization was under consideration. After the idea was presented, a creative manager raised her hand. She had a question about the change's impact on current staffing. Rather than answer the question, the VP demanded, "Why should you know that now?" The room became eerily silent.

The VP glared at the poor woman, who had merely asked what everyone else in the room was thinking. Fortunately, the VP of sales stood up. He told the group, "We don't yet know fully what these changes will do to the organization. We do know that we must make these changes to ensure the organization's competitive position in the market. And I personally promise that we will notify staff as soon as we determine if these changes will necessitate cutbacks."

Notice that the VP of sales did not remind the staff members of his position of authority. Instead, he focused on regaining the employees' confidence.

Upward Negotiations

In negotiating with your own manager, the situation is reversed—you are the person with less authority. On the other hand, the same rule applies—WIIFM. Your manager will be concerned with how the decision is received by upper management, the manager's peers, your peers, and perhaps other staff members. How can you position your request so that it addresses all of those concerns?

Presenting your need to mirror a strategic business objective or address a problem that currently puts your firm at a disadvantage would be ideal. But, whatever the reason for your request for staff, money, or time, it should be presented from management's perspective—as an investment from which it will either make money, save money, or increase productivity. Present your need in the form of a clear statement of expected results.

Let's assume that you are proposing a systems improvement for the customer service area. Your organization's goal is to improve its bottom line through new product development plus changes in existing product lines. The system you have in mind will bring data about customers up on the screen. These data will allow your phone reps to identify potential purchasers of the new products, information about existing product changes, and the history of customers, including former purchases that they no longer order. With these data, your reps can handle incoming orders, alert customers to changes in old products that they might want to reconsider, and tell them about new products that they might want to purchase. This system could help your firm increase market share in several product lines plus support new product introductions. You will emphasize this result when you make a funding request of senior management.

Customer Relationships

In negotiating with a customer, you will be using more traditional negotiation skills, although here, too, it's important for you to be aware of your customer's needs. Your own parameters for flexibility may have to be extended, but keep in mind that the final settlement must benefit both of you.

Traditional negotiations may be done between two organizations, usually for financial gain. The intent might be to win a contract to supply a customer, to purchase product at a specific quality and price, or to agree on delivery of goods or services. Negotiations are also done to reach formal, legally binding agreements with a regulatory or other government agency. Finally, managerial negotiations may involve discussions with union members about pay, terms of working conditions, and work output.

As with less traditional negotiations, the first step is to identify all your objectives. Once you have determined your goals, prioritize them into three groups.

1. Those that are your ideal
2. Those that represent realistic targets
3. Those that are the minimum you must fulfill to feel that the negotiation has not been a failure

Abandon any totally unrealistic objectives before you even sit down. Likewise, identify issues that are open to compromise. If you have to give in at any point, it is helpful if you know which objectives you are willing to yield on first. Express all your goals as statements prior to the session. This will make it easier during the actual negotiations to be clear about your desires.

Let's assume that you are meeting with a potential customer. In negotiating the sale of a product or a service, you have the advantage of being informed about what your company has to offer. Further, you should have studied the customer's firm to be familiar with its wants and needs. Just as you have identified your own objectives in the negotiations, you should try to identify the opposition's goals. Prioritize these, as you did your own. Also, consider the opposition's weaknesses. For instance, if your customer has few vendors from which to purchase product and needs immediate delivery, and if your firm can meet the customer's delivery needs, you may be able to raise the purchase price.

If a customer has an idea about how his or her needs should be met that does not follow your existing procedure, explain why your method can get the same results faster, better, or cheaper. If not, find out whether your company can concede to some degree to the customer's wishes.

Depending upon the product being purchased, you might try the "puppy approach." Those who sell computer software and hardware, for instance, use this ploy, offering customers a trial period during which they can test the product or service. If you have ever acquired a new pet, you will appreciate this tactic's name. Once you have a new kitten or puppy, would you ever seriously consider giving it back? No. Likewise with most major products. Even if you never thought you needed that new printer that does hundreds of copies in only a few minutes, within a few weeks you will find yourself unwilling to live without it. Vendors know this. So, even if a trial period will cost them, they agree to it because usually such a deal results in a sale.

Negotiating with Peers

Today, you and peers may find yourselves in two new situations. You are representing your firm in forming alliances with other organizations, which will involve you in a traditional negotiation. Perhaps you may find yourself on one side and your peer on the other, negotiating with each other for necessary resources—money, people, or time. Even the most successful organizations have limited resources, which means difficult decisions have to be made about their allocation. You may have to go to a peer to get help to complete your own work.

Let's look at these situations, beginning with partnering with peers to build relationships with other firms.

Before you enter into this kind of negotiation, you need to be clear not only about the best possible outcome for your firm but also the absolute bottom line (that is, the worst possible outcome for you, but a deal your organization could live with if it had to). You also need to know the concessions you can make and the limits of your authority.

Listen carefully during the meeting. You know what your firm wants. Now you have to determine what the other side wants. Ask as many questions as you need to understand their position. It'll be too late once a deal is struck, so don't be afraid to speak up when something isn't clear to you. Using complex language or confusing arguments may be part of the other team's strategy, and they may be hoping you won't admit that you don't understand. Don't fall for their ruse.

In your negotiations, you can expect give-and-take on both sides. Be prepared to trade concessions, but be careful not to go overboard. Say, slowly, "Well, I guess we might be able to. . . ." when the other side offers the very concession that you want.

Not all will go as you want. To close the deal, you may even have to settle for your bottom-line position—an outcome you can live with if you really have to. Monitor progress throughout the negotiation session. At regular intervals, stop to summarize what has been agreed on so far and what issues remain. That way, everyone will have the same understanding at the same time.

At the end of the session, summarize the agreement, point by point, to ensure that there are no disputes.

I mentioned the puppy ploy. There are other tactics and tricks of seasoned negotiators you should know, like:

- *The bulldozer.* This entails taking the initiative in a big way, right at the start of the negotiation, then making one assumption after another and pushing hard. If that's the other side's strategy, don't let it intimidate you.
- *The friendship tactic.* You have yet to agree on anything, yet the team from the other side comes into the negotiations behaving as if your team and they are old buddies. Don't fall for this. Just as you are there to negotiate the best deal for your organization, they are there to do the same for theirs. Hold on to your ideal outcome for as long as you can, and don't be tempted by the convivial atmosphere.

- *The tough stand.* The threats may be covert, but the implication is that if you don't become an ally with this firm, you could become an enemy. If you and your teammate have done your prenegotiation preparation, you have considered all the possible outcomes. Don't be so frightened that you submit unnecessarily.
- *The cool approach.* The other team dismisses or glosses over your concerns. The concerns may, indeed, be important to you, which is probably why the other side is trying to lull you into a false sense of security. The other side knows it will make a better deal if the discussion doesn't take this direction.

It may surprise you to know that a peer may use these strategies in negotiations with you. After all, your peer wants to come out well in negotiations with you, just as another firm would.

Such negotiations with peers come about as you look for support to complete a project or implement an idea. Your request for staff or funds has been turned down. Money is scarce. Management is willing to help fund a portion of your project, but you will need to get help from other areas of the organization to complete the work.

In such circumstances, you first need to ask yourself, "Is there a department or division within the organization with the resources—people or money—to do the work?" The second question: "If there is, would it give me the hand I need?"

Consider what this other department or division would get out of your project. If there is no direct benefit to the other operation, then you may need to do a little horse trading. Horse trading can be done over coffee or lunch, even standing by the network printer—today's water cooler. It is an informal negotiation in which you approach the other manager, describe your problem, make an offer, and wait to see if the manager agrees or not. It won't always be a fair exchange. If you are giving something worth one thousand dollars, you may think you should get something worth one thousand dollars back. But a more accurate measurement of a good horse trade is *if you get something you want.*

Let's look again at our database scenario.

Let's assume that Kevin, who heads up another division of the company, has a staff member, Jim, who in a previous job oversaw setup of a system similar to the one you plan. Jim has nothing to do with systems development, but he has told you he would be willing to provide the assistance your department needs if he just had the time. Maybe you can help Jim find the time, assuming Kevin is agreeable, and thereby get Jim's help on the project.

So you make it a point to ask Kevin to lunch. First, however, you find out what you can trade Kevin for Jim's time. What would Kevin's objections be? Better, what could you offer Kevin for help from Jim? Could the outcome of your project favorably affect Kevin's operation? Assuming that Kevin is agreeable, could someone on your staff do some of Jim's work? If not, what other options do you have? Would you have to go to a third manager to borrow a substitute Jim, calling for further horse trading?

Let's assume that Jim's work can be done by one of your staff members, and while Kevin believes his division won't benefit from your project, he thinks his group could benefit from marketing assistance. You happen to have some friends outside the organization familiar with the targeted market who might spend some free time with Kevin's marketing staff.

During lunch, you explain to Kevin the purpose of the project and how Jim could help. You have your bargaining chips—either a staff member to help make up for the time that Jim spends on your project, or marketing advice and counsel via your outside network. If you can mention to Kevin that being a team player will be well received by senior management, you might want to do so.

Before discussing your idea with Kevin, you should also check with your own manager to be sure that whatever deal you strike will be acceptable. During your meeting with Kevin, communicate senior management's support of your project. Give him further reason to want to get involved.

Kevin is a nice guy who is likely to agree to one of your two offers. But don't take advantage of the situation by doing a power play, bulldozing your way through. Fast talking might get you what you want, but at the expense of future cooperation or impairment of your reputation. Besides, those who don't think they got a fair deal may come back and renegotiate for higher stakes.

Kevin agrees to let you have Jim, but only for a month, at the start of the project. In return, he wants access to your external network and help in doing Jim's work over a two-month period. At first, you are sufficiently annoyed to want to stop negotiations and consider alternatives, maybe even consider other ways to complete the project without a systems expert. But you can't allow the heat of negotiations to cause you to lose sight of the project's need. Remember, as the person seeking help, you are in the weaker negotiating position. So you accept. You will go along with providing the extra month of help, even if you don't think the deal is fair.

The bottom line is that you and Kevin have both won.

Let's look at some of the reasons why the negotiations was successful.

- You were open to changing your position—you agreed to give more to get what you wanted.
- You heard Kevin out. He alerted you to a deadline Jim had that could interfere with his helping you unless he had additional assistance. So he offered an alternative solution—with which you were agreeable.
- You knew your objective but were flexible about how you would reach it. You didn't think to yourself, "I need to achieve A; to do that, I will do B and C." Rather, you thought, "I need to achieve A; help me to figure out what I will need to do to get that." You tried to understand Kevin's objectives, concentrating on his goals, not his demands or your own need to out-trade him.
- You didn't expect Kevin to be concerned about your needs. While you began by explaining your needs, you allowed Kevin to turn the conversation around to discuss his needs and addressed those to achieve your own.
- You asked yourself if the results were in the best interest of your organization. Nobody wants to be involved in a deal that is going to upset their own manager. You made sure that your own supervisor would be happy with any deals you struck. Further, you made Kevin aware that senior management would be pleased about his collaboration.

In the end, neither you nor Kevin can be seen as a loser. Kevin had you make a further concession, but in that you both came away with something that will help you, you both gained from the negotiation. Everyone won: you won, Kevin won, and—in the end—your organization won.

Let's assume that you have to negotiate with another manager, someone less agreeable than Kevin. Manny is indecisive initially, requiring you to check back and even undertake more horse trading before you get a final answer, which might be yes or might be no.

If you make your offer and it is refused, don't become insistent or threaten. Such a response will only create further resistance. Instead, ask questions to clarify the objections. Is the manager's objection that he doesn't need a horse at all, or is it that he doesn't need a roan or a bay—but a pinto would do nicely? Maybe you have a pony, and he needs a Morgan, a real workhorse. Perhaps right now, he can't make a deal—he hasn't the resources to spare—but might be able to do so in a month when circumstances change.

Probe to better understand Manny's situation. "What is the problem? Why can't you do this?" Most importantly, ask, "What if we . . . ?" which may reopen the door to negotiation by making him, not the solution to your project's dilemma, but a part of the problem-solving team.

Go further, still, and ask the person for advice. Manny may have an answer you and your project group haven't considered. Maybe this manager can become a horse trader for you if he is able to share the glory of a successful project.

Let's say that, no matter what you offer, Manny refuses. While you are disappointed—maybe even angry—you need to keep the outcome from souring your long-term relationship with Manny. After all, you don't know all the pressures he may be under.

■ Did You Know?

In negotiations, how you phrase your offer is as important as what you say. Here are some words and phrases that will aggravate anyone with whom you are negotiating.

- *"You don't understand."* Nobody likes to be told that. The phrase immediately translates to them as, "You're too stupid to understand."

- *"I want. . . ."* Unfortunately, in negotiations, while it is worthwhile for the other party to know what you want, the reality is that most people don't care. And telling what you want gives away an advantage in the give-and-take.

- *"It can't be done that way."* Try, instead, "Have you considered . . . ? Then offer an alternative solution.

- *"I won't,"* or, *"I refuse,"* or, *"I will never. . . ."* These are words you may have to end up eating.

- *"How could you?"* Your intention may be to make the other person feel guilty. Even if it works, it won't impact the final outcome of the negotiation except in a negative way—nobody likes to feel guilty.

- *"That's beside the point,"* or, *"That's irrelevant."* You may be right, but it is better to let the other person finish and then bring the discussion back on track.

- *"You would be better off. . . ."* The other side is not going to believe that you know better than they do what is in their best interests.

Rather than build a wall between you and Manny by venting about his lack of cooperation and collaboration, go back to the drawing board to see if you can identify someone else with the skills to help you. Maybe you need to send out members of your project team to identify likely opportunities for horse trading. (Keep in mind that you may have animals other than horses to trade; maybe someone needs a goat, a cow, or even corn, and you may have some in your silo.)

Never give up. In making deals, you have to maintain a positive attitude. Those you negotiate with will sense your self-confidence, and it will influence how they respond to you.

The Right Attitude

Whether the deal is with staff members, superiors, peers, or customers, if there are some rules, beyond WIIFM, they are these.

- *Remain unemotional.* Stay calm, cool, and collected at all times. Don't let the give and take of the discussion cause you to overreact.

■ Tips

- While you don't want to come across as a wimp, you shouldn't appear too tough, either. The other side may break off negotiations and leave if you give the impression that you are inflexible. Seeing your behavior, others will think you are more interested in getting your way than in negotiating the best outcome for everyone.

- Don't lose your temper over the little things. Know what is important and worth fighting for.

- Don't oversell the advantages of supporting your idea or project. Hyperbole breeds distrust.

- If the opposition has more than one representative, and there are differences in opinion among them, probe gently to see if you can use that weakness to strengthen your position.

- Check your body language to see that you aren't revealing too much. Develop a poker face. Keep your thoughts to yourself as well. Silence is golden during negotiations.

- *Be sincere.* If you are horse trading, the other person needs to know that you can be trusted to keep your word.
- *Be self-confident.* Old-time horse traders did their homework before negotiations to exude self-confidence.
- *Be flexible.* You have to be willing to change your negotiating plan if you want a change in the other person as well.
- *Be congenial.* The best horse traders keep the atmosphere friendly and nonadversarial. The point they want to make is, "By giving me what I need, you will get what you want in turn. How about it?"

■ How Do You Rate?

How do you stand in terms of your negotiating skills? Here are ten statements. Which reflect your approach to negotiating with others?

1. I research the other party before I enter into negotiations.

2. I am clear about my goals when I negotiate with others either inside or outside my organization.

3. I have a flexible attitude toward negotiations.

4. I believe that both sides can leave a negotiation session feeling satisfied.

5. I am polite at all times.

6. I communicate my points logically and clearly.

7. I can be objective and put myself in the position of the other party.

8. I avoid making the opening offer.

9. I show emotion only as part of a tactical gesture.

10. I periodically pause to summarize the progress that has been made.

See Also

Camp, Jim. *Start with NO . . . The Negotiating Tool That the Pros Don't Want You to Know.* Crown Publications, 2002.

Volkema, Roger J. *The Negotiation Toolkit: How to Get Exactly What You Want in Any Business or Personal Situation.* AMACOM, 1999.

20

Time and Space Management

As a new manager, you may be tempted to plunge into every assignment. This is understandable. A lot of experienced managers do the same. But there is a danger in working this way. You lose sight of your priorities and wind up trying to juggle so many tasks that ultimately you drop something or make a costly mistake.

Of course, your situation is understandable. Time has always been a resource in short supply, but never has it been so scarce as in today's lean organizations, in which fewer managers are being asked to do as much or more than was done in the past. Just because you are new at your job, you can't expect senior management to go easy on you.

On the other hand, you can't let your workload get the better of you.

I can't give you more time to get your work done, but I can share some tips to enable you to use your time more effectively. I can also offer some ways you can better organize your work space to manage those stacks of paper that, regardless of the promised "paperless offices," seem to find their way onto every flat surface.

Let's start with the issue of time management.

Stop Firefighting

Have you ever noticed how every job you are given is marked "urgent"? Every one of these may be urgent to the individual who gave it to you, but you have to consider the work in relationship to the other tasks your group needs to finish. Yes, you could put in longer hours and even work weekends, but as you will read in Chapter 22, that's not a good answer for the long term.

Let's start with how you should handle those last-minute jobs—you know the ones I mean. It's Friday, it's 4:30, and one of your firm's top executives strides into your work area with a stack of invoices that he says needs to go to customers by the end of the workday. Before you say a word, count to ten.

Taking a breath or two before responding should keep you from saying something you will regret all weekend, and it will give you time to think. You might ask, "Do these invoices have to mail tonight? Can the work wait until Monday morning?"

You would be surprised how many times the other party will answer, "Sure, just get them off my hands," or something like that.

On Monday, you would look at the work that needs to be done and reshuffle assignments so that the stack of invoices is the first work handled. You might also contact the mailroom and ask that the letters be taken to the nearest post office immediately.

But let's assume that this is one of those times when the work really does need to get done right away. Consider: Do you have enough staff, with the right skills, to lend a hand to the order processors to complete the work by 5:00 PM? Are there others in the office you can ask to help? Finally, if you complete the work at 5:00, will you be able to get the letters processed by the mailroom staff? If the mail clerks agree to work overtime, is there a post office nearby that will be open after 5:00? No, then could you deliver the orders on Saturday morning so they would still reach the firm's customers on Monday?

Next week, you will want to talk to your own manager about instituting a policy that avoids a recurrence of the situation. A rule that requires all customer invoices be handed in for processing before 3:00 PM would make sense. But for now, you need to get the letters out.

Your goal is not to find yourself fighting one fire after another like this. When crises arise, you have to learn to stay cool, calm, and collected and handle them. In time, as you become more familiar with the work, you should be able to determine what warrants a frantic pace and what can be done in due time— and respond accordingly.

Prioritize Your Tasks

Even after some time in your job, if you still have some confusion about what your priorities are, don't worry—you aren't alone. Even the most experienced managers feel that way. Priorities can change daily in today's ever-changing workplace. So, periodically, you may want to meet with your manager to discuss where you should be putting your major effort. Make sure your employees, too, are aware of the department's priorities. One way to do this is to tie priorities and employee performance together in the standards or goals set as a part of the performance appraisal process, allocating X proportion of the final rating to each priority based on its importance. The standards you and your boss set for you can be the blueprint for developing your staff members' goals.

Before you begin your conversation with your manager, here are some questions you might want to ask yourself. Bring the list with you, too, during the goal-setting meeting to compare your answers to your manager's.

- How is my operation expected to contribute to the company's strategic plan?
- What is seen as the department's key roles or responsibilities?
- In what ways can we support other areas of the business that are critical to the strategic plan?
- How can we better service internal clients? External clients? Contribute to the organization's image as a high-quality, high-service business?
- Do any problems—with people or work—require immediate attention?
- What is the department not doing that senior management would like it to do now or in the near future?

Answers to these questions will ensure that your focus and that of your entire operation is on issues critical to the company on a macro basis. On an hour-by-hour basis, they will also act as a compass to direct your attention to tasks associated with the bigger picture. Too much attention can easily be given to busywork and not enough to results-oriented tasks—a case of too much sawdust and not enough boards.

Once you know which activities and issues are important to the company, you can plan each workday better. Maybe you most enjoy talking and meeting with customers. But if your customer reps are having problems with the current telephone service or one or two reps are not as familiar as they should be with company product, then your time is better spent making a case for a new telephone system or training your reps. Maybe you would prefer to fine-tune an idea you have for a new product, but differences between your product managers may demand you pay attention first to their interpersonal relationships.

When you've done these more important tasks, you can work on that new product idea or make some calls to customers. These tasks are important, too, and they deserve your time. But don't waste previous minutes on insignificant chores. Treat time as an asset for which you want a return on investment for every minute.

Know that your management ability won't be measured by the quantity of time you spend on the job. Time spent on chores that could have been delegated to staff is wasted, with no return. But hours spent on projects tied to profit improvement issues or safety, service, or quality are well invested.

Don't just think through how you will spend the day. Write your priorities down for each day. That way, you are less likely to get distracted. At the end of the day, or in the morning before work (but always during nonworking hours, when you can concentrate), write down everything you have to do during the coming day and when you're going to do it. Don't be too ambitious. Try to be as realistic as you can. Leave some room for emergencies and interruptions.

A priorities list is very different from a to-do list. A to-do list is just that—a list of all the tasks you must, ought to, and could do. A priorities list orders your tasks in terms of importance.

The size of an assignment isn't indicative of its importance. Some small tasks can be essential. But no matter how critical, these smaller chores can be easily forgotten—sometimes not only due to their size but also because of how we become responsible for doing them. We walk through the office, visit with a peer, or meet with a customer. In the course of our travels, we may be asked to provide some information essential to someone else's report, to call our distributor to check on an upcoming shipment, or to sign off on a mechanical we have been asked to review. These tasks can easily slip our mind. To be sure that they don't get neglected, keep in mind that earlier tip and carry that small notebook in which you can write down reminders.

If possible, try to complete one priority before you start another. Say you have three things that need to get done today, three things to be done by week's end, and three to be done in a month or so. Take the three "today" items and determine which is most important. Start in on project one and stick with it until it's done, touching nothing else. Then go on to project two and follow the same procedure. If you get stuck at a certain point by circumstances beyond your control—for instance, you are waiting for a call—move on to the next project. But drop it and go back to the previous work as soon as you get the information you need to continue.

If you are relatively new in your job, you may need some help in determining how to prioritize your work. Here are some guidelines to help you.

- *Which jobs and deadlines are mandated from above?* These are important assignments but not always urgent. On the other hand, if your manager is pacing up and down in front of your desk waiting for an action file, you should go get it, even though it may take you away momentarily from an assignment that is both urgent and important. Taking care of the problem gets rid of the distraction and will free you to focus on that urgent, important work.
- *Which jobs, if not done soon, might create bottlenecks in your area or impede the work of departments that you serve?* As a general rule, these assignments fall into the category of urgent *and* important (if not to you, then to others).
- *Which jobs will have a major impact on your reputation with either internal or external customers?* These jobs are important. Ask for details to determine if they are also urgent.
- *Which tasks can be postponed or rejected?* Neither important nor urgent, these tasks can be shelved until later. Routine tasks often can be postponed until the next day.
- *Which tasks can be delegated to employees, and which ones should you do yourself?* When you delegate tasks, you need to make sure that your employees know the priorities you have set for them and your reasons and expectations for the work's completion.

Work delegated is more likely to be completed on time if your employees know its importance as well as its time frame. Fail to do this, and you will wind up reprioritizing delegated work that your employees let slide, taking time away from your own duties to do the job yourself. So spend time with your employees, describing not only the work but its importance either to your work unit or to the firm.

Divide and Conquer

Some managers may set priorities yet fail to get work done on schedule. They know what needs to be done but still put off doing the most important work because the task seems too difficult or is overwhelming. They need to divide large or difficult tasks into smaller, more manageable parts and start on one subset of the bigger job right away. Doing anything to get started, no matter how small, is the key to eliminating procrastination.

Starting a task is also helpful because an unfinished task is more of a motivator than a task that hasn't been started. As each small part of the job is completed, one's involvement and commitment increase.

Some people can't focus on big projects unless small, insignificant work has been completed. If this is the cause of the problem, often it is better to finish the small tasks as quickly as possible and then turn to the major project, rather than force yourself to work on the bigger, more important task. Too often, managers tell me, they can't truly commit to the more important work until they have done those less important tasks that continue to haunt them. Yes, this is contrary to advice about the need to prioritize tasks, but too often we waste time playing at the main project because our mind is still on those little bitty tasks.

Start important tasks when you can give them your full concentration, like very early in the morning before the workday really starts and you get pulled in many directions. Tell your staff that you should not be disturbed while you are at work on the assignment. Actually, because scheduled activities have a better chance of getting done, just scheduling when you will work on a project increases the chances of your completing it on time.

Don't forget to set a deadline. Put that deadline in writing and post it where you will be constantly reminded of it. Even share your commitment with others so you will be further motivated to get the work done.

Don't forget, either, to reward yourself when you have completed the task. If you think you might procrastinate over a project, then determine what you should give yourself (e.g., a special lunch, new clothes, or an afternoon off) for completing it and follow through with the reward when you've gotten it done.

Managing Interruptions

If you are a typical manager, you will be interrupted as often as eight to ten times an hour. That means that over the course of the day, you could easily be interrupted dozens of times.

Too many managers consider such interruptions a part of the job, and they believe that nothing can be done about them. This is partly true and partly false. Interruptions are likely a part of your new job, but that doesn't mean you have to accept each and every one of them.

Reducing the number of interruptions often demands an adjustment in attitude; that is, you need to accept responsibility for controlling them. Admittedly, you won't be able to control them all. But you can control some. For example, you can't control when someone calls you, but you can control whether or not to take the call. You may not be able to prevent people from popping into your office, but you can influence how long they stay.

Let's look at some specific actions you can take. We'll begin by reviewing some steps you can take to minimize telephone interruptions.

- *Use voicemail to screen incoming calls.* Those calls that can be handled by others should be forwarded to them.
- *Establish quiet hours to work on tasks that demand your complete attention.* They may be critical projects that demand your attention, or they may just be your day-to-day work that would pile up if you allowed interruptions.
- *Tell those who call you regularly when you prefer to receive calls.* Most people will cooperate and try to call at the preferred times, especially if they realize their chances of getting you at that time are much better.
- *Get through the social small talk as quickly as possible.* Get right to the point and stay there.
- *Bring calls to a prompt close.* Tell long-winded callers that you have a pressing appointment or deadline.

If most of your interruptions are from drop-in visitors, here are some steps to take.

- *Close your door.* Regular quiet time will allow you to concentrate on tasks and accomplish a great deal in a short time. If your office is a cubicle, see if you can arrange the furnishings so your back is not facing the entrance. This way, you won't inadvertently encourage drop-in visitors by saying hello to someone who passes by. People are also unlikely to stop by to chat if they see you busy at work.
- *Encourage the use of appointments rather than unscheduled visits.* Go to the other person's office if the individual must see you; you'll have more control of when you leave.
- *Stand up when someone comes in and remain standing while you talk.* Visitors won't stay as long if you remain standing while they are in your office. The same technique can also shorten staff meetings. Stand-up sessions in hallways, reception areas, and conference rooms tend not to last long.

- *Set up a schedule that enables you to meet with each of your staff members and cover a variety of subjects at one time.* I am an early bird, so it helps that my own manager is also an early bird. We get together before 9:00 about three times a week to discuss new assignments and progress on existing projects. I also see him at other times, but these early-morning meetings save him from being interrupted by me during the day—and save me from having to stop what I am doing to visit his office.
- *Learn to say no when someone asks, "Have a minute?"* Practice saying no, and, as important, learn to recognize when no is the appropriate answer.

If you still find yourself suffering from one interruption after another, you may want to determine why so you can put an end to the problem. Record the nature of interruptions for several days. When do they occur? Are they telephone calls or drop-in visits? How long do they last? Who is involved? What are they about? How important are they? An interruption log is easy to keep and will offer amazing insights once you study the results. You are likely to see patterns.

For instance, you will probably notice that a few people interrupt you far more than average. They should be bunching things together for you. You may find that many different people call you about the same things. Perhaps you need to find a better way to communicate information. You may see, too, that you socialize far more than you realize.

Whatever patterns you find, you will be able to break your interruptions into definable problems and tackle them one at a time.

Learning to Say No

Perhaps one of the most effective techniques for saving time is the ability to say no graciously. Unless you concentrate on tactfully but firmly saying no, you will find that you spend most of your time on other people's priorities.

Remember that you can't please everybody. The way you spend your time is bound to make some people unhappy.

Sometimes, there are trade-offs. For example, occasionally it is less time consuming to accommodate someone than to explain why you don't consider the person's request important. Of course, there are always some requests that you can't turn down, like those from your manager, even though you might make clear the implications for higher-priority activities. You may not win all the time, but if you have done your homework and can honestly identify work you should focus on first, your manager may agree.

Unfortunately, many managers, especially when they are new, find it very difficult to say no. To keep you from winding up with far more work than you can reasonably handle, here are some replies that may get you off the hook.

- "Sorry, I can't. I'll have to decline. But let me offer a suggestion. . . ." You're tactfully saying no.
- "I'll get back to you about that in a minute" This gives you time to think of an excuse that will work with the individual.
- "I know I've helped out before, but that was before I realized how much I am responsible for getting done here." This gets you out of trouble if you have previously said yes and, consequently, others assume that you will say yes in the future.
- "I wish I could lend a hand, but I have to finish . . . , then . . . , and I still haven't even started . . . or. . . ." Articulating your priorities should convince the party to go elsewhere for assistance.

These tips will save you time. But I'm not done yet. If you really want to reduce job stress and get a greater sense of accomplishment, look at how you can reorganize your work area to maximize your productivity.

Let's Look at Your Office

A crowded office may be evidence that you have a lot of work, but it can also distract you from concentrating on the task you are doing. Consequently, it is a good idea to practice the lean-management principle on your office space.

> ### ■ Did You Know . . . ?
>
> The term *deadline* comes from the American Civil War, specifically Andersonville, the infamous Confederate prison camp. Thirteen thousand Union prisoners died there—many of them because of "deadlines." The prison guards established a protective boundary, called the deadline, between themselves and the captives. The guards warned the prisoners not to cross the line. To do so meant death. Nevertheless, many of the prisoners did go over—and were shot. Some crossed by mistake; others went on purpose.

To begin with, keep work surfaces as clear as possible at all times. Cluttered desks can be distracting. Come into the office early and go through your desk drawers and put them in some order. There should be a place for everything, and everything should be in its place. Set up a system for keeping up to date with all the paperwork that winds up on your desk.

Deal with urgent items immediately. Set aside some time each day to go through all nonurgent items. Get into the habit of either handling, filing, delegating, or throwing away the documents that you receive, depending on the nature of the material.

If some paperwork requires more than a simple reply, write it down on your master list of things to do and file the document until you can get to it.

If possible, your work space should contain only those files to which you refer regularly. Keep these near your desk, preferably so that you do not need to stand to reach them. The files that you look at rarely should be in a special storage space or, if this is not available, an out-of-the-way corner of the office.

Now, let's look at how you should organize the items you put on your shelves. Books and magazines that you seldom use yet want to keep should be stored at the top and bottom of your bookcase. Place books, notebooks, and mag-

---

■ Tips

- Question deadlines that are unrealistic. Likewise, don't set deadlines for your employees that are unrealistic or, worse, deadlines that, loosely translated, mean, "Whenever you get around to it—even never, if you don't feel like doing the job." Loose deadlines like that are as useful as no deadlines at all.

- Clean up daily. Never leave a mess for the morning.

- Put a clock in your office where it is visible to both you and your visitors. You will be more aware of how you use your time and you can always point to the clock and tell your visitors, "Well, I guess we have to get back to work."

- Do not sit down if you are followed into your office. Stand and finish the conversation. As soon as you sit down, the other party will do the same—and a brief conversation will be unnecessarily extended.

azines to which you refer regularly on the second and third shelves where they will be more accessible. If these shelves become crowded, rethink their position in your bookcase and your office. If others need some of these books or materials in binders, consider having a bookcase outside your office that can serve as the department library.

What about paper—printed e-mails, reports, correspondence, and the like—that you want to keep? File them. To minimize filing, organize your folders by project name, and stuff the file folders with as many papers as will fit. This advice runs contrary to conventional teaching, but it makes good sense. There is less

■ How Do You Rate?

Yes or no, which of these statements reflect your time management style?

- I limit the duration of my telephone calls.

- I close my office door when I want some quiet time to devote to planning or other important tasks.

- I cross my name off the circulation list for magazines, newsletters, and reports I don't have to see.

- The meetings I run finish on time.

- I delegate tasks to employees rather than do work they could do as well.

- I encourage staff to write reports of no more than one page.

- I make a list of things I will do each day.

- I follow up on work I have delegated.

- I clear my desk of all paperwork.

- I discourage unnecessary interruptions.

Ideally, you have said yes to each of these statements. If not, add those areas for improvement to your to-do list.

chance of misfiling, and there are fewer folders to handle when you retrieve or put papers away.

For that special document—the one that you always seem to need but can never find—set aside a special folder.

Tear out or photocopy articles from magazines that suggest ideas. Put them into a special ideas file.

These small changes in how you work will ensure that you make a positive impression on superiors, peers, and employees who visit your office. But, more importantly, they should improve your efficiency. Time is one of our most valuable resources, and you don't want to take a haphazard approach to managing it.

Admittedly, it will take you time to learn how to use time effectively, but the learning process is a good investment that could pay handsome rewards.

■ See Also

Cook, Marshall J. *Time Management*. Adams Media Corporation, 1998.
Douglass, Merrill E. and Donna N. Douglass. *Manage Your Time, Your Work, Yourself*. AMACOM (updated), 1993.
Olsen, Jeff. *The Agile Manager's Guide to Getting Organized*. Velocity Press, 2000.
Pollar, Odette. *365 Ways to Simplify Your Work Life*. Dearborn Trade, 1996.

21

Living with Stress

You live in stressful times. You are surrounded by technology that is always changing yet demands that you remain skilled in its use. The competitive marketplace is more cutthroat, and your organization is counting on you to help it outdo its competitors. At the same time, your organization has become leaner. All you have to do is to look at the newspaper to become aware of what is happening in the job market—you know downsizing could happen to you just as it has happened to millions of other managers.

Whether the economy is good or bad, organizations are operating in a no-overhead economy, where individuals who seemingly aren't contributing to the bottom line can be downsized, delayered, or otherwise rationalized out as the need arises.

On top of this, you are expected to build, support, and lead your team; coach and counsel to build a top-performing staff and fire employees who don't meet expectations; disseminate communications in all directions; create a realistic budget and stay within it yet do more than you anticipated when you developed it; reduce downtime; increase productively; satisfy—no, delight—customers; and find new and better ways to get everything done. Is it any wonder that you feel stressed at the end of the workday?

Understanding the Nature of Stress

Stress doesn't come solely from feelings of frustration, anger, or depression. That's negative stress. Good stress, on the other hand, is the emotion that comes from completing an exciting project or a new assignment. Bad stress can lead to health problems like headaches, upset stomach, insomnia, high blood pressure, or stroke. Likewise, good stress—if you experience too much of it.

Because stress can add anticipation and excitement to your life, as well as leave you tied up in knots, your goal in stress management isn't to eliminate it but rather to learn how to manage it to optimal levels. You want to find the amount of stress that motivates but does not overwhelm you.

A graph can depict optimal stress. The X axis is stress, the Y axis is performance. An inverted U is the area of best performance. Where stress is low, you may find that your performance is low because you become bored, lack concentration, and are demotivated. Where stress is too high, your performance suffers from all the symptoms of excessive short-term stress. Your goal is to keep yourself in the area of best performance, sufficiently aroused to perform well without being overstressed or unhappy.

There is no single optimal level of stress for everyone. What is distressing to one person may be a joy to another. You may thrive in a job in which you have to develop new products or make risky investments, whereas another person might find it satisfying to have a routine position with little variety. Even where two people both find a particular situation pleasant, each may have a different physiological or psychological response over time. Stress resiliency is a function of three factors.

1. Your physical condition (physical health, fitness, stamina)
2. Your mental condition (mental health, emotional control)
3. Your personality (how you deal with the world, which includes your self-confidence and your responses when situations don't go as planned)

If you are experiencing stress symptoms, you have gone beyond your optimal level. You need to lessen the stress in your life, while also improving your ability to manage it.

The good news is that feelings of stress are self-induced; that is, they are caused not by external events but by the way you look at and interpret those events. Nothing in the world is inherently stressful—neither that overdemanding boss nor that pile of unfinished work. They only trigger feelings of stress when you look at them as representing some sort of gap between what you want and what you have and see the gap as a reflection on you or your circumstances.

So stress is in the eye of the beholder. Epictetus, the Greek historian, said, "People aren't disturbed by things but by the views they take of them." You don't even have to be looking at a situation to see it as stressful—just thinking about it can distress you. Further, over time you have been conditioned to look at some situations as stressful. So your response is habitual. You don't even realize what is happening—you just automatically, unconsciously react.

The good news is that nothing can cause you stress if you don't allow it to. You can control how you look at, think about, and respond to events—even situations over which you have no control—because you have the power to make conscious choices and to take action that supports your choices. For instance, you can choose to look at a corporate reorganization as a threat to your department or as an exciting opportunity to explore new markets or fund improved operations.

Daily Stressors

Some causes of stress (stressors) are physical; others are emotional. Before you can learn how to cope with stress, you need to identify the stressors that cause you to feel anxious or uneasy.

- *Excessive overwork.* Overtime for a significant period—paid or unpaid— can be stressful. In time, it can even cause burnout. An increased feeling of emotional exhaustion, burnout may end in loss of interest and motivation in one's job, even excessive use of drugs and alcohol.
- *Task demands.* Managerial positions are particularly stressful because of deadlines, performance evaluation responsibilities, and decision-making activities. Boundary-spanning activities can also be demanding, as they require dealing with myriad people with different backgrounds, interests, and demands.
- *Confusion over role demands.* When responsibilities and roles aren't clear, stress can occur. Over time, these stresses, like excessive overtime, can lead to burnout. Differences between an individual's values or beliefs and those of leaders within the organization are another cause of stress.
- *Physical environment.* A poor work environment can add to feelings of stress, especially if it is in conjunction with long hours. Think of some cubicles that are about the size of walk-in closets, or office environments in which employees freeze in winter and perspire in summer.

- *Interpersonal demands.* Differences with others can make the job less pleasant. In time, interpersonal conflicts can mean severe pressure on the body and spirit.
- *Unclear expectations.* If nobody knows what senior management *really* expects, you may feel stress.
- *Tough times.* The competition is tough, and you need to find ways to retain market share. Or the economy is bad, and you need to find ways to survive.
- *Bureaucratic decision making.* Fifty-nine people have to review, comment, and sign the proposal you just wrote.
- *Unrealistic expectations.* Your manager wants to look good and, therefore, asks you to do the impossible.
- *Talent retention.* It's a skill war out there, and your best workers get job offers. You want to keep these individuals, but your firm won't give you the resources to do so. Maybe it doesn't even have them to give.
- *Making hard decisions.* It's hard to keep the loyalty of peers/employees when one has to make decisions that will have a negative impact on their lives.
- *Antagonism.* People are out to get you, or so it feels.
- *Failure.* Expected results don't appear, no matter how hard you worked for them.
- *Unfair decisions.* Internal politics earn another person the promotion you deserve.
- *Organizational infighting.* The battle of egos takes precedence over organizational needs.
- *Work overload.* You are managing three crises at one time.
- *Directional shifts.* Just when you get a system going, you are asked to shift direction and begin anew.
- *Diminished returns.* You make a mistake and fall from senior management's grace. No longer are you a member of the inner circle.

It is wonderful if you are passionate about your work—passion is the hallmark of an outstanding manager and leader. But passion without some detachment can lead to self-destruction. So learn how to keep a measure of emotional detachment when you encounter any of the situations described above. All are sources of chronic stress.

Most people aren't as aware of these sources of stress as they are of an acute stress experience, like a near car accident. But a long period of chronic stress can be very dangerous, leading to serious illness, severe personal ineffectiveness, and even death. It is possible to graph this long-term stress. The X axis is sustained stress and the Y axis is performance. Initially, you will encounter hard work, but you will be positively challenged. After a period of time, however, you will begin to feel seriously tired. Performance will begin to decline as high stress continues. If the high level of stress continues without relief, you may experience burnout and even some serious stress-related illness.

As a manager, you have two responsibilities related to stress. You need to keep burnout from happening to your employees, and you need to find ways to reduce your own feelings of stress.

Helping Your Employees Cope

White-collar employees may suffer from the stress of too little responsibility and not enough control over a heavy and tedious workload. A plant worker may become ill as a result of boring, repetitive work.

To make their workdays more satisfying, provide your workers with regular feedback and the information they need to do a good job. Say thank you regularly, and give your employees a sense of control over their work situation by involving them in decisions—don't let them feel powerless.

If you can't provide money as recognition for a job well done, then consider other forms of recognition for top-performing employees. Also, make yourself accessible so they can alert you to problems—whether personal, like a family situation, or operational, like an unrealistic deadline.

In short, be alert to employees' needs for help. Most importantly, if you see one of your employees is evidently tired and suffering from work overload, look for ways to reduce that person's responsibilities. If you suspect that an employee is putting in extra hours from fear of being laid off, provide reassurance if you can. Be on the level about the situation, even if the person leaves your company before you were ready.

Aware of the impact of stress on their employees, management increasingly is working to find ways to reduce stress or to help employees who experience high doses cope better. For instance, efforts are being made to identify those employees most at risk from stress and to promote stress awareness in in-house publications. Some companies have instituted policies that forbid employees from remaining after 7:00 PM, despite their workload. We are also seeing more employee assistance programs (EAPs) being offered, as well as physical fitness programs to provide an outlet for feelings of stress. Companies with such programs report absenteeism down by as much as 60 percent.

Managing Your Own Feelings

What can you do about your own feelings of stress?

To help minimize stress from work, the best advice is to pace yourself. That's what successful managers do. They go into superdrive for a period, then slow down for a time, then speed up once more, and at the end of the day take a break.

If you feel stressed out while at the office, take a walk around the block. If you don't want to leave the office, at least step away from your desk—say, walk over to the copier. The object is to get away briefly from that stack of paperwork or long list of e-mail.

Try to avoid high-pressure lunches. Instead, seek out on-the-job friends to share your meals with. It's less stressful on your digestive system and may even give you a chance to get another viewpoint on a situation or to vent, both of which are important in these high-stress times.

Watch what you eat. Eating well can help to reduce your stress level. Avoid foods high in saturated fats, such as meat, cheese, butter, and eggs. Eat steamed, baked, or broiled food rather than fried. Reduce your daily intake of caffeine by replacing coffee and tea with water or juice. In between meals, eat a crisp, raw carrot if you feel the urge to snack. Chocolate may make you feel more energetic in the short term, but you're likely to experience a serious energy dip after the sugar high.

Drink at least eight glasses of water every day.

When you return from lunch, don't worry about a project you need to get done. Instead, plan how you will get it done. If it will take more than a single afternoon, ask yourself, "When is it easiest for me to do a task? When is it toughest?" Adjust your work schedule so you do the most stressful tasks when your energy is at its highest.

Let's assume a problem arises in the office, and you solve it, but you have to reschedule all your other work. Don't become upset. Remember, you can't control events, but you can control your reaction to them. The same applies to a career setback. Recognize that you are neither the first nor the last person to be in such a situation. You can only do your best. There is even a positive side to failure: it teaches. You cannot learn important lessons unless you take risks, and some failure is inevitable in every achieving person's life. The founder of IBM said that he judged people by their failures. If they had never failed, they hadn't tried enough difficult things.

A support network can help you through stressful times. Honest communications with friends and family can strengthen you when you're under emotional stress. It is especially helpful to talk to people who have faced the same challenges. Such conversations put your situation into perspective.

Tombstone Tactic

When you face what seems to be a huge and overwhelming problem, ask yourself the following questions:

- *Is this really a problem at all?* Think about it for a minute. Is it actually an opportunity to do something well? If it really is an impossible problem, then most other people would probably fail at it or give up. If you can do better than that, then it could be a major triumph for you. If you take the problem on but fail, at least you will have learned from the experience.
- *Have others dealt with this problem?* If others have had to cope with the situation, seek them out and ask how they handled it. Most older or more experienced colleagues probably have insights into such a situation, even if they didn't personally experience it. Ask them in confidence for advice.
- *If you've got lots of problems, can you prioritize them?* This will enable you to regain a sense of control over the situation, which can reduce your feelings of distress.
- *Are you overreacting to a problem?* When you look at each situation as a matter of life and death, you can develop tremendous feelings of stress. Ask yourself, "What is the worst that could happen if I don't complete this project or schedule? Would the world end?" No. "Would I lose my job?" Unlikely. "Would my manager think less of me?" Perhaps, but taking more time might also produce a better-quality end project, which might be well received. Sometimes all you need to do is to alert your manager sufficiently in advance that, "I may be delayed in completing a project because. . . ." Frame your own questions to evaluate potentially stressful situations and keep overreaction to a minimum.

If you find it hard to keep situations in perspective, here's an eye-opening exercise that should help. Draw a picture of a tombstone. On it, write the issue from which you are experiencing distress. "Died [date] because his boss told him he should not have included X in a meeting event, although X had asked for the meeting to be held," or, "Killed in a turf war because a colleague got all the credit for work she had done," or, "Dead from overwork, remaining at his desk until 1:00 AM to complete. . . ." Whatever you write, it can't be worth the emotional upset you are experiencing.

Don't try to be perfect or outdo everyone. Trying to be perfect in everything is not only self-defeating, but it's stressful. The reality is that we can't always do outstanding work no matter how much we might wish to. Sometimes, we have to "settle" for good work if we can then do several other, equally important jobs well.

Besides being realistic about all you can do, be realistic about your career expectations. Stress often is the result of a mismatch between an individual's career expectations and the job environment. Venting your frustration and exercising may relieve some of the tension that comes from the situation, but the only real remedies are to seek advancement elsewhere or to learn to live with your situation. Talk it out with friends and family. Don't let your frustrations bottle up inside you.

Think Positively

Don't listen to internal negative thoughts. Instead, try to develop a positive outlook. Begin by making yourself aware of your thoughts when under stress. Normally, you might not even know that they exist. Examples of common thoughts are worries about how you look to others, a fear of consequences, self-criticism, and feelings of inadequacy. Let's assume you make a mistake and send out the wrong report to someone. Your self-voice might be telling you, "Only you would screw up like that." You can quiet the negative self-talk and tell yourself, instead, "Oh well, nobody's perfect," or, "This, too, shall pass," or, my favorite, "I may not be perfect, but I'm almost perfect."

Some people have learned to counter their negative thoughts with positive affirmations. You can develop affirmations based on clear, rational assessments of the facts and use them to undo the damage that negative thinking may have done to your self-confidence. Here are some affirmations to start you off with.

- I can do this.
- I can achieve my goals.

- I will learn from my mistakes. They increase the basis of experience on which I can draw.
- I am a valued person in my own right.

Turn off negative thoughts, calm down, stop berating yourself for a simple mistake, and recognize your true worth.

What if you discover that a negative thought may be right? You really can't handle a specific problem. Then work on the problem to eliminate or neutralize it. Don't let stress take control of the situation—you take control of it.

Avoid Stress

You can reduce the stresses you feel, too, by changing stressful situations when you can. What incidents or situations regularly contribute to your feelings of stress? To find out, keep a stress diary. In it, note how you feel throughout the day—good and bad. When stressful events occur, write down the nature of the event, when and where it occurred, the factors that made the event stressful, and the outcomes of the tasks you were doing when you were under stress. After a few weeks, analyze the information.

You should be able to identify those instances when stress made you feel bad. Now that you understand what events trigger unpleasant stress, you can make an action plan to deal with them. Some elements of this action plan will be steps to contain, control, or eliminate the problems that are causing you stress. Other parts may be health related, such as taking more exercise, changing your diet, or improving the quality of your environment.

Exercise Regularly

Regular exercise is a vital weapon against stress. As well as ensuring a strong heart and circulation, it is also a very good way to relieve tension. Some sports,

■ **Did You Know . . . ?**

Stress-related problems are thought to cause half of all premature deaths in the United States.

■ **Did You Know . . . ?**

New managers experience stress due to lack of confidence in their ability to handle their new position. On the other hand, high-powered executives may revel in their heavy workloads, even brag about their responsibilities, but studies have found that they do so to disguise their own fear of failure.

---

such as tennis and golf, combine physical exercise with social activity—in itself a stress minimizer. Whatever you do to exercise, don't overdo the activity at first. Otherwise, aching muscles may discourage you. Besides, exercise for short periods has been found to be better than the occasional long session. Aim to do at least 20 minutes of exercise a day, but any exercise is better than none.

If you can't go to a gym or exercise class, build exercise into your daily routine. Use stairs, not the elevator or escalator. Walk all the way to work or, if that is not possible, take a bus or train for part of the trip and walk the rest. Don't have your paper delivered, but go pick it up at the neighborhood stand instead.

Also, look for a pastime that is as refreshing as sleep. A hobby won't just relax you—if you are good at it, it will boost your self-esteem. After a tough workday, in which nothing went right, you can head for your hobby and lose yourself in your painting, embroidery, photography, or carpentry. Whatever the outlet, don't let work keep you from it, either. Build time into your schedule for engaging in your hobby on a regular basis.

Assess Your Work Environment

Yes, your work environment can contribute to your feelings of stress. So you need to check out your surroundings to see how you can make your workspace more pleasant. Remove the clutter from your desk. Papers, files, and books are best stored on shelves, not on your desk, leaving more workspace. Large pieces of paper are best for writing notes; scraps get lost. Keep a pad on your desk to use. Records of phone calls are useless if you can't recall when they occurred, so date your notes. Old newspapers should be thrown away.

Check how the furnishings have been placed. If you can, rearrange the layout of your office or cubicle to create a more relaxed environment. Arrange your desk so that those things you use most often are most accessible. Position your

■ **Did You Know . . . ?**

The Japanese have officially recognized stress as a killer. *Karoski* is death from stress due to too much work.

computer so you don't need to twist around to use it. Family photos or a plant will make your surroundings more relaxing.

Bring in some CDs and listen to music—use headphones if you need to. Some managers bring a radio to their office and tune it to their favorite station with the volume set low. They have found this keeps them relaxed, productive, and enjoying their work.

You personally may be unable to make some changes, but you may want to discuss them with your office's managers because they can reduce stress and improve productivity. For instance, you may want to remedy noise or air pollution. Both can make the workplace more stressful. Check lighting, too. Natural light can lift moods and prevent eyestrain.

What about the temperature in the office or plant? Is it consistently comfortable, or do your employees complain that they are too cold or too warm?

Once you have made these changes, see how they work. After a month or so, give yourself an emotional audit. How are you doing in reducing the stress in your life?

■ **Did You Know . . . ?**

You can use stress to improve your performance—the good stress, that is. If you are not feeling motivated toward a task—maybe you are bored by it or too tired to focus on it—then you may want to psych yourself up. Focus on the importance or urgency of the work, or set yourself a challenge and reward for completing the work; e.g., I'll finish this job before 4:00 PM and leave immediately thereafter. Your intent is to reach your optimal stress level, not exceed it.

■ **Did You Know . . . ?**

Business travel can be very stressful. Flyers are three times more likely to experience stress-related disorders than most managers.

■ **How Do You Rate?**

The first step to beating stress is determining if it is a problem for you. Here's a self-assessment to measure its impact on your life. See how many statements are true for you. The more that reflect your situation, the more your need for stress-reduction strategies like rest, relaxation, a little exercise, and counseling.

- When things go wrong, it is usually my fault.

- I bottle up my problems, then feel like I want to explode.

- I focus on the negative aspects of my life, not the positive.

- I feel guilty if I sit down and do nothing for an hour or so.

- I feel rushed even if I am not under pressure.

- I feel anxious when experiencing new situations.

- I don't like to admit when I am overloaded with work.

- My work tends to take priority over my family and friends.

- I won't leave the office until I finish all outstanding work.

- I find it difficult to say no to demands on my time.

■ Tips

- Stress is infectious. It is stressful to live and work with people who are suffering from it.

- Relieve pressure by discussing work problems openly.

- Go for a jog or swim over lunch to alleviate stress.

■ See Also

Maher, Barry. *Filling the Glass: The Skeptic's Guide to Positive Thinking in Business.* Dearborn Trade, 2001.

Carlson, Richard. *Don't Sweat the Small Stuff at Work: Simple Ways to Minimize Stress and Conflict While Bringing Out the Best in Yourself and Others.* Hyperion, 1989.

Hutchings, Patricia J. *Managing Workplace Chaos: Workplace Solutions for Managing Information, Paper, Time, and Stress.* AMACOM, 2002.

Newman, John. *How to Stay Cool, Calm & Collected When the Pressure's On: A Stress Control Plan for Business People.* AMACOM, 1993.

22

Balancing Work/Family Needs

Since the events of September 11, 2001, more people are questioning the allocation of their time. Whereas in the past, they often gave up personal time to their work, now they are wondering if their jobs are getting in the way of their lives with family or friends.

Technology has both helped and hindered. E-mail, a cell phone, and the Internet may give us the potential to work flexibly. On the other hand, they also make us accessible when we aren't in the office, like on vacation. A series of studies of vacation plans by the American Management Association showed that for the last two years, executives have given up on longer vacations, opting for long weekends to stay in touch with the office. Those who said they took lengthier vacations arranged to call into the office on a regular schedule. Some managers even reported that this practice was required by their firms.

Consequently, even during vacation, we don't seem able to leave our jobs, although our health and relationships with family and friends would suggest that we should.

Too many of us have worked hard to gain "success" but we have given little consideration to what success means. You may be on the first rung of the career ladder, for instance, but do you have a good home life? How much time can you spend with friends? Leisure time? Success is not just about hard work and the respect that comes from being committed to your work. At least, it isn't for most people. There are many rich, accomplished people with big bank accounts who do not actually feel successful or fulfilled. Success is a state of mind, which means that defining success for you may demand some personal soul searching.

Brian Dyson, CEO of Coca Cola, used this analogy to describe the situation in which many managers find themselves. "Imagine life as a game in which you are juggling five balls in the air," he said. "Name them work, family, health, friends, and spirit. Then imagine that you are juggling all of these in the air. Work is a rubber ball. If you drop it, it will bounce back. But the other four balls—family, health, friends, and spirit—are made of glass. If you drop any of these, it will be irrevocably scuffed, marked, nicked, damaged, or even shattered. It will never be the same. You must understand that, and strive for balance in your life."

This issue isn't solely for women anymore, if it ever was. Men and women are both taking on multiple roles. Men are doing more of the care responsibilities and women are working more. Research suggests that fathers feel they miss time with their children.

It isn't only time with kids, either. With people living longer, more workers are experiencing care demands for elderly relatives. The fact that women are now having children later in life means that families may face caring responsibilities at both ends of the age spectrum.

As a new manager, you may see this issue of work and family balance as unimportant to you. Let's assume you are 25 and married. You are trying to find your professional niche, trying to get on the fast track. You are busy and decide that you will take care of this thing called work/family balance "mañana."

But what happens? You get older. You are now 30, you have a 3-year-old child, and you have either found a good track or are still looking for one. If you are doing well, your work is taking up much of your attention. If you are doing poorly, you believe you need to put in more time. You decide that you'll take care of your private life mañana.

Five years later, you are 35. Yes, you have made it to your first goal—you've gone from being a first-line manager to a middle manager or maybe even a senior manager. You have every reason to be proud of your career, but every so often you feel a little empty. Because you can't pin down the cause of your anxiety, you let it go.

By the time you reach 40, you discover something that many men and women also realize at around that time: the experiences given up to build their careers can't be captured today. You can't recover the relationships that you didn't have with your children when they were young or moments you should have spent with elderly relatives before their death.

Realizing the futility of thinking that tomorrow you can recapture today, and understanding how much is at stake, may help you better organize the present.

Clarification of Values

Ask yourself, "What matters to me?" If you want to be truly happy, you need to give your life meaning—hopefully beyond work—and start living your life focused on what matters to you. So far, we have talked about your career and the skills, abilities, and knowledge you will need to succeed. But let's look now at the bigger picture, which includes not only your position within your organization but also your life as a whole. Picture the key people in your life—partner, family, friends, and colleagues. How do your relationships with these individuals reflect your values? If you could be the ideal partner, what would that entail? If you could be the ideal parent, what would that mean? What kind of son or daughter? What kind of friend or manager?

Have you succeeded at work at the cost of relationships at home and with friends? Are you so wrapped up in your position that you have no time for leisure activities? I'm not suggesting that you put aside your work or career goals but rather that you add some additional goals related to your family, friends, and your own development (not professional but personal development). It's important to have goals that represent all aspects of your life. Focusing on one to the exclusion of all others might mean that you consistently prioritize your work above your family. Your role as a spouse or parent might suffer if you spend too much time and energy on your career or hobby. Friendships can be lost if you don't have the time for a night of bowling or simply a beer after work.

In Chapter 1, we discussed planning as it relates to your job. Use the same concept of SMART goals to devote time to the other relationships in your life. You may want to spend time with family and friends, but the key to implementing good intentions is to create and follow an action plan. The end result will be more balance between your personal and professional lives.

Family Ties

Don't just promise yourself that you will spend more time with your partner and kids and parents. Schedule time together in which you and your family pursue mutual interests. Don't take your office worries along, either. A poor work-life balance can have a detrimental impact on your personal relationships. If you can't leave the stress of the office in the office, it can affect your private life.

For instance, let's assume that you have a child. Make a goal to spend at least one hour a day with your youngster. Consider this time a priority. Some evenings, you may have to take work home, but don't let it interfere with quiet time with your partner. Limit the number of evenings when you bring work home to two or three. Save Saturdays for your family and friends. If you are a dedicated hobbiest, put aside some restful, creative time over the weekend as well. Don't let an excessive workload keep you from enjoying your life. Besides, I can assure you that time spent on your family and yourself will improve your ability to deal with stress in the office and your job performance.

Simplifying Your Life

You may be reading this and laughing, thinking that this author knows nothing about the workload you carry. On the contrary, as an author and full-time editor with family and friends, I'm well aware of how difficult this transition will be to you. I am proposing that you change your life, setting new priorities and making time for them by rethinking what you do now. Perhaps a little simplification can help you find the time you never seem to have for being alone or with your family.

Work-life balance is not impossible. Difficult, yes. Fraught with trade-offs, no question. It doesn't come by working harder to get more done in less time. By the end of each day, by juggling your responsibilities and commitments, you only wind up asking yourself, "Whom or what did I neglect today?" Rather, balance demands that you make a list of how you spend your time, identify those things truly important to a full and happy life, and delegate or dump the rest. If you are like the rest of the world, you have become too busy to think strategically about what is important and build a plan around it. Before you get caught up, look at how you spent your time.

Truth is, we can't have everything. Rather, we need to determine what we want, then rightsize our lives to achieve our wants. That may entail something as extensive as toggling between intensive focus on work and intensive focus on a nonwork life, giving all of ourselves to our jobs for a time, then cutting back (maybe quitting altogether) for a season to focus on our families. It may demand rethinking how we work, like working part-time, telecommuting, or starting up our own business from home. Once we allow ourselves to think of alternative work options, we may, surprisingly, find a way to balance work and family in a manner that not only gives us time for our own lives but improves what we do or how we do it.

Sometimes, however, such alternative work options—rightsizing our lives—are not available or are unacceptable to us. If our time with family and friends is critical, then we need to rethink our business priorities. The solution may be to back away from heavy involvement in our profession and pour ourselves into our families, hobbies, and other interests. This doesn't mean quitting our jobs. Rather, it means stepping off the fast track and seeking a less intense work life. If your current job doesn't allow this, then a change in position, even with lower pay, may be worth the increase in free time.

There are other work options than a 9-to-5 job. Let me share these.

Flextime

The most popular flexible work option, it allows you a flexible starting and quitting time within management limits. For instance, if normal working hours are from 8:00 AM to 5:00 PM, you might be allowed to start at 6:30 AM and leave at 3:30 PM, or 9 AM to 6 PM, or whatever start/stop time works best for you while still being acceptable to your employer. The advantage of flextime is that you would be present at work yet still have time for family or other obligations.

Telecommuting

For the most part, you would work at home, although you might be expected to come into the office for staff meetings and meetings with prospective clients.

Compressed Work Week

You would put in 40 hours but in fewer than 5 days. The most widely used arrangement is ten-hour days for four days a week. Another arrangement is called 5-4/9. This is a week of five nine-hour days followed by a week of four nine-hour days, giving you a day off every other week. As you can see, you gain an additional free day, but you need the stamina to work nine-hour and ten-hour days.

Part-Time Hours

You might choose to work fewer days per week or a shortened work day of five, six, or seven hours to make the difference between stress and sanity and allow you to juggle your work and personal life. With fewer hours on the job, you may find yourself with more energy to get the work done. On the other hand, if you would like a full day off during the week to be with a young child or an elderly family member, or just get some personal time, a four-day week can be a desirable option.

Job Sharing

If your job demands don't allow anything less than five days a week and you want more time for yourself, you might consider sharing job responsibilities with another person. For managers and others in high-level career paths, job sharing is an attractive work option, because it keeps the individual on the career track while still providing free time for family or other personal needs.

If you see these solutions to work/family balance as too drastic, you may want to make small changes in your life toward better balance.

Leave Your Work Behind

Differentiate between work time, family time, and my time. You may discover to your surprise that working fewer hours actually enables you to produce more focused work. Do you have a mobile pager, cell phone, e-mail? Turn them off.

Learn to Say No

Saying it is not difficult. It's not feeling any guilt after you said it. Focus on the important things that you can get done because you said no to something that wasn't important to either your professional or your personal life.

Learn How to Set Limits

This is along the lines of saying no. But setting limits for how you will respond to demands from both your work and your personal life will prevent you from overcommitting yourself. Then stick to them.

Delegate

We have mentioned delegation elsewhere. But it's equally important in trying to balance work and family. When you free up some of your time, you have the opportunity to focus on both tasks at work that only you can do and commitments to family, friends, and yourself.

Rethink Your Outlook

A balanced life is as much a mental attitude as a physical state. Put aside the pressures of the office and find time for laughter, a moment of kindness, or other good feelings.

Care for Your Family

By family, I mean your spouse, children, parents, and friends. All can be your bedrock, the support that helps you manage the other areas of your life (like work) more successfully. Don't neglect them, giving them attention only when there is a problem. Schedule quality time with them on weekends and evenings.

Relax Regularly

Some people practice meditation, others read quietly, and still others take long, hot baths. Some individuals prefer more active and social types of relaxation like playing sports, going to the movies, or enjoying a meal with friends. Relaxing regularly will boost your health, enable you to enjoy life more, and even improve performance at work.

Manage Your Time

If your goal is to achieve a better balance between work and life, setting unrealistic deadlines defeats the object. So learn not only to pace your work—pace events in your life as a whole.

Encourage Leisure

Take time to put the zest back into your life. Play golf, learn how to play tennis, build model ships, or sew. After a stressful workday, doing something different is invigorating.

■ Quotable Quote

"Time is the coin of your life. It is the only coin you have, and only you can determine how it will be spent."—Carl Sandburg

■ See Also

Fletcher, Winston. *Beating the 24/7: How Business Leaders Achieve a Successful Work/Life Balance.* John Wiley & Sons, 2002.

Glanz, Barbara A. *Balancing Acts: More Than 350 Guilt-Free Creative Ideas to Blend Your Work and Your Life.* Dearborn Trade, 2003.

Merrill, A. Roger and Rebecca Merrill. *Life Matters: Creating a Dynamic Balance of Work, Family, Time & Money.* McGraw-Hill Trade, 2003.

Networks, Mentors, and Political Know-How

In Chapters 10 through 14 on communications, I talked about the importance of interpersonal communications. If you are to advance beyond your current position, you need to perfect that skill. It's critical to creating or becoming a part of professional networks, groups of personal contacts you can use to help achieve job and career objectives. Networks may be internal or external. Those within the organization involve peers to whom you might turn for information or a helpful hand. External networks include people outside your organization—either former colleagues or contacts you've met at business or community events—to whom you may turn for help either with business or career goals.

Mentoring will also help you with both work-related concerns and career issues. A mentor is essentially a business coach. A mentor can be a senior executive within your organization, a supportive executive outside your firm, or even your own supervisor, who has chosen to give you extra attention because he sees great potential in you.

All together, these relationships add up to political savvy and enable you to stay on top of your current job—and position you for promotion when the opportunity arises.

Turning to Your Network

Let's assume that you are a sales manager. When you were promoted, you discovered that regional sales reports were only issued quarterly. Times have changed, and you realize that such reports need to be issued more frequently—say monthly. To increase frequency, you need support from the systems division. Unfortunately, the head of that division has a long to-do list, and your project has been relegated to the bottom of the list. But let's say you lunch with someone who is a friend of the head of systems. Should you mention your problem to her, and she in turn mention it to the head of systems, you might find your request at the top of the list. Your request is especially likely to move up if you can point out the advantages to the sales operation of having monthly data, and even advantages to your friend's operation.

You may not get exactly what you want, but the head of systems may have some other options that will enable you to achieve your objective.

This is only one way that building positive collegial relations will help you. You may be a team leader or be asked to complete a project that demands access to information a fellow manager has, or be required to hold a meeting that involves people from outside your department. Important to any of these responsibilities will be your ability to get, easily and readily, the participation of all the people you need. Don't assume that because your request is good for the organization, everyone will be eager to help. Not so. Having strong collegial relationships are at the core of your network and organizational savvy that alerts you to where to go for help will enable you to mobilize those key decision makers, get critical information, or reach advisors who can give you important direction in your task.

Outside the organization, the same networking and influencing behaviors will provide opportunities for promoting the company and getting key information to improve your organization's competitive position—not to mention promoting your own abilities and desire for advancement.

In the past, networks inside and outside the organization were just something that happened. But given the importance today—to both your job and your career—of building and sustaining a network of contacts and the subsequent power base it gives you, networking demands rigorous attention. Although your job description doesn't likely include networking or the related political responsibilities we will discuss in this chapter, it might as well—they are very much a part of a manager's competencies today.

So how do you get started in creating an internal network?

Building an Internal Network

Let's say that your organization holds annual meetings with its staff, and you are invited. The meeting involves managers from various facilities and operating areas. You may know a few of the attendees, but most of the managers are strangers. You have two options. You can revert to your childhood behavior of hanging out with your friends, those managers you know and already have good collegial relations with, or you can mingle with those managers you don't know.

These managers don't have to be individuals who represent areas of the business that impact yours, although certainly you should make it a point to introduce yourself to those people from parts of the business that do influence your own unit. But the point of the exercise is to get to know and be known by as many people within the organization as possible. The more people you know and, over time, add as friends (network), the more available will be information and help to you and your employees. Don't forget, too, that circumstances change. Someone who may have nothing to do with your department today may have a significant impact on it—or on you and your position—tomorrow.

Here's another way to expand your contacts within your organization and, thereby, grow your collegial network. Check out your Rolodex or Palm handheld. Have you gone through it lately? Take the time soon to go through the names and numbers you've collected and take stock of how many of these people you still know. You will undoubtedly be able to divide people into these categories:

- People you talk to frequently
- People you talk to occasionally
- People you never talk to but may want to in the future
- People you have completely forgotten about

Now make another category: people in your organization whom you do not know but would like to know.

Click on the corporate directory on your company's intranet. Go down the list and copy the name of each manager or employee you should know. Place the list within view. At the next managerial meeting, business retreat, or company social event, find an opportunity to introduce yourself to as many on the list as possible. Engage in some small talk to create a bridge between you both so you can contact the person later if you need the individual's help. You don't want to come across as pushy—just friendly. If you can help with a current problem, bring up the situation and offer to share your experience or resources. Suggest that the person call you after the meeting to obtain the specific information needed.

To meet those not at the meeting, take a walk around your organization and introduce yourself. Most people will not turn their back on someone from their own organization who says something like, "I've heard you were an expert on. . . ." or, "I heard you did a great job on. . . ." or, "I'm Michael/Michelle, I work in production."

The managers who are best at networking listen more than they talk. They give others the chance to express their needs, which helps them to build that bridge to future communications. But what they hear may also help them with a current problem. A two-way exchange of information also enables both parties to close white space, to explore issues they may both be considering, find ways they can work together to help each other, and discover problems with ideas they are currently considering.

Karen's Dilemma

I can't emphasize enough the importance of thinking of internal networks as reciprocal. Let me tell you about Karen.

Karen is a new office manager in a discount retailer. One day, as Karen went over her firm's inventory records, George, the division manager, walked in. "I've got good news for you, Karen," he said. "I've received approval to have a new data management system installed. It will enable you to better track inventory. You will be able to monitor sales and purchase products as needed, rather than guess about what the outlet needs. To get the final OK, all I need from you is a report detailing exactly what system you want and a rough estimate of total costs."

"But, George," Karen replied, "costs can vary so widely depending on the software. Is there a budget figure you can give me as a guideline?"

"Well, not exactly. But Keith is familiar with various inventory management programs. Maybe if you talk to him, you can get an idea of how high they run."

"Um, okay George. I'll get back to you as soon as I can."

"Better push a little on this, Karen. The budget for this quarter is going to have to be completed by next Thursday. That means I need your report by Tuesday. You have one week."

George left Karen trying to take stock of her situation. On the one hand, she was excited about getting permission to install an inventory management system. But on the other hand, the prospects did not look good for actually getting final approval in the budget. She needed more information, and she needed it right away.

Karen decided to see if she could base her proposal on what Keith knew. He had told her at a corporate meeting that he had installed a program like the one her operation needed. He would be familiar with the costs and the applications she would want.

But when Karen approached Keith, his response was very cold.

"You know, Karen, I seem to recall that I asked you for some help with the proposal for a new product line, but you didn't seem to have any time. Well, right now I'm a bit swamped myself. The best I can do for you is to give you the number of the software producer I ultimately selected in my last job."

"Oh, please Keith. I hate talking to salespeople before I know exactly what I need. Why don't I buy you some dinner, and we can discuss it in a more relaxed environment?"

"Gee, you really are desperate. Well, I'll get back to you on it. I'll talk to you later."

Karen felt as if she was at Keith's mercy. How could she get herself out of this mess?

Fortunately, Keith was a team player and came through. He suggested they go on the Web, review the various firms, and consider the pros and cons of each one's offerings.

When Karen told me what had happened, she admitted that she had created her own problem. She had met Keith and had offered to introduce him to his new colleagues but then forgotten. She had left her new peer high and dry and only went back to him when she needed help. He could very easily have ignored her request because she hadn't fulfilled her obligation to a new peer, let alone lent a hand when he needed it.

Her situation was even worse, she told me, because Keith wasn't the only individual with whom she had neglected to build a collegial relationship. "In truth, I hadn't made any effort to build a support system to which I could turn for information, inside or outside the organization," she told me.

The lesson taught Karen just how important cooperation among fellow managers is. She also realized how important it was for her to gather expert sources so she would not find herself without people to whom to turn for help.

Sustaining Your Network

As you build your network of colleagues, recognize that networking is a give-and-take relationship. If someone within your network needs your help, render it. If you need help, ask for it.

E-mail makes keeping a network relationship alive and well a lot easier than in the past. Actually, you don't need to move out from behind your desk. You can message the engineering manager in the downtown facility or that colleague from Brussels you met last year at a corporate annual meeting. True, there is a time commitment, but the benefit—expanding your access to information—is well worth it.

How do you measure the quality of an existing network relationship? Is it enough to talk to someone frequently? No. That doesn't guarantee that the person is as valuable a contact as you might assume. It's not enough just to know someone and be on friendly terms. A truly valuable contact meets all or some of the following criteria:

- The individual will call on you when in need of your help or on hearing that you need some assistance.
- The individual is trustworthy enough to give you advice on a project based on personal experience or to listen quietly as you vent about a problem.
- The individual is knowledgeable and skilled in an area that is useful to you.

It is possible to talk to someone daily yet never truly get on a comfortable basis. Cultivating individuals to build a network requires that you take the next step toward achieving personal rapport. You don't need to become fast friends, but you should extend your conversation to, say, sympathizing with the difficulties of your contact's operation and, maybe, revealing some of your own vulnerabilities. You might express some of the problems you encounter that your contact may well be able to connect with.

Even if the two of you aren't from the same functional discipline or business, you may discover a different type of bond that will cement your relationship and make it valuable to both. It could be a similar life experience, or it may, more possibly, be that you have compatible styles of dealing with stressful or high-pressure situations. Only by letting down your guard ever so slightly, will you will be able to reveal your own style and, therefore, open the possibility of a business relationship that will work for you in the future.

Are there some people whom you know and talk to occasionally but don't know well? Why aren't they a part of your network? Occasional contacts can often slip by without being recognized for their importance. Yes, you know Darren in shipping, but will Darren go out of his way when you need a favor? Certainly, all coworkers appreciate being treated respectfully and fairly. But when your dealings with someone at work are minimal, try to make a favorable impression each time you do speak. Remember, too, that networking is a two-way street. It's not enough to recognize that someone is useful to you and to treat the person courteously in the hope that you will be appreciated. Look, also, into how you can make the relationship truly reciprocal, and even go as far as offering a service or favor to prove that your relationship is equally beneficial to the other person.

In any network relationship in which you have lent a hand, don't expect an immediate payback, whether in the form of assistance, information, or the name of another person who can help. Often, the return isn't in the same form as the help, anyway. Certainly don't leave the person you helped with a feeling of being beholden. That attitude will only tear down the bridge you are trying to build, not strengthen it. Rather, you should behave as if your assistance was a gesture of help to a colleague, nothing more. But recognize that in the process, you are selling your worth to members of your network, and the long-term payback could be unlimited.

As I said, networking is a reciprocal relationship, so you shouldn't be embarrassed about accepting help from another. Actually, not using your network for that purpose can put that bridge between you and your colleague on as shaky a foundation as your not lending help when the need arises.

Just as such networks are valuable to you, they are equally important to staff members. So encourage them to build their own networks. Organization networks shouldn't begin and end with you. Find opportunities to have your staff members meet with employees from other operations within your business. Describe what each group does and identify how each can help the other.

How well do you model the behavior you want your employees to practice? To answer that question, put yourself in the shoes of your fellow managers and answer each of these questions about yourself. Do you:

- Listen as well as talk when you chat with your colleagues?
- Introduce yourself to strangers you meet at a corporate or an industry meeting, rather than hang back with your pals?
- Break the ice with questions or small talk when surrounded by strangers?
- Visit with colleagues, during which you listen to their concerns and thoughts, or are such visits made solely to ask for something?
- Stay in touch with colleagues from various parts of the organization, or are colleagues more likely to hear from you only through a holiday card or when you need their help?
- Begin phone conversations with, "Am I calling at a good time?"
- Ask your network partner if you can use his or her name in making a further contact, or do you just do it?

- Show a willingness to give help as well as to get it?
- Become a pest, calling over and over again to remind someone of a promised favor?
- Know how to say thank you?

Outside Networks

Incidentally, while I have focused on building internal networks, recognize that your network shouldn't end at your corporate door. Actually, the value of your network—and, consequently, your worth to your colleagues and company—increases when it includes other managers in your field, in your industry, in your town, in your state, your country, and around the world. Whenever you meet with a manager who impresses you, add that person's name to your list of contacts. Scribble some notes about the circumstances in which you met.

Outside contacts can be met through such sources as professional organizations, business and management seminars, and trade shows. If you consciously work to develop an open and friendly demeanor, you will increasingly make new contacts and widen your network.

Practice the same kind of bridge building with these individuals as you do with your internal network. At least every quarter, call those people in your outside network to reestablish contact, find out if you can help them—or if they can help you—and reaffirm your networking relationship.

In the next chapter, I will discuss how to leverage this external network to advance your career. But let me point out here that a network that contains members from both within and outside your organization is critical to building a power base within your organization.

As you have read this chapter, you may have acknowledged the worth of internal networks, but you may have dismissed the value of external networks. From some perspectives, networks have a bad reputation. Many newer managers see them as political contrivances, an extension of the phenomenon known as the "old-boy network," in which "fat cats" help other "fat cats" make money. But from my perspective, nothing is wrong with networks per se—it is their purpose that makes the difference. If you see networking as supportive to your business and personal goals, then I would argue that networks are a good thing.

Likewise, so are mentoring relationships.

Finding Yourself a Mentor

Finding a mentor provides you with access to insights, information, and contacts that came with experience that you are yet to have. Increasingly, companies are installing mentor programs that bring compatible first-time managers and seasoned executives together, partnering someone who has "been there, done that" with a first-time manager, so the younger individual gets the benefit of the older one's experience and knowledge.

Other than concern that other employees will see the mentoring relationship as a sign of favoritism, there is no reason why the mentor can't be in the chain of command or even the immediate supervisor of the protégé. Most structured programs bring individuals from different parts of the organization together, however, to offer the younger manager a broader perspective than what would be available with the immediate supervisor.

Should you take advantage of your company's mentoring program? If your firm doesn't offer one, should you make an effort to find a mentor? The following individuals can benefit from a mentoring relationship:

- Those who are facing the challenge of learning new skills and/or operating in new ways
- Those who have been promoted to more demanding jobs
- Those assessed with the potential to be on a fast track to the next level of management
- New hires who, as first-time managers, need not only to adjust to the management ranks but also to learn how to operate within their new organization.

In other words, someone like you, who wants to excel in your current position and have a safe harbor where you can stretch yourself professionally and increase employability without risking your reputation. If your firm doesn't offer a structured program, you may want to find a mentor on your own. If so, keep in mind that there are drawbacks to an informal mentoring partnership—for instance, the mentor you find may not be the best teacher for you or may fall out of favor with senior management, taking you out, too. Consequently, consider these questions before you take the first step in creating a mentoring relationship.

- *Does the individual have a reputation for training and coaching others?* Some managers may want to be mentors and may even have the contacts outside the organization to help you make the next career move, but they may lack interest in helping you with your current job.

- *Would the mentor have the time and information that could help you?* You need someone who will be available when you need advice and has had experience in areas where you need coaching.
- *Would the mentor see you as a threat in time?* Right now, the prospective mentor might see benefits from such a relationship, like access to information otherwise not available and an unofficial assistant who can oversee projects. But in time, as you increase in visibility, will this individual feel threatened?

If you have had some association with your prospective mentor, you should be able to answer these questions. If not, check out the office grapevine. If you believe the relationship would work, find an opportunity to speak with the individual, perhaps asking for help with a problem you have. Alternatively, you might ask the individual about a successful decision he or she made. Most senior executives in your firm are likely to give you time. If the conversation goes well, the executive may ask you about your career aspirations and may offer to be available if you need help. You might also ask if you can return occasionally for guidance if you run into a problem.

So the relationship will build. Neither of you may ever use the label *mentoring relationship,* but that is what it will evolve into. At one time, executives were scared off by the time commitment that mentoring demanded, and consequently protégés were discouraged by management gurus from using the term, but as companies have recognized the worth of such relationships, in time the executive might even use the term personally.

The tool in Figure 23.1 can offer your mentor or supervisor a look at your development needs or career aspirations.

Cultivating a Power Base

There will always be politics in large organizations. But the political games of the past aren't as likely to work in today's integrated, boundaryless organizations. You know what I'm referring to: those fat cat executives we now see primarily on the Turner Classics channel. Today's companies are looking for team players, who use their relationships with colleagues and those outside the organization for the benefit of the organization. Today's corporations are no more likely to reward those who curry favor or try to get on the good side of Mr. Suc-

FIGURE 23.1
Helping Your Mentor or Boss Better Understand You

	What You Like to Do	What You Don't Like
What You Do Well		
What You Don't Do Well		

Use this template to help your mentor or boss better assist you with your career. You can give it to an employee to gain insights into his or her development needs or career aspirations.

cess than those who limit their interactions to the people identified in their job descriptions but otherwise hide themselves away in their office. Those managers who will be rewarded will be those who bring about change, and change is not something one person can accomplish alone.

Power today comes from a willingness to share credit, a desire to lend a hand as well as get a hand, and give access to information as well as get access to information. This kind of power stems from the feelings of trust that you earn when you:

- Show you share the glory with those who helped you achieve your goal.
- Demonstrate that you can be trusted not only to lend the hand you promised but also to keep confidential those things told by a peer or manager.
- Give access to your outside network to help colleagues without expecting them to give you credit. It may not be what you know but what someone you know knows that can help a fellow manager. The assistance will be readily accepted—and likely reciprocated—if it is clear that there are no strings attached.

- Establish a successful track record. No matter who is in your network, you need to have a reputation for getting results.
- Refrain from taking sides. No matter which side you take, and no matter who wins, you eventually lose. At some point, the loser may be in a position to influence a decision affecting you, and that person may have a long memory.
- Allow a colleague on the other side of a negotiating table to walk away with something. To do otherwise is to win the battle but ultimately lose the war.
- Build a reputation of truthfulness. Never lie to win a point or get the resources you need. If you think individual managers' memories are long, the corporate memory is even longer. There will always be someone who remembers how you misled to win your point.

You won't be perceived as someone a fellow manager wants to add to his or her network if your own reputation has been sullied by broken promises, turf battles with colleagues, or an inability to keep information confidential. Also, don't think a record of misdemeanors against fellow managers will be unknown at another corporate facility. Tidbits like that are fodder for the managerial rumor mill; don't think there isn't one.

To benefit the most from an internal network, let alone an external one, you need to undertake some soul searching. Think about the relationships you are developing. Are you building a healthy network or not? Look at the questions here. Hopefully you can say yes to each and every one.

- When you visit with peers, do you listen more than talk?
- Do you go to lunch with different people on a regular basis?
- Do you ask questions to get to know colleagues as individuals as well as to understand their role in the organization?
- Do you respect any and all confidences?
- If you have associations with people who outrank your manager, do you use these relationships to benefit your boss?
- Have you identified people whom you can help and followed through with that assistance?
- Are you respected? What about your words—are you guilty of empty flattery?

I was told about a manager who was very friendly and outgoing. But over time, those who worked with her discovered that her flattery was empty. She might promise to help others, but she never delivered on her promises. She always found herself too busy. "I'll call you," she would tell a friend, yet she never called. Once people got to know her, they came to realize how little worth she added to their business network.

Clearly, relationships can be a great source of power, but the wrong ones can be heavy liabilities. In this instance, the manager was known to tattle on peers and to set up situations with her "valued friends" in which they suffered and she came out a winner.

How would your peers measure you?

■ How Do You Rate?

Networking and mentoring can help you build a power base that ultimately impacts your career. How effective are you in managing your career via networking and mentoring relationships? Answer yes or no to these questions.

- I use the grapevine to keep up on events within my organization.

- I use my friendships within the organization to know what the key players are doing.

- I network with key players both within and outside my organization.

- I network not only with those who think as I do but also with those who challenge my ideas.

- I have a mentor within my organization.

- I have several executives within my organization to whom I can go for advice and extra coaching.

- I am a mentor to an employee with potential.

- I make an effort to become involved in projects that will gain me visibility with higher ups in the organization.

- I have joined a professional organization because I believe it will advance my career and introduce me to others in my field.

- I volunteer to serve in my community to meet leaders in business and thereby become more visible outside my firm.

How well did you do? We're looking for yes replies, of course. The more yeses, the more you are positioning yourself for promotion—see the next chapter.

▪ Tips

- Share credit. When something goes well that involves your work unit and someone else's, express your appreciation to the other person for your mutual success.

- Being a friend of a friend is probably the quickest way to develop mutual trust and cooperation—and to join a new internal or external network.

- Remember the old saying: "You never have a second chance to make a first impression." Keep this in mind when you introduce yourself to others. Effective networkers project a demeanor of self-assurance that draws others to them.

- Ask good questions and listen. For instance, say, "I need some advice. Can you help me?" Such a question will generate a positive response from your contact. We all like to believe that we can help others.

▪ See Also

Dobson, Michael and Deborah Singer Dobson. *Enlightened Office Politics: Understanding, Coping with, and Winning the Game—Without Losing Your Soul.* AMACOM, 2000.
Gallagher, Richard S. *The Soul of an Organization.* Dearborn Trade, 2002.
Nierenberg, Andrea. *Nonstop Networking: How to Improve Your Life, Luck, and Career.* Capital Books, 2002.

24

Career Planning

It is easy to get so caught up in the day-to-day routine that you forget about developmental and career advancement needs, particularly in today's organizations where there are so few chances for job promotion. But when opportunities arise—and they will even in the leanest companies—they will go to those who are best prepared for them. That means you should not allow the pressures of the job to distract you from your own professional development and career planning. At the very least, you should be keeping on top of the changes in your field. Whatever it is, change is probably occurring so rapidly that it is easy to suffer from professional obsolescence.

Today, training is a lifelong endeavor and it is your responsibility. No matter how sophisticated your company's training operation, staying abreast of ever-evolving developments in your field, your industry, management, and technological applications is your responsibility, not that of your organization.

Avoid Obsolescence

Fortunately, it is easier to grow professionally today. While attendance at a seminar or course at a local university may be the first thing you think of to satisfy development needs, there are other ways to avoid obsolescence. There are home-study programs. There are business books and articles relevant to your field and industry. Don't forget general management books and articles, either, because they will keep you on top of new management trends, thus helping you to understand developments occurring in your own organization, the reasons for them, and the implications—including career issues. That knowledge can be translated into a more serious action plan for career advancement or development.

Increasingly, e-learning programs are available. If that isn't your learning method of choice, check out organizations that offer classroom training or organizations that offer blended learning—a combination of classroom instruction and e-learning.

If the opportunity for formal training arises, take it. If you seem open to new knowledge and eager to learn, management is likely to make such opportunities available to you. If you then take the information you have learned and apply it, more such opportunities will come.

Build the skills beyond those you need to do your job by involving yourself in a volunteer organization within your community. Besides leadership skills, involvement in civic groups will give you experience in working with people, making presentations, and developing and using the facilitation skills you need in team structures.

To measure your efforts at lifelong learning, take the test at the end of this chapter.

Your Career Plan

Take a piece of paper, work through the worksheet in Figure 24.1, and list your answers to these questions—what are the skills in which you have greatest proficiency? Your favorite tasks? The work climate in which you are most comfortable? Given the realities on that piece of paper, what next job would be most satisfying to you? How likely are you to get such a job now? Over a period of time? Does getting this job entail a move outside your current field, or will you have to job-hop from one company to another to achieve your objective?

Don't forget to study career or job patterns. Will the ideal job for you still be there when you are ready for it? If so, then begin to develop an action plan that will gain you that position in the timeframe you have identified.

Does that job exist in your current company? If it doesn't, don't forget to include in your plan learning experiences in your current situation that will bring you closer to your goal. If you want to be in charge of product development, for instance, but new product development efforts are few and far between in your organization, then look for opportunities to serve on teams whose purpose is to

FIGURE 24.1
Career Planning Worksheet

1. Career risks I see in the next ___ years.

   _____
   _____
   _____
   _____
   _____

2. Career opportunities I see in the next ___ years.

   _____
   _____
   _____
   _____
   _____

3. Prioritize risks and opportunities.

   Risks   Opportunities

   _____   _____
   _____   _____
   _____   _____
   _____   _____
   _____   _____

4. Action plans to address those risks.

   Risks   Plan

   _____   _____
   _____   _____
   _____   _____
   _____   _____
   _____   _____

5. Action plans to maximize those opportunities.

   Opportunities   Plan

   _____   _____
   _____   _____
   _____   _____
   _____   _____
   _____   _____

develop new products or services within your own organization. Work your way up to team leader of a new-product effort. Each success will help make your name more familiar to those who do product development for a living—and closer to your chosen dream job.

If your job goal entails leaving your current position, then your career plan should include the following:

- The position you want (your goal)
- Short-term jobs (assignments you might take to achieve your goal)
- Action plan
- External network contacts to let others know about your interest in working elsewhere
- Headhunters
- Your assets. These are the attributes that describe your character, like accurate, articulate, calm, collaborator, committed to your job, decisive, dynamic, friendly, hardworking, lively, methodical, optimistic, organized, proactive, quick to learn, responsible, sensitive, or steadfast.
- List of industry contacts to alert
- Define success in your own terms. For instance, how much time do you want or need to spend with your family? How often do you see your friends? Do you like variety or routine in a job? How important is it that your work has some value to the community? Would you thrive on challenges? What about input from others—would you mind having other people tell you what to do or veto your ideas? Would you mind relocating? How much money would you want?

A career plan for a promotion would take into consideration a key fact: advancement is the result of a successful mix of three characteristics—competency, visibility, and opportunity. Having the right skills, abilities, knowledge, and attitudes isn't sufficient to get you a new position. You also need to be visible to those who make the promotion decision. Maybe even more importantly, you have to be in the right place at the right time (although you may be able to set up circumstances so you create the right place and the right time).

You may also have to make some tough decisions about your personal management style or values if you choose to stay in your current organization. If that organization is undergoing changes in style and values, you will have to make dramatic shifts in your management approach (e.g., from manager to team leader) if you want to stay. You will have to adapt your interpersonal communication and leadership styles to reflect the new organizational design and work process.

Your Boss

So far, in discussing your opportunities for advancement, I have been focusing on your capabilities. However, your manager may be an obstacle to advancement in your organization, no matter how strong your skills, abilities, and knowledge. Your manager may be an insensitive boss who, intentionally or otherwise, bawls you out for minor mistakes and takes credit for your achievements, while neglecting to praise your efforts, or, your manager is an incompetent boss who lacks creativity and has trouble making decisions, or, your manager is someone who has one new assignment after another for you and is extremely open to new and better ways of getting the work done—provided the ideas are his. What do you do then?

You need to learn more about your manager—strengths and weaknesses—and take the tasks your boss dislikes and shore up weak areas so your manager looks good to the next level of the organization. Of course, you need to be diplomatic about this, helping in a subtle manner so your manager won't feel threatened. Likewise, you can offer to handle tasks that your manager thinks are a waste of time yet you see as worthwhile, and you can make an extra effort to support your manager with projects that she considers a priority.

If you're new to your position and the organization, you can start off on the right foot with your supervisor by determining how much he or she likes to be kept informed, how he or she likes to be informed (written or verbal), and how involved he or she wants to be in decisions. Keep in mind that your manager is your supervisor—neither a buddy nor a close confidant. You may work closely together, but that doesn't guarantee you become friends. With some managers, the best you can hope for is professional respect. It doesn't hurt, however, not to give your manager reason to dislike you.

To obtain high regard from your manager, you need to learn not to respond to every slight and even to go out of your way to defend your manager's position when it makes sense. Such behavior will position you well professionally. Others will come to learn about you from the manager as well. Consequently, your name will come to the mind of either your manager or others in senior management when career opportunities come up. Good managers know which employees to keep in the background and which ones to trust and, therefore, recommend for promotion.

Performance Assessments

Even if your relationship with your manager is great, you shouldn't assume that your annual appraisals or quarterly updates will reflect the good work you do. Unfortunately, too many managers give only perfunctory reviews. Consequently, you need to take a more active role in your assessments. Prior to each review, prepare a minievaluation of your own, one that compares how you've done against what you were expected to do. Armed with your own self-appraisal, you can then take more control during the performance review sessions with your manager. Point to concrete accomplishments. If your efforts made a difference to either the unit's contribution to profits or cost savings, you can almost be sure that your manager will write them up, because they will make her look good as well.

If your manager sees you as someone who can represent him and the department in a positive way, then your manager may also recommend you participate in a crossfunctional team where you can gain the kind of recognition that could, in time, lead to a promotion. But be patient. Today's leaner organizations don't offer the opportunities for promotion that companies did in the past.

What if, despite your best efforts, you get passed over for a promotion or don't get the raise or bonus you expected—or even are demoted? Such setbacks occur in most people's careers, so you shouldn't let it devastate you. Confronting the decision maker won't undo the decision and will only make you more upset. Instead, try to look at the situation objectively. Consider what happened. If you lost a promotion, was the other person better qualified? If you didn't get the raise or the bonus you expected, were your expectations unrealistic, or is it just that money is short right now? How realistic was your goal?

The World of Work

Actually, staying where you are is a goal in itself in today's world. So you need to go back to your career plan and determine whether a promotion is realistic right now.

If a promotion is unlikely, would a lateral move put you on a new career path? Could that path eventually lead to the job goal you identified in your career plan? How about a zigzag plan that moves you through the organization?

We tend to think of advancement as only upward, but promotion isn't the only way to advance. Making a lateral move, or several lateral moves over time, makes your capabilities known to senior officers other than your current manager, and that visibility can pay off in the long run. A lateral move also gives you first-hand experience of working in different areas of the business, a plus in today's integrated organizations.

All this information about advancement may be premature if you have only recently moved into a managerial position. You may have much to learn before you feel ready for the next rung up the career ladder. This shouldn't preclude consideration of your career. You must accept a reality in today's business world that through no fault of your own, no matter how good your managerial skills, you may find yourself out of a job. Just as promotion comes from being in the right place at the right time, so termination happens from being in the wrong place at the wrong time.

Defending Your Job

Let's assume that your company, like many, has done some downsizing. To evade a pink slip, you might want to do the following:

- *Become a trusted advisor to your manager.* Become irreplaceable. Be key to helping make decisions and get things done. Make your boss a success. As a trusted advisor, you become indispensable to your manager and your organization.
- *Look busy.* I'm not being cynical. But when work slows down, it is critical that you stay in the mainstream of the remaining workflow. Seek out projects. Ask people if they need help. Make it clear to those around you that you want to be busy. Don't see the time as a paid vacation spent at work.
- *Get in early and stay late.* Even if the workflow in your company diminishes, staying late sends a strong message that you are busy, that you're ready to pitch in, and that you can be trusted to do whatever it takes to get the work done.
- *Become more important to your customers.* Servicing your customers' needs, beyond the confines of your relationship with them, is an essential component to success in any economic climate. In bad times, when customers are reevaluating their relationships with suppliers and service providers, those who add value will be most likely to win out. This may mean working with your customer or client to understand their broader strategic goals and to introduce them to other people or companies that can help them achieve those goals.

- *Figure out how to save money.* Every company is looking for ways to help their bottom line by cutting expenses. Doing your job in a more cost-efficient manner is an important way to add value.
- *Become a valued coach and mentor.* People bring value to their companies, not simply by performing the job that they have been assigned but also by helping other employees perform their own jobs better.
- *Be confident.* No matter how hard you work, how late you stay, or how much value you add to the company, it will all go unnoticed if you project insecurity and fear. Of course, false bravado wears thin quickly, so confidence must be backed up with real skill and commitment. Nevertheless, an assured demeanor will take you far.

Just in Case . . .

I don't want to earn the reputation of a Polyanna. So let me say that while maintaining this upbeat attitude, you should also have an up-to-date resume. As I said, no matter what your level, skills, or loyalty to the corporation, always have a survival plan. This plan can take one of two directions: it can find you a comparable job or promotion in the same career track; or it could move you toward what I have labeled *Career Plan B,* the job you dream about. In my life, I've met many younger managers who had secret careers in their hearts—from an editor who wanted to become a lawyer to a consultant who yearned to be a soccer player. No kidding. Both used layoffs to see if they could achieve their goals. The consultant had a bum knee so he is back behind a desk, but the editor completed law school and now practices in San Francisco.

What helped both individuals was that they had active support networks that helped them not to take the layoffs personally. They might have felt like clamming up and suffering in silence, but this is a time to talk, and they had family and friends who were there to talk with them about what had happened and what they were going to do about it.

In essence, they made downsizing a new beginning rather than an ending. Yes, they went through the four stages of coping with job loss—denial, anger, depression, and acceptance—but they were able to get through the shock to recognize an opportunity on the other side.

■ How Do You Rate?

Answer yes or no to each of these questions.

- Besides this book, how many other management books have you read this year?

- Have you attended a training program in the last 12 months?

- Have you volunteered to be a part of a project team in which you could demonstrate your capabilities?

- Have you set up a meeting with the staff of a colleague's department or several colleagues' departments to find out more about how each of your operations work?

- Have you attended an industry conference or joined an association related to your industry? Are you a member of an organization that is related to your field?

- Have you become involved in some civic or community activity that allows you to meet with managers from other companies? Are you regularly practicing your networking skills outside your organization?

- If someone asked senior management who was on top of the new office technology, might you be named?

- Have you looked for opportunities to perfect your oral communication and writing skills? Maybe written an article for that trade association's magazine? Offered to speak at an industry conference? Perhaps taken a committee membership position that allows you to influence industry events?

If you haven't done any of these things, include them on your to-do list. Better yet, add them somewhere on your personal priority list. Admittedly, self-development requires an investment of personal time, but businesses are constantly changing, and you will need to change just to stay even, let alone be a part of your company's future focus.

Besides maintaining your worth in the job market with a self-development plan, do some research to determine what jobs will be growing, or even be here, five years from now. Where are new jobs emerging that might interest you? Equally important, which jobs are disappearing? You don't want to build your career plans on the rocky foundation of a job market that is slowly shrinking.

> ### ■ Tips
>
> • If you want to achieve your goal, you have to take an active role in managing your career.
>
> • Even if you are just starting a new job, it is not too soon to start thinking about the next rung on your career ladder.
>
> • You may be happy at work, but you should still keep an up-to-date resume. You never know in today's job market.

Draw a Mind Map

As you think about your career, consider a spider diagram to stimulate your thinking. In the middle of the page, write your career plan. Now, think about what is important to you. Write the things of most interest to you on a branch labeled "Goals." Next, consider the impact of achieving your career goal on your time with friends and family (F&F). Label another branch "F&F" and indicate your conclusions on that branch. Next, ask yourself how you will achieve your goal. On the branch labeled "Training," note what you would have to study to achieve the goal. Keep going, naming one branch after another depending on those elements important in your life. Once you have your drawing completed, you will have a pictorial representation of your action plan, something that often has more impact than a written list of pros and cons.

> ### ■ See Also
>
> Citrin, James and Richard A. Smith. *The Five Patterns of Extraordinary Careers: The Guide for Achieving Success and Satisfaction.* Crown Business, 2003.
> Dobson, Michael and Deborah Singer Dobson. *Managing Up!* AMACOM, 1999.

Index

Share the message!

Bulk discounts
Discounts start at only 10 copies. Save up to 55% off retail price.

Custom publishing
Private label a cover with your organization's name and logo.
Or, tailor information to your needs with a custom pamphlet
that highlights specific chapters.

Ancillaries
Workshop outlines, videos, and other products are available on
select titles.

Dynamic speakers
Engaging authors are available to share their expertise and insight
at your event.

Call Dearborn Trade Special Sales at
1-800-245-BOOK (2665)
or e-mail trade@dearborn.com

Dearborn™
Trade Publishing
A **Kaplan Professional** Company